GINA N. BROWN

Lucy McGee's Moment of Truth

First published by NovaHeart Media 2021

Copyright © 2021 by Gina N. Brown

All rights reserved. No part of this publication may be reproduced, stored or transmitted in any form or by any means, electronic, mechanical, photocopying, recording, scanning, or otherwise without written permission from the publisher. It is illegal to copy this book, post it to a website, or distribute it by any other means without permission.

This novel is entirely a work of fiction. The names, characters and incidents portrayed in it are the work of the author's imagination. Any resemblance to actual persons, living or dead, events or localities is entirely coincidental.

Gina N. Brown asserts the moral right to be identified as the author of this work.

Gina N. Brown has no responsibility for the persistence or accuracy of URLs for external or third-party Internet Websites referred to in this publication and does not guarantee that any content on such Websites is, or will remain, accurate or appropriate.

Designations used by companies to distinguish their products are often claimed as trademarks. All brand names and product names used in this book and on its cover are trade names, service marks, trademarks and registered trademarks of their respective owners. The publishers and the book are not associated with any product or vendor mentioned in this book. None of the companies referenced within the book have endorsed the book.

All rights reserved, including the right to reproduce this book or portions thereof in any form whatsoever. For information, bulk book purchases, or speaking engagements, please contact NovaHeart Media: novaheartmedia@gmail.com or www.novaheartmedia.com

First edition

ISBN: 978-1-9995741-0-9

Cover art by Kathleen Lynch

This book was professionally typeset on Reedsy.
Find out more at reedsy.com

*For the Brown family
and
Robert Bryan Crockett*

Acknowledgement

Thanks to my family for their ongoing support of all my projects: Christina Brown, Dale Brown, Reisa Muir & Al Muir, Connor Muir, Tanya Brown & Ric Hamilton. And in loving memory of my father Floyd "Brownie" Brown, the original storyteller in our family.

Special thanks to Robert Bryan Crockett, for encouraging me through endless edits and not letting me give up early on; then imploring me to wrap it up when I couldn't stop rewriting!

Endless thanks and gratitude to Cathy Jacob and Kelly Hennessey, co-founders of our writing group Word Salad. In addition to many years of sharing our writing, cheering and egging each other on, as well as attending many retreats, both read my novel in advance and provided excellent feedback. Also, to Sylvia Rowlands and the Rowlands family for their lovely home, Terra Rosa, where we held many writing retreats.

There were also people who provided support and/or inspiration: Renée Hartleib (excellent editor), Elizabeth Peirce (amazing proofreader), Norrie Matthews, Kathleen Lynch, Reena Davis, Glenn "Glenner" Reid, Susan Miller, Nancy Laberge, Shaylyn MacAulay, my cousins Anne Crocker and Gail Bugden, Nancy Dorey and Rob Upward.

Chapter 1

2016

Lucy

Deep in Lucy McGee's purse, a ringing and vibrating phone jolted her back to the present. She groped around the cavernous bag and pulled out her cell, hurrying toward her car for a meeting across town.

Lucy glanced at the call display and recognized the country code from France, followed by a string of numbers. Puzzled, she stared at the phone, neither answering it nor sending it to voicemail.

The fifth ring demanded action.

When she said hello, she heard a woman's unmistakable voice: accented, yet exquisitely polished, conveying that English was one of many languages spoken. Worse, Lucy thought she sounded calm–*over calm* if there was such a thing. She shaped each word with chilling precision, sending Lucy's vitals into a frenzy. Maybe Lucy was reading too much into her tone, but the woman rattled her.

"Lu-ceee?" said the woman in a velvety French accent,

emphasizing the final syllable.

Lucy wished she could rewind thirty seconds and send her to voicemail. This was the last person she wanted to speak to. They had never met in person, yet this woman and her husband had turned Lucy's life on its head twenty-seven years ago. If she hung up, Lucy knew she would call back, or worse, show up on her doorstep. She had already learned the hard way that Elise's gale-force will was fearless, mowing down anything in her path.

"Who's calling, please?" Lucy said, yet she knew who was calling. She was buying time as she cursed herself for answering the call. There was a slight pause, as if the woman were choosing her words carefully. "It's Elise… Elise Morin," she added.

"Yes, I remember your name from the custody documents," said Lucy, unable to stop the sarcasm from sneaking out of her mouth. As she arrived at her car, Lucy climbed into the driver's seat and closed the door to protect passersby from a potentially heated conversation. She was curious about why Elise would be in touch after decades of silence. Lucy clung to grudges, stashing them in a corner of her brain–yet ready for recall in an eye blink. This was the oldest and biggest in her slagheap of grudges, and she recalled every stinking detail. "What can I do for you?"

"It's about my son," said Elise.

"You mean *my* son," said Lucy, squeezing the words through her taut vocal cords.

"Yes. My son, your son… perhaps we say our son, *non*?"

"Okay. What about Daniel?" Anger churned inside Lucy as she recalled the cruel injustice of the past, with little chance to defend herself at twenty-one. Lucy thought she knew a lot

CHAPTER 1

more about life than she did. She recalled the legal wrangling, the intense shame and sorrow, with everything over in a flash. Elise and Jacques got custody of her little boy. The rest was a blur. It was as if these decades-old memories had happened ten minutes ago. She neither forgave, nor forgot. Instead, she gradually admitted defeat and moved on with her life by hiding the fiasco.

"He goes by Max now... Max Daniel Morin," said Elise.

Well, bully for her. Lucy wasn't ready to call him Max just because Elise decreed it so. In her mind, he was still the sweet little baby Daniel that Lucy held in her arms. Now in her fifties, she had learned how to present persuasive arguments without giving in to her emotions. Over the years she had rehearsed obsessively what she would say to this woman and her husband if given the chance. She knew it by heart, like a fine Shakespearean soliloquy ready to move a rapt audience.

As a trained but non-practicing lawyer, she had mastered the art of staying calm as she described the injustice heaped on her when she was young and vulnerable. The speech was so moving, she knew it would rouse listeners to a standing ovation. Lucy opened her mouth... and froze. Damn it! She couldn't recall a single syllable. What happened to her earth-moving speech of the century? Why did this woman have such an effect on her? "What is it, Elise?" she asked.

"Max has a life-threatening medical condition," Elise stated.

"What do you mean?" said Lucy, suddenly gripped with fear. As Elise launched into her story and impassioned plea for help, Lucy learned there was a medical crisis that 'only she could solve' as Elise put it. At first, Lucy's cynical mind wondered if Elise was manipulating the situation–this woman was capable of such deeds. Yet Lucy sensed this was different.

Instead of venting three decades of angst at Elise, she listened to what the woman had to say.

When Elise finished, they ended the call without a resolution. Daniel's situation shocked Lucy; it was not at all what she expected. After making her case, Elise begged her to say yes on the spot. Lucy said she needed time to consider such an enormous request.

Lucy's mind zigzagged with thoughts. There were implications, enormous implications. Besides helping Daniel, she also realized she could atone for her act of poor judgment at twenty-one that denied her a lifetime of inner peace. There were major physical risks to consider and numerous medical tests to go through before it was a possibility. But she was strong and mostly healthy, so she could handle curveballs. Hell… life's curveballs were her specialty. Yet, there was a catch. There was always a damned catch: she hadn't told her husband or children about Daniel and the unwed mother chapter early in her life. Her heart sank as she thought about the domino effect. Revealing the story would spark enormous chaos in her daily family life and not revealing it could set off even bigger problems, possibly catastrophic. Either way, she'd lose.

As she stared at the dashboard of blinking lights in the car, she thought about earlier that morning when she was reading a self-help book, one of many stockpiled on her shelves. She read them dutifully, full of hope to improve her life, yet found they never yielded the desired results (or maybe she didn't follow instructions). This time, she had read a quote that hovered in her head all day, refusing to shove off: "If you keep on doing what you're doing, you're going to get what you get." It sounded like a simple homespun homily, yet it summed up

CHAPTER 1

her entire life.

Her chest pounded with the same discomfort she felt at her weekly spin class from hell. She took a deep breath and counted to four as the air went in, then released it in three counts to slow it down. When things settled, she thought about what she needed and boiled it down to two things: a fail-proof plan and a trusted friend to help her. There were only three people who knew her past story. Her two parents–fueled by her mother's religious outrage about the situation–were a no-go, she knew. While her father supported Lucy when her mother was out of earshot, he wasn't the right one to help now.

That left only one person who had stood by her through the mess. Joanne Cambridge was her oldest friend, and Lucy cringed for letting their friendship lag in the past few years, but it would not stop her from asking for help. That's why she loved her non-judgmental friend. In this situation, it was Joanne's ability to think and plan before making a decision that would help her most. Lucy needed time to consider how to respond to the earlier conversation with Elise, and what she would do about it. If she was going ahead, she needed Joanne by her side. There was way too much to think about, and her thoughts swirled around until they collapsed in a big heap.

A meeting reminder on her cell jolted her out of her thoughts. Either it was giving her a fifteen-minute reminder of a start time, or the meeting was now starting. Cringing, she checked the car clock, which always ran seven minutes fast (she secretly wondered if that clinched the deal when her husband was buying the car). All fired up, she tried to calculate the timing: was she running seven minutes late, or seven minutes early? She was never early, but she lived in hope. Whatever. She sighed, pushing the ignition button and easing into the morning traffic. What a way to start the day.

Chapter 2

Lucy

After the meeting across town, Lucy returned to the office, answering a stream of questions from eager team members as she walked the pathway to her desk. She managed an under-funded environmental non-profit, which focused on changing behaviors and attitudes, not impressing visitors with décor. The office consisted of mismatched furniture and worn-out office chairs cast off by the company next door, and stacks of bankers' boxes that seemed to multiply overnight.

She sat at her desk and yanked on the sticky bottom drawer until it opened far enough to wedge in her bulging purse. Stacks of environmental reports all awaited a thorough reading and little yellow polka-dot post-it notes reminded her of a zillion things she was supposed to do. Her days vaporized in a flash of meetings, calls, texts and communications. Normally, Lucy thrived on the breathtaking pace of shifting from one issue to the next about climate change, oceans and sustainability. Except today. Lucy's head churned with the conversation she had earlier with Elise and the news about Daniel, or Max as he was now known.

Her thoughts drifted to McGill University in Montreal and her second year there when a weekend fling changed her life. One minute she was a partying university student, the next a twenty-one-year-old mother facing endless decisions, legal wrangling, and shame. Endless shame. There was the dreaded call to her parents in Nova Scotia to tell them the news. After fumbling through a rehearsed speech with her mother on one line and her father on the extension, there was an eerie silence. Her mother then berated her for two minutes straight without taking a breath. She warned Lucy about the wrath of God about to befall her–and the terrible humiliation for the family at church if anyone got wind. She finished with a stern warning not to come home "until it was safe"–whatever that meant. Her mother hung up without saying goodbye, leaving Lucy alone and afraid. Shaking and frightened from the call, her best friend Joanne held her, promising to help Lucy whatever she chose to do. And what Lucy would learn was that the knock-on effect of her decisions would ripple through her life no matter what she did to hide things.

For the rest of the week, Lucy couldn't shake the thoughts about her son in France, whom she hadn't seen in nearly twenty-seven years. The minute Elise and her husband Jacques had gained custody of the boy, they slammed the door of connectivity in Lucy's face. While she saw him take his first steps in Montreal, she never got to experience the things any parent would expect to see as a child grows up: the first day of school, learning to ride a bike, becoming a teenager and graduating from high school–the list of non-memories was painful. Yet Lucy thought about him on all those occasions, wondering about every detail of his life.

Lucy only cared about helping Max. Many things in her

CHAPTER 2

life had turned out great, like her husband and two children in Halifax. However, there was still a lingering burden from her past that refused to resolve itself; and she wondered if she could straighten out the past without ruining her future. The more she thought about it, Joanne was her best hope to solve her crisis. Lucy knew exactly where to find her on the weekend: the Halifax Seaport Farmers' Market.

***

On Saturday morning, she got on her bike and headed for the back streets. She blurred past Halifax's group of tree streets: Beech, Elm, Poplar, Chestnut and Walnut and continued along the north side of Citadel Hill, coasting past the old Town Clock for a quick time check. Crossing Spring Garden Road, she dipped into the back alley of Dalhousie University's school of architecture, to avoid the traffic gridlock. In less than ten minutes she was across town at the harbor front. The sprawling Farmers' Market buzzed with early morning shoppers. Fresh basil and baked bread scents drew in crowds strolling the waterfront. She twisted past the cars waiting to park and made a beeline to the bike rack.

Sweating from pumping across town, she welcomed the cool harbor breeze until it chilled her skin. Goosebumps arose on cue. She rustled in her knapsack, pulling out a jacket, thinking how crazy it was to wear it on a summer day. In Nova Scotia, multiple seasons were a daily occurrence. One minute the scorching sun would be interrupted by an autumn fog bank, then whisked out to sea by a sou-westerly wind, returning the climate to summer. Every season was a never-ending chore of adding and peeling off layers, followed by an endless rotation of jackets with a two-week wearing period.

The market, looming larger than a football field, pulsed with people. Her impatience bubbled up as she worked her way through the people on weekend time: stroll, pause, talk, saunter, repeat. She side-stepped the chatting couples who blocked the entrance, the strollers and the children larking about. Lucy scanned for Joanne. She noted most of the women surrounding her looked a lot like herself: jeans and sneakers or rubber boots, hiking jackets, recycled tote bags and graying hair, with more salt than pepper these days.

She climbed the middle stairway for a panoramic view and watched people milling. Five minutes later, she spied Joanne hovering in her natural habitat: the cheese booth. Lucy hurried down the stairs and moved toward Joanne among the clutch of cheese lovers. The smell of geriatric blue cheese clung to the air; and to Lucy's nose smelled like the back alley of an ice cream shop on a sweltering day.

Lucy admired Joanne for her ability to focus intently, while she herself had the attention span of a gnat. Her friend looked official and serious, as if someone had appointed her to the world's most important role, like chair of the hors d'oeuvre committee for the Last Supper. Joanne even looked the part, wearing a casual, yet high-quality blazer on a Saturday when many wore sweats and hoodies. Her light brown hair, cut in a perfect bob at her shoulders, reflected golden highlights in the sun that poured in from the harbor windows.

Lucy watched Joanne sniff the samples, spear a cheese cube with a toothpick and pop it into her mouth. She would then tilt her head sideways and stare into the distance, as if it would help her decide if she liked the taste. Then she'd raised her eyebrows slightly and pick another. Lucy leaned in and lowered her voice. "That's our finest aged blue, Ma'am. We call it 'Grandpa's Reeking Socks'."

Joanne twisted her head sideways and laughed. "Lucy!" she yelped over the din while they hugged. "What brings you here?"

"Maggie's soccer team is having a bake sale. I'm buying tea biscuits, putting them in a nice basket and calling them hand-crafted scones."

"Cheater," joked Joanne.

"I didn't say *I* made them. There's a reason Pops called me Loosey Goosey Lucy. I learned my best tricks from him." Lucy leaned over and poked a piece of cheddar with a toothpick. "How's life? Still doing HR?"

"For now. I'm dreaming of a three-day work week… or less."

"You don't mean retire?"

Joanne smiled. "I've got big dreams, baby. If I only knew what they were."

"No kidding," said Lucy. The background noise bubbled. Lucy glanced at Joanne and a train of thoughts charged through her head. She wondered how she should handle this delicate request with her friend. Should she lay out the entire story with every painful detail, then ask for Joanne's help? Or should she hint at her dilemma and wait for Joanne to offer? That would be like old times, when Jo could nearly read her mind and be ready with a perfect solution. Except Lucy had dropped the ball on their friendship over the past couple of years.

She squirmed slightly as she thought about not getting back to Joanne's last phone message. It was just a catch-up call, but Lucy hadn't gotten around to calling back. No excuses, she just hadn't. But now she needed to renew things. "Want to grab a coffee?"

"Okay, but I have to buy my stuff first. I don't want to get side-tracked with Lucy antics."

Lucy slipped her arm through Joanne's. "How about coffee first and then shop? My treat," added Lucy before her friend could argue. She caught Joanne's trademark stink-eye aimed directly at her, which meant she was onto Lucy, but still prepared to go along with the plan.

"In that case, I'm getting a double-ass latte," Joanne said, stepping around a child wailing and kicking on the floor. "And a bagel."

Lucy and Joanne sat on the benches of the wide stairway where people gathered to sit. Sipping coffee and sharing a bagel, they watched the local musicians play, while joyful kids danced, free of any concerns about moving to the rhythm. After a song ended, parents handed money to their children to place in the busker's fiddle case.

"So how are the kids?" said Joanne.

"Great. Love them to bits, but Riley has turned into a basement dweller who emerges long enough to inhale the fridge contents and return to his cave."

"Is he still at university?"

Lucy rolled her eyes. "He started with a BA, then added computer science with multiple minors, which he's now finishing online. He also has a side-hustle with his buddies developing a computer game or app. Says they'll be rich soon."

"And Maggie?"

Lucy beamed, thinking about her daughter who was so clever and mature for her age. "She started university this year and is applying herself, unlike me, as you may recall."

"You were lucky you were so damn smart."

CHAPTER 2

Lucy sipped her coffee and watched kids running up and down the staircase. She wasn't ready to spring any news on her yet; she needed time to build up to it. "And how are Emmaleigh and Gretchen?"

Joanne smiled. "Emmaleigh's great, you know what she's like. Still making the world a better place." She paused briefly. "Gretchen, well, she's still struggling."

Lucy knew Gretchen was a more delicate topic. "I bumped into Kaye Phinney at a fundraiser a few weeks ago. Remind me: was she in our Home Ec class in high school?"

"That's right," Joanne said.

"I didn't know she lived near you. Well, I vaguely remember her, to be honest."

"Our kids went to school together. She's helped me a lot with Gretchen," said Joanne.

"Yeah, she updated me about her bulimia—."

"Anorexia," said Joanne. Lucy caught Joanne's annoyance for mixing it up. She either hadn't listened fully to Joanne the last time she asked about her daughter, or maybe her memory was slipping. She had noticed that a lot lately, and it worried her. "Jeez, that must have been awful. How's she doing now?"

Joanne perked up. "She's improving and there are signs of—"

A noise caught Lucy's attention, and she glanced up to view a hulking shadow hovering over her. She forgot Joanne was in the middle of a sentence. "Dr. Doofus," said Lucy, emphasizing the second syllable.

"Miss Train Wreck 1985," he shot back.

"Hi Darryl," said Joanne. Darryl turned, surprised. "Hey Jo. I didn't see you there. Big mouth was getting all the attention." He returned to Lucy. "I guess you didn't get the memo, Lu," said Darryl.

"What?"

"You forgot to age like the rest of us. Right Joanne?" Joanne raised an eyebrow, but Darryl continued. "You still look like Bonnie Raitt with your long red hair and rockin' attitude."

"And you don't look bad for a guy named Darryl who claimed to move here from L.A." said Lucy.

"I did."

"Right. Lethbridge, Alberta."

"Admit it, you thought I was hot when I was from L.A."

"Oh please," groaned Lucy.

"Still working with Tree Huggers Unanimous, or whatever it's called? I've heard you on the radio, giving politicians the gears."

"Somebody's got to protect the environment," Lucy replied half-heartedly, trying to figure out how to wrap up a conversation with a guy who loved to talk and used to have a major crush on her. Bad combo. She worried Darryl could interfere with her plans with Joanne. She scanned the crowd and spotted the woman velcroed to his arm in all his social media posts. "Hey Darryl, is that wife number three?"

Darryl looked startled as a stern woman with a busy hairdo walked toward them. "Got to run," he said, taking off as if his shoes had built-in rockets. He beelined to his wife's side, slipped his arm around her waist and guided her deep into the crowd.

Lucy watched Darryl disappear with his wife. She turned to Joanne. "Shit, if she teased her hair anymore, they could charge her with bullying."

"Guess he didn't want to introduce us," said Joanne, adjusting her coffee cup. "Then again, maybe she noticed the

CHAPTER 2

lingering tension between you two from high school days."

Lucy groaned. "Darryl? Me?" She noticed Joanne shooting her a look. "Well, she has nothing to worry about. Enough about past embarrassments," Lucy said, poking at the foam in the latte cup. Should she say something now? It was hard to bring up such an unusual topic in a hurry.

"How's your Mom these days?" said Joanne.

"Still blaming and saying, 'I'm not impressed' in response to anything I tell her."

"See her much?" Joanne asked, twisting off a bite of bagel and popping it into her mouth.

"I go weekly, under protest. And she gives me grief for something," said Lucy. She wished it didn't have to be that way, but she and her mother shared a tense relationship that had begun in her childhood and gone downhill from there. Lucy turned to Joanne. "Do you ever long for simpler times?" She figured this was her best chance to introduce her plan–not every detail, just enough to get things rolling.

"Every day," said Joanne.

"Remember university? Partying late in the bars, eating at Fairmount Bagel at two in the morning and no weekend plans."

Joanne tore off another piece of bagel, passing it to Lucy. "Here's to Montreal bagels. They absorbed the booze, didn't they?"

"Know what I found the other day? Photos from our trip to Europe," Lucy said, waiting to see Joanne's response. She looked surprised. "Did you know it was thirty years ago?"

"It feels like yesterday," said Joanne.

"Remember the LuLu and JoJo Show?"

"You got us in deep with that slime-ball club owner," said

Joanne, laughing and munching.

"That's why we're good together–I get us into shit, you get us out of it," Lucy added, trying to point out Joanne's attributes.

"Guess that makes me the boring one."

"Hell no. I couldn't have traveled with someone like me. Seriously, we'd be dead by now," said Lucy.

"It was fun."

They both sat quietly, watching the people herding their wayward kids, sharing snacks and listening to live music. Lucy reflected on their time at university in Montreal. It was so far away, yet her friendship with Joanne was like no other she'd had in her life. Without sisters, Lucy and Joanne leaned on each other. While Lucy's brothers loved her to bits, they were either teasing or protecting her.

In Lucy's mind, Joanne was more like a sister. She took a breath, wondering if she should blurt out the new medical situation facing her son in Paris. On the one hand, it was a natural thing to raise with her, after all they had been through. But this new development… it felt entirely overwhelming to Lucy. She could hardly cope with what was coming at her, let alone pull Joanne into it. First, it would dredge up memories of unhappy times the two of them had been through in Montreal with Lucy and the baby. It was a memory so upsetting, neither of them could discuss it without reliving the terrible pain they shared. In addition, Lucy felt guilt and shame for allowing the outcome that changed her life.

They had only talked about it a few times in the past twenty years, once on a weekend get-away where they'd sat on a dock on the lake and cried all afternoon. The other was during an afternoon at the beach, but Lucy ended the discussion after only a couple of minutes–she just couldn't cope.

CHAPTER 2

Now, things were different and happening fast: she needed to go to Europe, in case her son needed her. Yet, she might not be a suitable candidate to help, until she completed a series of medical tests. So why stir up a bunch of emotions for nothing with Joanne? However, she still needed to hedge her bet. Either way, she wanted to go to Europe. And if it turned out to be just a vacation, so much the better. Lucy looked sideways at Joanne, sipping her latte. "You know what, Jo? We should go back."

"Where?" said Joanne. "Europe?"

Lucy nodded. "Just us."

Joanne raised one eyebrow. "With all our family commitments? Not going to happen."

"Not with that attitude," said Lucy with an edge before she could catch herself. Joanne was always the sensible one to crazy Lucy–and mostly that was good. But just once, she wished Joanne would ignore the caution button. She was springing an idea on Joanne that sounded far-fetched given all their commitments. Yet somehow it had to work. "At least consider it before you say no."

Joanne sat up. "Sorry, I was too fast to find fault with your idea. How long were you thinking for the trip? Not three months like last time, I hope!"

Lucy had piqued her interest, so she had to play this exactly right. "No, more like three weeks and a few cities like London, Paris, Amsterdam or Barcelona. But we'd fly instead of night trains," laughed Lucy.

Joanne paused. "Now that you mention it. Could be a cool trip."

"Tell you what. I'll even sweeten the deal," said Lucy. "We can use my travel points for the flights over and back." Lucy saw Joanne's eyebrows raise slightly.

"Are you sure? Those flights will be pricey," said Joanne.

"I just got notice that unused points will expire by next year, which is very annoying. We have thousands. And Dave's idea of a long-haul trip is a four-hour drive to Prince Edward Island for a weekend. The man doesn't do vacations."

"That's generous, Lu. Could I think about it some more?"

"Sure," said Lucy. She could tell things were turning in Jo's head. "No pressure, Jo, but let's keep thinking about it, okay?" Lucy saw Joanne nod and felt it was a perfect time to wrap up. They gathered their cups and bags and deposited them into the bins. "I have to deliver these biscuits to Maggie. So glad to bump into you. Talk soon." They hugged for a moment.

Lucy picked up her bag. She was annoyed with herself for not raising the situation with Max, but she didn't have time to get into the complexities of it all. It would be a long, heavy conversation. Plus, it was a deep emotional strain for her to even talk about it.

"Hey," said Joanne, her hands on her hips and her eyes stern. "What about our shopping?"

She knew Joanne's chiding was a shared joke, because Lucy had a habit of not following through on what she committed to do. "I'll call you Jo," she said, blowing a kiss to her friend. She saw Joanne shake her head and turn back to her shopping, while Lucy made a beeline for the exit.

Chapter 3

Joanne

She cranked the volume and smiled as the song filled her body with driving rhythms. Joanne bustled around the living room, singing along when she could remember the words. She tidied in bursts, with little attention paid to her dusting. After bumping into Lucy at the Farmers' Market a week earlier, her thoughts had returned to European travel. Lucy had that effect on people. She attracted them by serving up spontaneous and memorable experiences. Everybody wanted to be part of her whirling wave of energy. In a way, it was typical for Lucy to disappear out of her life for chunks of time. Yet when they got back together, they picked up where they left off as if they had seen each other just the other day.

The two established their buddy relationship early in childhood, even though Joanne's parents warned her about Lucy's free-wheeling behavior. On a lazy summer's day while Joanne lounged in a hammock reading a book, Lucy would arrive out of nowhere with exciting ideas and plunge them headlong into hair-raising adventures.

Unable to resist, she would fasten her seatbelt for the ride because she could never dream up such fun. And when trouble appeared, as it always did, Joanne slipped into her role as the responsible one. By sounding sensible and articulate with outraged neighbors, she pulled them out of endless scrapes. Lucy anointed her the "designated adult" at a young age.

Joanne was waiting for the perfect moment to raise the idea of traveling to Europe with her family. While she liked the idea of going on a trip, she wanted to make sure it didn't disrupt her family life. In fact, she couldn't remember the last time she went somewhere on her own, except for a few weekend workshops.

First, she thought about telling Gretchen. If she were having a bad day with her anorexia and health issues, they would discuss nothing. Her husband Peter had become depressed and withdrawn as he tried to cope with his daughter's illness. Worse, he didn't like change, so he wouldn't like her traveling for a few weeks while he stayed with Gretchen. The problem was obvious: he didn't have the emotional capacity to deal with a condition that rarely showed signs of improvement. Her daughter Emmaleigh would offer to stay in a heartbeat, but she was a young adult now on her own who was juggling many community projects. It didn't seem fair to ask. Everything felt messy. She'd let a week slide with no action.

Beyond her household, there was also her father to consider. He wasn't faring well on his own. If she asked her brother Jake to be the caregiver for three weeks, she pictured him fussing and complaining as if doing her the biggest favor ever (while she did it the other forty-nine weeks of the year). In the past, he'd agree and then forget to drop by. Their father refused to move into assisted living, and Jake sided with him, leaving Joanne with the caregiver responsibility.

CHAPTER 3

She believed their joint refusal to address the growing problem lay in the unstated belief that he'd pass on before it got too bad. Meanwhile, Joanne was arriving at her father's place to find the kettle boiled dry on the stove and a tub of melted ice cream in the cupboard.

Joanne wondered if she should forget Europe and focus on her family's needs. Yet she wanted to go, and she needed a break from her life. Lucy did these things without suffering any guilt. Why couldn't she be more like her friend in these situations?

Lucy had been in touch on and off all week, texting digital photos of great pubs and cafés in Europe as an enticement. They agreed to meet up for another chat on Saturday after lunch at Lucy's place. Joanne knew that when Lucy was on a mission, she didn't let things linger. She knew it would disappoint Lucy that she hadn't finalized plans, but she would have to deal with it–Joanne needed to do it her way.

***

She ate lunch and got ready to go over to Lucy's. As she prepared to leave, she stood at the bottom of the stairs as she usually did when heading out of the house. "Gretchen, honey?" she called in her gentlest tone to her daughter, who spent a lot of time in her room. She waited for her voice, but only heard the grandfather clock pendulum lumbering back and forth on the landing. While no response was common, she hesitated to keep shouting in case she was asleep.

Joanne inched up the stairs and glanced into her room. Her daughter lay on her bed, an exposed leg dangling over the side that resembled a long twig about to snap. Whenever they ran errands, Gretchen wore cut-off denim shorts, revealing legs like two pale straws with hinges at the knees. Passersby stared at the pair because Joanne was double the circumference of her daughter. She sensed their judgment as if to ask, "How could you let your daughter get to that point?" To which she wanted to reply, "I wish I knew."

It wasn't from lack of trying. Joanne had set up appointments with three different health professionals for Gretchen, and she found reasons to reject them, even though they were all amazing and helpful. In frustration, she told Gretchen she had to see someone, but she was welcome to find one of her own. Gretchen finally agreed to a woman from the earlier sessions, but often cancelled her appointments or didn't show up when she didn't feel like going. For Joanne, life was one step forward, two back.

She tilted her head sideways and smiled at the inert horizontal body staring into space. "Gretchen, honey?"

Gretchen looked at her and said nothing. Joanne was used to these exchanges, but they still unnerved her. "You okay?"

"Uh huh."

Joanne turned around to leave and glanced back. "It's a sunny day out there. Want to cycle to Lucy's with me? There's an amazing view of the harbor from the bridge."

"I'm good," said Gretchen, resuming her all-encompassing task of gazing at the ceiling.

Joanne dreamed of convincing her daughter to go out into the world again but wanted to avoid a scene. Whenever she asked her a sensitive question, a twisted pain burrowed through her chest, like a screw turned so far into a piece of wood it emerged on the other side.

"I'll be back before dinner," she called out. Some days she wanted to shake Gretchen and tell her to buck up and get on with life, but mostly she dreamed of holding her until her mysterious affliction went away. How did this terrible situation start, and when would it end? Did she do something that caused her daughter to become anorexic? Joanne felt responsible for the entire situation but couldn't figure out how it got this way.

Patience and unconditional love, she learned, was the most effective way to help. Yet progress was slow, and tiny signs of hope were quashed by giant steps backward. Every time she felt discouraged, she reminded herself to hang in there and be strong. "There's fruit salad in the fridge if you get hungry," she said, grasping for ideas of what might appeal to her.

"Fat chance," said Gretchen.

Joanne chuckled as she headed downstairs, wondering if her daughter's dark humor might be a sign of feeling better. Buoyed by her tiny gesture, Joanne smiled as she headed out the door and got on her bike.

She pulled up in front of Lucy's home in the West End–which they called the "Euro Zone." Six streets gathered in a cluster: Berlin, Edinburgh, London, Liverpool, Cork and Vienna. Summit and Seaforth interrupted the theme–which she nicknamed the latter street "Seafroth", to make it sound bubbly.

A British fortress city settled nearly three hundred years ago, thousands of mature trees lined Halifax's streets. Joanne loved the "city of trees" as it was sometimes called, its spacious streets adorned with maple, oak and beech trees and their shimmering emerald leaves. They stood tall and majestic with long branches leaning in to form a cathedral at the top, offering a canopy of shade in the summer sun. Lucy's mid-century home, with its crewcut lawn and flagstone walkway surrounded by orange day lilies, resembled a vintage house from a 1950s Sears catalog.

She stood outside for a moment looking at Lucy's place and wondered if this European trip was just a crazy idea. While she had vacation time available and money wasn't an issue, the timing sucked. Gretchen's issues flared up suddenly, usually at the end of the week or the weekend, which meant trips to emergency when the doctor wasn't around. This created tension between her and Peter, and she didn't need more of that by announcing a trip that would take her away from Gretchen. Certainly a break would help her rejuvenate.

Yet there were other concerns. For someone suggesting a spontaneous European vacation, Lucy seemed to have specific dates in mind. A tiny voice in the back of Joanne's head reminded her Lucy was notorious for tacking on additional activities, throwing plans into chaos. Even Lucy's offer to use her travel points rattled her. While Lucy was beyond generous, and it was entirely characteristic of her to offer her something like that, Joanne worried about the logistics. Would Lucy even remember to book the flights? That was usually Joanne's job.

Should she confront Lucy right away? While Joanne loved the thought of traveling, she also knew that once she said yes to Lucy, the plan would gather momentum like a tidal wave preparing to wash ashore and the only hope would be to run like stink toward higher ground.

Chapter 4

Lucy

The dog barked and raced up the side of the sofa to his look-off spot out the window, which told Lucy somebody was at the door. She walked through the hallway and swung the front door open during an eight-part doorbell ring that sounded utterly pretentious for a modest home in Halifax.

"Thought I was at Downton Abbey for a second," said Joanne, stepping inside.

"It's amazing what you stop noticing once you move into a place."

The cat and dog raced to the door in competition for Joanne's heels. "Bugger off, Pepper," Lucy ordered as he climbed over the cat to reach Joanne's feet. She tried to move Pepper away, but he ignored her pleas when guests arrived–the porch was his territory. As Joanne kicked off her sandals, the dog licked her toes.

"It's time for a shower when a dog is partial to the smell of your feet," joked Lucy, trying to make light of her pet's poor manners.

Joanne laughed. "I swam in the ocean earlier today, so he

was smelling salt. They say a dog's sense of smell is fifty times greater than a human's."

Lucy snapped her fingers to get Pepper under control. "So, why are they attracted to peoples' feet? Shouldn't they run in the other direction?"

"Another of life's mysteries, along with bathing suits labeled two sizes smaller than our clothes. When you finally squeeze into one, you can barely walk, and your compressed torso resembles one of those wrestler suits." Joanne looked around taking in the interior. "Fine improvements here, Lu," she said.

"You haven't seen the renos?" Lucy realized that could only mean one thing: she hadn't been exactly hospitable to Joanne in the past few years.

"Last time I dropped you off, I didn't come in."

"How rude of me," said Lucy.

"Nah. It was late, and you were bubbly," added Joanne.

This was Joanne's code for Lucy having a few too many glasses of wine. Lucy waved her in. "That means you haven't seen our mini-renos from last summer. Anyway, as you know, this was the living room, and we knocked out a wall. Being married to a sound man results in a large stereo with amps and speakers everywhere that want to rock-and-roll."

"How is Dave these days?" said Joanne.

"Let's see… he is either working… or working. I'm joking, he's great," Lucy said smiling as she thought about Dave. They were super busy with jobs and life, but still got along well, even though they sometimes communicated by notes on the counter and texts. Flare-ups erupted, followed by a few days of arguing about who was right or wrong, but life went on.

Lucy described their marriage and child-rearing as free range–everybody did their own thing and when they got together as a family of four, they focused on the moment and had fun. It worked for her. Sometimes she envied Joanne's calm family, where nothing erupted. And yet… her daughter developed anorexia, while Lucy's kids were doing great. She wondered how she got so lucky. "Check this out," said Lucy heading out of the kitchen and dining area.

Joanne followed as she guided them through each room, chatting non-stop, then she continued toward the back of the house. The glass walls on two sides revealed an outdoor flower garden in full bloom that had never received the touch of Lucy's hands. She was infamous for ignoring houseplants and then wondering why they died.

"This is my new and improved office," said Lucy, swinging her arms wide, as if hosting a TV makeover show. The afternoon sun beamed through the skylight, tinting the room a deep goldenrod.

She noted Joanne's eye locked on the large painting behind Lucy's desk, with vibrant orange and yellow sunflowers swaying in the afternoon sun.

"You still have that?" Joanne said.

"Uh huh," said Lucy.

"Really? How come?"

Lucy raised one eyebrow. She wondered why Joanne was even asking about it. But then again, she hadn't seen it in a long time, and it took up a large space on the living room wall in the apartment they shared in Montreal.

Joanne returned her gaze to the sunflowers. "Doesn't it remind you of…?"

"Not too much."

"That's an interesting way of *not* putting it," said Joanne.

Lucy studied the painting, taking in the breadth and depth of it. She remembered Jacques arriving in Montreal as a visiting professor and how he had noticed her at his lectures (well, maybe she peppered him with questions afterwards).

In no time, they were arguing over legal topics at a café, which morphed into a weekend at her apartment. Over a glass of wine, he suggested creating a special painting to remember the weekend. They picked up the canvas and paint supplies around the corner, plus some booze. They were set.

She shivered inside–no man had ever made her feel that way before. First, he was thirty-two to her twenty, which made her feel more mature. Up to that point, most encounters were with university guys after playing caps at someone's apartment. Romance was not part of the scenario; rather, it was fueled by drunken hormones.

Jacques was different; he was sophisticated and confident. He romanced her in slow motion, because, as he said, kissing her forehead, "there is no rush". She clung to every syllable as he explained he had been painting sunflowers at his family's estate in France all his life.

It took them the entire weekend to finish the painting and he smoothed over her flowers to make them perfect, leaving her with a stunning painting and a reminder of their fateful weekend. Little did they know that there would be a much bigger reminder of their only encounter together, now coming back into her life.

Lucy noticed Joanne waiting for a response. She had zoned out thinking about the painting. She didn't want to admit how much that canvas reminded her of a special time, even though Jacques eventually made her life hell. "Isn't it funny how you can have a large painting staring right at you for years and you forget it's there?" Lucy asked, trying to de-emphasize its importance. "It's from another time and place. I suppose I should get rid of it," she added.

"Funny, when people say they *should* do something, it means they don't really want to. Is that what you are trying to say, Lu?"

Lucy turned away from the painting. "Care for a glass of wine in the garden?" Relieved that Joanne gave her a shrug, Lucy led them back to the kitchen and hustled around the space, juggling wine, dips and glasses.

She handed Joanne items on a tray to carry to the garden. Once outside, Joanne gasped at the outdoor border laced with tiny flowers and ground cover. Behind them, bigger flowers lit up the garden. "Wow, here's a skyscraper lily. And these are friso lilies, check out the deep rose color."

"Translation please!" Lucy said. "I wish I had your talent. The gardens at your place look like a magazine spread."

"Thanks," said Joanne. "It's in our blood."

"True. Except your talent with flowers and gardens blew everyone else out of the water. Does your grumpy cousin still run the flower shop in Dartmouth?"

"Yep. Bev is running it into the ground as we speak–no pun intended."

"Not surprising," said Lucy, scooping a cracker full of dip and popping it into her mouth. "I stopped there a while ago. Tell her the 1970s called, they want their dyed blue carnations back."

"You know," mused Joanne. "I've got an idea about that shop…"

Lucy knew Joanne wanted to talk about that family flower shop in Dartmouth, but she could talk for a long time about the place she should have been running instead of her cousin.

Lucy didn't want to get side-tracked because they had things to sort out. "Here's to returning to our natural habitat–sitting outdoors with my bestie on a summer day sipping rosé." The hand-cut crystal glasses released a sweet tone as they touched. "That's way smoother than that Crackling Rosie crap we used to drink when we were underage."

Lucy pulled out an aging photo album. She hadn't looked at it in years, and Joanne had only seen the photos once. Lucy had promised to get reprints and hadn't gotten around to it. The pages had stuck together, and photos were being devoured by the clear acetate cover. She had to pry each page apart, which added to their screams of delight and horror as it revealed additional photos.

"Hello, 1980s! OMG is it you, or Madonna?"

Joanne stared at the photo, her eyes popping. "Jeez, I had more jewelry than Mr. T, and my hair looked like a squirrel's nest."

"I've got the cropped, netted top, layered with tanks and tees," groaned Lucy.

"Your attention-seeking midriff served us well."

"I wouldn't be doing that now," she laughed, patting a slight bulge around her tummy. "That photo was twenty pounds ago, or a thousand bottles of wine ago, to put it another way."

"How do you figure that?"

"Well, I've averaged several bottles a week since my twenties, that's a hundred per year, multiplied thirty years. Shit… that's more like three thousand bottles. Even worse!"

"Embarrassing, eh?" said Joanne.

"I should have practiced better girth control."

"Well, I think you look great for fifty, Lu."

"Spoken like a true girlfriend." Lucy took a drink and set

it down. The afternoon was flying by. "Hey, Jo, have you thought any more about Europe?"

"All week. You know, ever since you mentioned going there, I've been thinking how much fun it could be. I need a laugh right now."

"To get a break from Gretchen?" said Lucy.

"I wouldn't put it that way. But it has been a rough go for a couple of years."

"How's Emmaleigh? And what is she up to?"

"Her latest project is called Labor of Luv. Have you heard?"

Lucy shrugged. "Nope. Do tell!"

"It connects local people with skills, knowledge or money to those who don't have them. Let's say you need a carpenter to help fix things around your apartment but can't afford it. Somebody with those skills will volunteer a few hours of time."

Lucy could tell Joanne was so proud of her daughter, she could gush on about her for hours. "Emmaleigh is simply amazing," said Lucy. Then she thought about the other daughter. "No wonder Gretchen struggles."

"Em invites her to be part of everything," said Joanne. "We tried to celebrate Gretchen's talents, but she's always been—"

"Kind of angry, eh?" said Lucy. "Could it be birth order?"

Joanne smiled. "Seems like it was a red flag. Emmaleigh somersaulted from my womb like an angel in satin pajamas. Gretchen battled the delivery the whole time–heels dug in and arms flailing, as if she were trying to go back."

"Maybe she was, or—" Lucy winced.

"What?"

"That was a tough name to get. You've got Emmaleigh, a name that's all grace and poetry. Then Gretchen. How did you decide on that?"

"Do you remember Peter's mother, Gretchen?"

"Now *she* was a Gretchen," blurted Lucy. "Right from the old country, right? I remember her barking orders at your wedding and criticizing everybody's outfits for being too floozy."

"Anyway, as you may recall, she died a week before the baby was born. Peter was so distraught he insisted we call her Gretchen. What could I say?" Joanne paused. "I nicknamed her Greta when she was little. She said it was a stupid name."

Lucy could see it was a sore point for her. "Maybe, that's just who she is. She has to find her own way to happiness."

"I'd do anything to help her," said Joanne, a misty tone draping each word.

"I know. There's still hope; she's only eighteen." Lucy didn't want Joanne to feel bad and focus on the negative. She topped up her own wine glass, while Joanne guzzled water because she was cycling. In minutes, they were laughing at each photo, recalling memories about their first trip to Europe. Lucy opened a map of Europe on her laptop.

They discussed which places they'd like to visit again once they figured out how long they'd be away from work and family obligations. Lucy proposed London, Amsterdam and Paris, with sound reasons why they'd want to go there. Fortunately, she knew that Joanne loved those cities, so they sounded reasonable for both. She also suggested a wild card city, either Barcelona, Florence or Athens.

"Now I have to figure out how to tell people at home and at work that I'll be away for three weeks," said Joanne. "How do you do it?"

"I travel for work, so they are used to me being away." said

Lucy. "If I may offer some advice, assume it'll be okay, and it will be."

"I haven't been away from Gretchen for three years," said Joanne.

"And Peter?"

Joanne held the glass by the stem up to the sunlight, looking distracted. "Could be tricky. We are not in a good place. In fact, I'm worried we might not make it."

"Whaaaat? Since when?" Lucy took in a breath. "Is this about Gretchen?"

Joanne nodded. "Yeah, he's having a hard time dealing with her condition. He missed two appointments taking her to the doctor, and I had to leave work to get her there. His breaking point was going to emergency for the third time." Joanne stared off in the distance. "He apologizes each time, but now we're arguing over the stupidest things."

"Meanwhile, I'm sure you're carrying most of Gretchen's problems."

Joanne's sense of pain spread across her face. "Peter can't cope with any of it. He doesn't understand anorexia at all. Says it's like watching his daughter die in slow motion."

"Wow, that's huge, Jo. I'm really sorry. Doesn't seem fair to you, either. I'm sure you are just as freaked out, but you keep going somehow. What about some counseling for Gretchen, or your whole family?"

"Oh, sure. We've gone through four so far. Gretchen rejects them, one at a time. But I'll keep trying," Joanne said, nibbling on another cracker. "It's weird. One day you wake up beaming and declaring that life is going well, then the next day the house of cards falls."

"Story of my life, my friend," said Lucy. The door opened

and Maggie walked out to the garden, calling out a big hello. Joanne rushed over and hugged her, then held her at a distance. "You're… so grown up," said Joanne.

Lucy joined them and put her arm around Maggie, hugging her at the waist.

"How did your bake sale go?" Joanne asked Maggie. "I saw your mother picking up stuff at the Farmers' Market."

"Bake sale—?" said Maggie, glancing at her mother.

"Look, this woman has to get going," said Lucy. "Are you sure you are fine for cycling?" she asked Joanne. She had been a little too generous with the wine over the afternoon.

"I've been guzzling water for the past hour," said Joanne.

Lucy hadn't really noticed, but she was glad Joanne was smart enough to keep an eye on things. She watched Jo put on her helmet and pull out on the bike. She hoped her friend could swing the trip to Europe. If not, she was in deep trouble.

Chapter 5

Joanne

She decided to visit her cousin's flower shop in downtown Dartmouth. Her heart was full of hope and her mind busy with ideas about what she might do for the next phase of her career. Joanne stepped out of her hundred-year-old house at the top of Old Ferry Road, so steep and twisty, it would have been perfect for an Olympic bobsled trail, except that it emptied into the harbor.

Over the past few years, she'd been contemplating a change from her role as a senior HR professional, a thought that filled her with fear and excitement. Each time she started daydreaming about doing something different (although she wasn't sure what that was), she would immediately worry about leaving a well-paying profession with significant benefits.

Many people in Nova Scotia didn't have those luxuries, so she hesitated at the thought of explaining why she'd give up a good job and break free of the golden handcuffs as she knew them. And yet, that yearning for a more meaningful career would not go away.

One day, she had driven by a billboard that said: "What would you love to be doing?", followed by "Why aren't you doing it?" She pulled over to think about it because she felt as if it spoke directly to her, and it wanted an answer.

Since she worked in HR, she followed her own advice and spent time thinking about what she'd love to do. After completing multiple career and soul-searching exercises, she laughed when the results came back: she had a passion for flowers. Not just selling flowers but creating beauty and harmony for others through flowers. Wasn't that curious? Right back to square one: the family business that she had helped with as a kid.

She floated the idea with her cousin Bev who had inherited the family flower shop, and hated every second of it, and expressed no interest in her ideas. Meanwhile, Gretchen's condition became the priority. Yet Joanne still thought about it. So, on a rare day off during the week, she visited the flower shop to see what was up.

She followed the harborside trail to view the skyline across the water. The morning sun ricocheted honey light from one glass tower to the next, and water diamonds sparkled on top of the waves. By early daylight, the harbor bustled with a daily parade of sailboats, cruise ships and fishing boats. The morning commuter ferry chugged back and forth between the two downtown areas.

Dartmouth was morphing into a lively business and residential destination, and Joanne pictured being part of it. Five years earlier, tattoo parlors and bars dominated the area, with barely a handful of customers. Decrepit drinking establishments on their last legs served withering ghosts from the past who had nowhere else to go during the day. Most taverns looked the same: an empty cave full of carved up tables and chairs wobbly from too many fights, and old carpets peppered with cigarette burns. Ashes, and last night's beer felt like squishy moss to walk on.

Then things changed. A few entrepreneurs with big dreams of shops and restaurants swapped places with tattoo shops. Enthusiasm fueled the first wave. New buildings followed, including a series of condos resembling a tall sailing ship, moored patiently in the harbor as if ready to set sail with the next southerly wind.

Joanne hadn't visited her first cousin Bev for several months and was keen to discuss taking over Henderson's Flowers, the family shop started by their grandfather. Joanne was born to the youngest of three Henderson brothers, William, who adored flowers, but was too low in the family tree to inherit the business.

Bev's father, Charles, was the oldest. He grew up helping in the family shop or taking orders as he described it. In his teens, he realized he was being groomed to take over the business. The only thing he detested more than roses was customers. He dreamed of heading off to sea, and it reminded him of where he'd rather be whenever he glanced out the shop window to the harbor. He resented working with his father, who ran a tight ship on land. Charles called it the "arranged business marriage" dictated by his formidable father. Even though it was clear the youngest was the child best suited to the flower business, his father would not budge.

Since the shop was a little gold mine, Charles didn't dare give it up. As soon as his father died, he asked his daughter Bev to take over. The tradition continued with the wrong person in the wheelhouse.

Joanne had grown up hanging around the family shop, pitching in during Christmas and busy seasons. She developed a knack for creating beautiful arrangements and loved seeing customers' reactions. Soon they were requesting her bouquets, and Joanne asked if she could work there when she finished school. Uncle Charles refused; he wanted to keep the money in his part of the family.

When Bev took over with the same lack of enthusiasm, her philosophy was simple: those who entered her shop could take it or leave it. Ditto for employees. Bev avoided investing in the business and modernizing the interior. Street traffic reduced to a trickle, except for last-minute shoppers and a few older residents who remained loyal to the family.

That morning, Joanne had big ideas as she arrived at Henderson's Flowers. Everything looked tired and dowdy, including the original neon sign that had burnt out most letters except for 'ow' in the word flowers.

Maybe this time Bev would consider a change. She tried the door. It was locked and there was no sign of life. Joanne stepped into the Seaside Café, the space next door. She sang out to her friend Holly, her voice joining in with the sea glass mobile jingling as the door opened. Holly was a good friend from high school who had operated a café next to Henderson's Flowers for a decade.

A sturdy woman, Holly always looked fresh, even when she worked ten-hour days. At work, her brown hair was always in a ponytail, wrapped with a scrunchie. Priding herself as a multi-tasker, she hurried through the café filling coffee cups, fetching muffins and chatting with customers.

"Hey, Jo. Looking for Bev?"

Joanne nodded. "Did she open yet this morning?"

CHAPTER 5

Holly shrugged. "Let's just say her advertised hours differ from her actual hours."

"What do her customers say?"

"What customers?"

Holly and Joanne filled coffee cups and sat at a corner table, while the hubbub continued. They shared news and concern for Bev, who had worked next door to Holly since the restaurant opened. She decorated the walls with paintings of the ocean by local artists, and jars filled with colored glass lined up in rows on the window to catch the light. "You've got this place looking nice," Joanne said, surveying the interior.

"Funny, I was thinking it might be a time for a change. After ten years, I need a refresh for my clients." said Holly.

"Such as?"

"I'd like a plant-based café with healthy meals and smaller portions. The only way I can make a'go of it is to expand the restaurant. But that means taking over space Bev uses. She talks about closing her shop but I don't think she's ready."

Joanne sipped her coffee and gathered her courage. Ideas pulsed and her heart pounded. "Know what'd be cool? Knock down the wall of Bev's shop and combine it with your existing space to create a refreshed flower boutique and café."

"With Bev?" Holly said, nearly choking on her coffee.

"No. I'm just in blue-sky mode. Assume she's out of the picture."

"In that case, continue."

"What about combining a health food café and a new style of flower and events space? A posy of fresh flowers on each table. Over here, we'd sell bouquets, arrangements, potted herbs and seasonal wreaths. In the restaurant, we could host talks on flowers, planting and seasonal tips."

"How about painting and drawing lessons? And then exhibit and sell the local paintings on the wall," added Holly.

"Brilliant idea," said Joanne. "Picture the outdoor café sign with botanical tulips or other flowers."

"Amazing. What would we call…?"

Bev trudged in, rattling the tinkling bell hanging on the doorjamb, making it sound angry. Her dour green outfit summed up her state of mind. Joanne looked at her cousin, who was close to her age, early fifties, though she looked much older. Her face drew downward, as if gravity had sculpted years of scowling.

She felt sorry for her cousin, who didn't seem happy but chose not to do anything about it. Joanne wished she could help, but also knew that Bev had to make the change, not her.

Holly and Joanne exchanged glances. Joanne blushed, even though they were doing nothing wrong. "We were brainstorming ideas for refreshing these two shops," Joanne said, smiling. She nodded at Holly and Bev, hoping for a positive reception.

"Why would you do that?"

"How about attracting new clients?" said Holly.

"I don't want any," said Bev. She helped herself to the gourmet coffee, loaded it with cream and sugar, and mumbled for Holly to put it on the tab. She slammed the door behind her.

"Wow, it's hard enough to make a go of it when you have loyal clients. I can't imagine how long she can hang in there," said Holly.

Joanne shrugged. "No kidding." She paused and looked at Holly. "I said I was dreaming, but I'm kind of excited. Do you want to keep talking in the future?"

CHAPTER 5

"As long as Miss Morose isn't involved."

"I'll talk to her. Maybe she'll reconsider selling," said Joanne on her way out the door. She figured there was no good time to engage with Bev, so she might as well try now. As she entered Henderson's and said hello to Bev, she looked around the shop. The air hung with a muggy mist and the glassed-in cabinet was fogged up, preventing clients from seeing what they cared about most: flowers. One wall featured an array of cheap basket arrangements with artificial flowers, garden frogs holding balloons, and gnomes with long pointy hats coated in dust. She smiled at Bev as she walked up to the old brown counter with worn-out patches near the cash register.

"What?" said Bev.

Joanne knew her cousin had little interest in keeping in touch. "How's work?"

"Same," shrugged Bev. Joanne wanted to poke her in the eye for filling every room with gloom. She tried another tack. "Well, I'm considering a different career."

"At your age? Better get a move on."

Joanne shot her a look. "If I can reduce my work week to three days, I'd love to work here."

Bev scoffed. "You mean, I pay you?"

"You know I've always loved flowers," she said, ignoring her question.

"I'll give you that. Aside from Granddad, you were the only one who cared about them."

"I still am, if it could lead somewhere."

"You want to own my damn shop, don't you?" Bev barked.

Joanne switched to her professional mode. "Maybe you could do something different. Something you love."

"Look, Joanne, you sniff around here now and then, hinting

about buying. I can't give it away; it's worth a fortune." Bev's ears glowed like red embers. "I'm not selling right now."

Joanne knew that was enough for one day. "I have to jet," she said, picking up a bouquet and placing a twenty-dollar bill on the counter. Bev raked the bill without a word. Joanne noted the selection that she called the Bev Special: a couple of shriveling roses, puffed up with carnations and baby's breath.

"See ya," Joanne said, smiling at her cousin. Maybe she wasn't selling now, but there was always the future. Joanne needed patience, and that was enough encouragement to continue with her dream.

She poked her head into the restaurant. Holly was busy serving, so Joanne gave her a sideway thumbs up, meaning that it may have gone well, but maybe not. They both laughed. "For a name, how about 'Botanica Café'?"

"Love it. Love it. Love it," said Holly, as she placed the plates in front of her customers.

"Talk soon." Joanne closed the door and headed home, mulling over what had unfolded. She thought about her life. When she had time, she spent hours poring through design magazines and online sites for inspiration, to the point where she could picture the shop in her head, right down to fine details.

The flower shop musings could go on for hours on a Sunday afternoon, until family issues flared up, such as her father's health or Gretchen's problems. Immediately, she would park her dreams.

Meanwhile, life was racing by. One minute it was spring, and she was setting up lawn furniture, then she was Christmas shopping. While she liked her HR career, there were no fresh surprises. Yet each time she thought about buying the shop,

CHAPTER 5

her nerves jangled. How much money would she need? What if her new venture failed? What would friends think? She carried a long list of "what ifs" in her head that blocked her from taking action.

On the home front, if she could get Gretchen to sit up and eat properly again, she'd be relieved. Lately, she had noticed Gretchen going out for the odd hour or two, saying she was helping Emmaleigh. Joanne wasn't sure if it was true but took her at her word to avoid triggering an argument. At least Gretchen was getting out of the house.

She walked home at a carefree pace, allowing her thoughts to flow. While Bev showed little interest in changing her situation, Joanne decided she could only achieve something by taking little steps. Holly owned a successful café, and they'd known each other since high school. A whiff of optimism bubbled up as she considered possibilities–even if the plans were preliminary.

Meanwhile, she thought about the European trip with Lucy and felt a surge of excitement. Where would they go: London, Paris or Amsterdam?

Joanne was most excited about Amsterdam because she had read about a new Van Gogh exhibition. Lucy would have a long list of wants. In addition, Lucy would attract intriguing characters and situations along the way. Joanne was too introverted, and she secretly admired Lucy's ability to create fun moments out of nothing. She had to admit, Lucy was behind their most fun and memorable moments in life, especially with traveling.

Before getting too excited, her thoughts landed with a thud as she faced a reality check. She had bigger concerns, starting with telling Gretchen and her family about her travel plans.

Chapter 6

Max

Gazing out the apartment window in the eighth *arrondissement*, his favorite neighborhood in the city, Max Morin watched a gentle mist settle on the streets of Paris. He returned to his laptop and pressed publish, then sipped his mug of green tea.

After learning he needed a new kidney and several years of dialysis treatments to keep him alive, he launched a blog, *Desperately Seeking Kidney*. His goal was simple: to locate a donor.

When his medical troubles began, he did not understand how many people had the condition. Through research, he learned there was a waiting list of 16,000 people in France. He despaired to think about how many years it would take to receive a kidney with thousands ahead of him.

Worse, people waiting for a transplant lacked a central place to gather for information about transplant updates. To help others in the same situation, he tracked his odyssey through a blog, documenting the highs and lows. He was frightened to think he might die during the process, but the urge to tell the story overrode his "what if?" fears.

He posted in English and French, his profile expanding daily with thousands of followers, including transplant hopefuls, families, and healthcare specialists. The blog informed people at various stages of a chronic kidney condition, and he wrote the truth, even when he knew the news wasn't good.

As he skimmed the comments, he couldn't believe what people were going through and sometimes felt overwhelmed. How could he help everyone who needed it? Certain people waiting for a transplant fared well, others hung on with slim hope, and many died before receiving one.

He felt the pain of losing another member of their community every time he read their story. Doctors sometimes wrote sharp comments below his blogs, but he didn't care–this was his truth. He decided no matter how difficult it was to run the blog, he couldn't give up. He knew that with his growing knowledge and storytelling abilities, his blog could serve as a touchstone for people trying to inform themselves about kidney disease. While he felt squeezed for time with his work as an architect, his home life and medical condition, he parlayed his public role as a blogger to raise awareness about the grim situation.

**

Max descended the steps and climbed into the car idling at the curb. He felt like each appointment was a replica of the last one, yet he maintained a positive outlook during the session, even though his nephrologist only offered the tiniest hope of receiving a kidney in the short term. Experimental drugs surfaced without consistent results–yet they pursued any possibility. Max visualized being released from the tether of weekly dialysis and refused to quit until it happened.

His mother, Elise Vincent Morin, stepped up first to offer a kidney but was neither a blood nor a tissue match. Max knew there were no guarantees with any potential donors. He was disappointed, but he spent more time trying to comfort her.

She vowed to find a live donor and applied herself to the task with her trademark doggedness. It amazed Max to watch her create a family tree and contact relatives. He had overheard a few conversations while visiting her, listening as she described her connection to them and her son's medical situation before launching into her unusual ask.

Elise offered potential donors the finest medical team at a luxurious private clinic. Max knew that when she called Jacques' family, there would be a universal dislike for her late husband as Jacques had avoided contact with most relatives. Only three in Jacques' family considered it. None was a match.

For Max and his wife Katarin, the wait for a kidney from a stranger dominated their lives as the disease worsened. He believed in following a strict health regimen. He ate organic food, exercised, slept well and reduced unhealthy habits. As his doctor observed, "What a shame. You are otherwise such a healthy young man for having a serious kidney condition."

While Max considered himself fortunate to have access to regular dialysis, every second day of treatment repeated like an endless loop.

He understood it was a short to medium-term solution, with dying a grim possibility on the horizon. Many people on the waiting list died before receiving a kidney. With updates on the blog, the shock of each person's passing grew to the point he could barely manage the volume of sorrow. Gradually he accepted the weekly tally with a shrug of sadness and defeat.

At home, he and Katarin organized their lives around the

possibility of a sudden transplant opportunity. If a person died and was an organ donor, the medical team needed to mobilize Max in minutes. Max knew the importance of keeping a packed suitcase and driving the quickest route possible to the clinic. His heart pounded whenever he saw particular phone numbers on his cell.

He'd answer within a single ring, adrenaline surging through his system, even though he knew chances were miniscule. He realized that staying optimistic served him best, yet a call from the clinic would remind him that someone died. Maybe it was a young person in a car accident, a suicide or long-term illness, he wouldn't know why. The thought rattled him: while he and his family would celebrate a new lease on life, the donor's loved ones would grieve.

He tried to convince himself, if the person was dead, he might as well have the organ. However, he couldn't shake the image of a mourning family. As he thought about it, he realized he was getting way ahead of himself so why fret about these things? The transplant world was a never-ending carousel of wins and losses.

***

Max spotted his mother's Jaguar XJ waiting outside his apartment. The tinted windows shielded the passengers from the glare of impatient drivers, honking as they swung around a car straddling the curb and street. He surveyed the black pearl exterior that remained pristine–not a single scratch in sight–a near-statistical impossibility for vehicles in Paris. Max figured Pierre was either the most talented chauffeur ever, or his mother swapped the car for a fresh one after any minor dent. Knowing Elise, it was likely the latter.

Max climbed into the rear seat and smiled at his mother,

who mimed an air kiss while talking on the phone. He knew the drill: work called her away often. He settled in and checked his cell for messages as Pierre sped along the back streets for the appointment across town.

Slim, elegant and self-confident, Elise represented Parisian women of a certain age who pulled off the look with ease. She wore a tailored linen suit with every thread accounted for, accented with designer gloves and handbag–everything a fashion triumph. Her crowning glory was shiny, chestnut hair coaxed into a style of careful insouciance.

After wrapping up the phone conversation, they chatted, catching up on news. When the cell rang again, she checked the display and apologized to Max, saying she needed to take the call.

Max knew she needed to take every call. Before he responded, she squeezed his hand and spoke with someone at the family vineyard. Max could never quite comprehend the extent of her abilities, juggling multiple tasks and making calculated business decisions with her patented shrug, while still canvassing the world for a kidney for her son.

The car pulled up in front of the specialist's office that had become a familiar destination over the past two years. Elise wrapped up the call and tossed the cell into her handbag. "We'll find a donor for you. I promise." She repeated the mantra every time they visited the specialist. Max believed that if anybody could deliver on that promise, it was his mother.

He kissed her on the cheek, nodded and climbed out of the car.

Chapter 7

Lucy

She climbed the stairs to Strange Brew, a pint-sized pub off Agricola Street. There were kitchen parties in Nova Scotia that held more people. Yet what they lacked in seating, the crowd made up for in conversational din.

Lucy strolled outdoors to the deck and picked a table for two. It was a perfect neighborhood microbrewery on a warm summer evening. Brittany, the server, placed a glass of Raspberry Wheat beer on the coaster and Lucy watched condensation beads trickling down the side.

She thought about the European trip and the double duty it needed to serve. First, there was the fun part–she and Joanne revisiting the past and hanging out together, like old times. And then there was the "medical excursion" that she needed to take for her son Max. It was a big one and it would shift the entire focus of the vacation, once that part of the agenda kicked in. Should she tell Joanne about the whole thing, or wait until they were in Europe? What if the whole kidney thing fell through and she had pulled Joanne into the mess for nothing? Maybe they could have some travel fun for the first ten days and then switch over to the operation.

Lucy figured she could pull the whole thing off without missing a beat. But would Joanne support all of this, or would she back out if she knew the entire story? Was it fair to Joanne? She had been Lucy's best friend since childhood, but Lucy knew she was pushing boundaries. Also, she could tell Joanne needed a break from the stress in her life, and maybe it was unfair of Lucy to deny her a full vacation.

Five minutes later, Joanne arrived on the deck, hugging Lucy and sliding into a chair in a single swoop. Brittany brought a menu for Joanne and went off to get her a beer.

"Your eyes look like puff pastries," said Joanne.

"Thanks. I'm on a run of bad sleep."

"That island dream again?"

Lucy nodded.

"With the insistent rowers and the unidentified parcel?"

"Uh huh."

Joanne shook her head. "That's been going on for years, eh?"

"Not as often, only every year or so." Lucy knew exactly why it was flaring up again. Whenever life become complicated and stressful, the dream came back. It was something she had learned to endure. She stacked the menus. "Enough about that. Hungry?"

"Are you eating?"

Lucy nodded. "My custom order."

"What?"

"Veggie burger, with bacon and cheese."

Joanne grinned. "Taunting vegans, are you?"

"One of my many talents."

Brittany arrived with the drink, joining the conversation

about the burger. "Lucy started something with that dish. Others are now asking for it. We need a name."

"How about the Paradox Burger?" said Lucy.

She giggled, turning her attention to Joanne. "What can I get you?"

"I'll have the chicken and avocado salad. Hey, Lu, can I have some of your fries?"

"Right. Make me order crap while you eat your health food. You know, way off in the distant future, you'll be embarrassed to find yourself in the hospital dying of nothing."

"I'll take that as a yes."

Lucy sipped the frothy head on her beer. "Any updates?"

"I told my family," said Joanne, beaming. "I got everybody's support for the trip!"

It amazed Lucy that even though Joanne was in her fifties, she still wanted approval from every member of the family. Lucy announced things and then waited to see if anybody was bothered and dealt with it when necessary. "Great. How did you manage that?" said Lucy, doing her best to respect their differences in approach.

"Emmaleigh offered to come back home and help Peter. Gretchen grumbled, but I think she sees how important it is to me. She'll be fine with Em."

"And work?"

"I have tons of vacation and a team that can run things without me. Boss wasn't thrilled with my taking three weeks off, but we're good."

"What about your Dad?" said Lucy.

"Well, Jake 'agreed' to look after him," she said, adding air quotes.

"Maybe it'll be good for them; they usually wait for you to

mop up the messes. Does Jake spend much time with him?"

"Very little and hopes I don't notice. Wait until he finds out how cranky Dad is on a day-to-day basis," said Joanne. "I rate my visits on the PMT scale."

"Which is?"

"The Plus or Minus Tally. One day I visit Dad and he's not complaining, pleasant even. That's on the Plus side. The next time, there's a cereal bag on the floor with rice puffs scattered everywhere. Then he's cursing mad and things go downhill from there. That's the Minus day," said Joanne.

"I hear you. When I take Ma to a medical appointment, she's nasty until we get to the clinic, then pours on the Irish lilt and acts sweet. The staff gush about how lovely she is. Heading home, it's a grump fest."

Joanne nodded. "Then, there's the 'revisionist travelogue'. Last year, Dad and I went on a cruise. The whole time, he complained about the food, the room and the activities. Said there was nothing to do."

"On a cruise ship?" said Lucy.

"He refused to start a conversation with people, then called them snobby. Thinks everyone should beg him to join in the fun, forgetting that they too are feeling shy. When they don't, he's peeved. Six months later, he tells everyone he had a grand old time. What's with that?"

"Beats me."

"And you? Any concerns in your family?"

"Nah. Maggie's busy at university. Riley is managing his career from the basement, and David has his business. They're used to me traveling."

"What about work?"

Lucy dismissed it with a hand wave. "Everything will be fine.

CHAPTER 7

I promised to check my email, in case something is brewing back home. Mostly, it's a non-profit that's ticking along." Lucy wondered if this was the time to expand on the additional angle of the trip and just get it out into the open with her friend.

"What?" said Joanne. "You drifted off into another world for a minute. What's on your mind?"

Lucy opened her mouth and paused. No, she wasn't ready. "Nothing, I was just thinking about all the details, the people and the office cooperation needed to pull off a simple three-week vacation."

Lucy knew it was going to be a far from simple vacation, but she didn't want to spoil the moment. "Remember how we barely planned our first trip to Europe then stayed for two months? Too bad we couldn't climb in a time machine and make it simple again."

"So…. are we doing this?" asked Joanne, lifting her glass.

Chapter 8

Lucy

The McGee family household: Now that was a weekly chore ranking low on Lucy's list of must-dos. She took the long route to her parents' place to delay a conversation that should have happened decades ago. She tensed up whenever she visited because of her lifelong struggle with her mother, Mary McGee.

Along the streets, she slowed down to admire architectural styles. Her parents moved to the north end of Halifax in the seventies. Populated by overworked and underpaid laborers, the houses ranged from simple and ramshackle to sturdy and modest.

In the seventies, kids roamed the neighborhood, racing through backyards and ducking clotheslines. Everybody watched them. Kids landed home for meals, then returned to the streets for continued fun and mischief.

The architecture represented a story of renewal, rising from the catastrophic Halifax Explosion in 1917 that leveled most houses, killing two thousand people and injuring ten thousand. Over decades, they rebuilt that area of the city, one

CHAPTER 8

house at a time. One hundred years later, it had transformed into the trendy Hydrostone community.

She stashed her bike in the bushes beside her parents' house and avoided looking at the repairs begging for attention on a house they had moved into and never upgraded. She wondered how on earth a family of six, with three rowdy boys, ever squeezed into that home. Back then, nobody complained about lack of space, including one bathroom; they just lived their lives.

The three McGee boys, Owen, Terry and Brian, settled domestic arguments in the house with regular brawls. When wrecking crews tore down an old place nearby, their father dragged home hardwood doors to replace the light balsa doors that the boys wrecked in bulk.

Despite their endless brotherly quarrels, Owen, Terry and Brian were a tight-knit trio, born in rapid succession. "Take on one McGee, you take on all" was their mantra. As teens, they were a formidable threesome known as "The Vice Squad" for their activities in the neighborhood which they promoted to make sure nobody crossed them. Lucy was born years after the "clump of brothers," as she called them. Owen summed up the family dynamic when neighbors moved in next door. When they heard there were three boys and a girl, the follow-up question was "Where does Lucy fit in?" Owen gave his sister a brotherly shove and joked, "She doesn't!" Lucy learned to hold her own with the boys, which gave her a hard-as-nails exterior.

The McGee house rocked with action and non-stop yelling. There were kids coming and going, pets waiting to come in or go out, and doors slamming–a typical household of the era.

Now as she walked past the garden, Lucy noted the perennials were getting no love or water, except from Mother Nature. They looked fed up with their annual blooming duties and huddled to one side. Weeds snaked around the plants, choking everything in their path.

Lucy and her brothers should have been doing more to support the house and garden, but she couldn't keep up with her own, never mind her parents'. Indoors, the décor resembled a fading interior from the disco era, including a rust-colored shag carpet and pole lamp.

She turned the knob, pushing hard with her shoulder to open the door that had been sticking since the day they bought the place. Angie the cat, whom she renamed "Mangy," emerged to see who was invading her territory. Mangy, a patchwork of threadbare fur, bore a permanent "Meh" air of indifference on her sour face, with no hope of ever going viral on social media. She showed only begrudging tolerance to those who fed her.

Lucy stepped inside the dank hallway that smelled moist even in summer. Stepping on the decrepit cat toy that held the world record for the most germs lurking in an object the size of a golf ball, she punted it to the oncoming feline with the tip of her running shoe (which she vowed to scrub later).

Once the cat recognized Lucy, she sneered and ambled back to her lair. "Welcome to the McGee household," Lucy thought. Somehow the cat understood she was her mother's least favorite child.

She stood in the hall at the archway and hollered hello three times, but the game show soundtrack drowned out her voice.

Lucy scanned the living room of her youth–so familiar and so depressing. Solemn Virgin Mary knick-knacks sat motionless on stiff white doilies dotting the room. Her

CHAPTER 8

mother arranged coasters on side tables, featuring Biblical verses intended to stir up guilt in her husband as he drank and smoked in his younger years.

With the same strict and unhappy Catholic upbringing and no interest in following his wife's religious fervor, Lucy's father, Lucky, refused to feel guilty. One night, after a few rums, he scribbled response verses on the back of the coasters. The first verse said, "To everything there is a season, A time for every purpose under heaven: Ecclesiastes." Lucky scribbled, "Eat, drink and be merry, Ecclesiastes. Sincerely, Lucky."

"Many are called, but few are chosen: Matthew." Lucky replied, "Well, Matt, you didn't call, and you didn't write. So, I guess I wasn't chosen." Lucy smiled each time she pulled out a coaster, wondering if her mother had ever noticed his cheeky retorts.

The focal point of the living room was a wall dedicated to a foot-long brass sculpture of Jesus, nailed again into the middle of the wall forty years earlier. Tired of waiting for her husband to drive in a single nail to hang her beloved inspirational artwork, Lucy watched her mother pound a large nail into the wall.

With a single blow, a hairline crack traced the vertical and horizontal direction along the wall. Lucy watched the crack expanding over the seasons, following the outline of the cross. Creepy metaphor, she thought.

Ignoring the television racket, Lucy wondered if there was such a thing as a game show channel–it ran every waking hour. Her father lit up as he spotted his daughter's arrival. Lucy thought his nickname Lucky was ironic, reflecting his philosophy rather than his lot in life.

He got the name during a gambling spree, with the proof

stowed in a cabinet. Lucky's prized possession was a baseball signed by Lou Costello, with three magic words inscribed on it: "Who's on First?". Lucy remembered a lengthy story about how he had acquired it in the 1970s, during a late-night card game with a visitor from New Jersey. Every time he rolled out the tale, his wife Mary rolled her eyes. Lucy loved the story and didn't care if it was partly fiction. She laughed as if hearing it for the first time, even though he embellished the details until it sounded like a great con movie.

Despite the nickname, Lucky's reputation was more as a rogue and charlatan (by his wife). Despite his faults, people adored his undeniable charm, which served him well in sales when he put his mind to it. He was artful in extracting money from people and making them feel happy as they handed over their hard-earned cash. The only problem was, he didn't put his mind to it often. He settled down over time, his health putting a damper on his shenanigans. But he still loved sharing a belly laugh with his daughter Lucy, who took after her father more than the McGee boys did.

"Here's our pretty young lass!" he sang out to Lucy, even though she was fifty years old.

Her mother glanced over from the show but did not acknowledge her daughter. "It's 'picket fence', you idiot," she shouted to the hapless contestant on the screen.

"What's new, my dear?" he asked, always asking for updates. Mary kept tabs on the show, but as a seasoned gossip, she followed several conversations at once.

"David got the contract again for the Royal Military March," Lucy said.

"Great," he said. "Is that the sound and lights stuff?"

"Yup," Lucy said, as she leaned over and kissed him on the

head before sitting down.

"David who?" her mother asked, eyes locked on the television.

"Baxter. You know, my husband for the past few decades," she said, unable to block her sarcasm. It slipped through her lips before she could stop it–even though her father had asked her to go easy on her mother since she was struggling with memory loss. It amazed Lucy how kind he remained, no matter what happened. "How are you two?"

"Wonderful," said Lucky. Lucy could tell from looking at him he was losing his battle against arthritis and a heart attack that left him weakened. He practiced the old Irish adage, "Never complain, never explain".

"Well, I hurt," moaned her mother. "But I know you don't care, Lucille. Nobody does."

Lucy had long since given up trying to get her mother to stop calling her Lucille. Further, she had no idea about her mother's ongoing ailments that were vague enough to sound dire.

"Sorry to hear that, Ma," Lucy replied on autopilot. She knew that even if she helped her mother to fix one thing, she'd find a new misery. It amazed her that her father could listen to the grumbling day after day. Throughout their marriage, Mary called him a misbehaving ne'er do well with a wandering eye, and it surprised Lucy that he stayed with her. She figured he'd either stopped hearing her endless complaining or he was angling for sainthood.

Lucy stared at the screen, waiting for a commercial break to talk to them about her trip and the situation. The volume increased as a man in white, surrounded by dancing starbursts, began hawking floor cleaner.

Lucky lowered the volume and smiled at Lucy. "How are my favorite grandchildren?" No matter which child was visiting, he'd call their children his favorite grandchildren.

"Great. Riley's figuring out what he wants to be when he grows up."

"Me too! Tell him I'm seventy-six years old and still trying to decide," he joked. "Boys take a wee bit longer to mature. Right, Ma?"

"They never do," she shot back.

He and Lucy shared a chuckle. Despite the many hardships he had heaped on his family with his spells of drinking, gambling and unemployment, Lucy adored him. She cut him slack, figuring that he didn't win the marriage lottery.

"And how's sweet Maggie?"

"Wonderful, Pops. She's self-directed and really has her act together."

"Unlike her mother," said Lucy's mother.

Lucy's irritation gathered momentum until she noticed her father's hand signal to calm down. In her younger years, these comments led to endless arguments. "Joanne and I are going to Europe," she said.

"That's fun," said her father. "A little vay-cay?"

"It's the thirtieth anniversary of our trip during college. Remember that?"

"I hope you won't act like you did back then," said her mother.

"Not quite as bad," Lucy said, winking at her father.

"All that drinkin', cussin' and behavin' like loose women," she said in her angriest tone, saved only for Lucy. "Disgusts me."

"You weren't there, Ma, so I am not sure how you'd know.

Unless…. you read my diary." Mary scowled and returned to the screen.

"Where are you going?" said Lucky.

"We fly into London, then we'll go to Amsterdam, Paris and decide a wild card city over drinks."

"A fun plan," said Lucky.

Her forehead beading with sweat, Lucy leaned closer to her parents. What was the protocol for drumming up pain from the past and then fanning even more emotional flames in the present? Lucy's son was born "out of wedlock" as her mother described it, when she lived in Montreal.

Her mother had told her not to come home to Nova Scotia until she dealt with the problem. Mary never asked about the baby, and on the rare occasion that Lucy raised his name, her mother shut down the conversation. Lucky would have side chats with Lucy, but they agreed it was best not to raise the topic in the household.

That left Lucy with a gaping hole in her life story: her parents knew about the baby, but her husband and two children didn't. It happened long before they were part of her life. Now life had shifted, and her first-born son needed her help to survive. "Ma, Pops, I have something to tell you…"

"And here you are abandoning your family for this travel lark," said her mother, hurling the words like a cannonball across the room. "Shame," she added.

'Shame' was her mother's favorite word. Lucy tensed. "They're close to adults now and have their own friends. Besides, David will be there."

"I'm not impressed," said Mary.

"You never are," said Lucy. She pushed back another urge to confront and realized with dismay this was the only trait she had inherited from mother. It bothered Lucy, but she struggled to change this behavior.

"What did you want to tell us, Luv?" said her father, nodding to continue.

She stared at her mother. Even though Lucy was a non-practicing lawyer who, by instinct, didn't back down, she still stumbled with her mother.

"Well?" said her mother, with incredible impatience built into one syllable.

"Maggie is doing great at university," she switched in at the last moment. It was hardly a topic that warranted muting the television during her mother's show.

"Must get that from her father," said Ma.

Lucy watched her father's eyes narrow. She knew he didn't believe that was her big news. If there was one lesson her father had taught her when she was a teenager tagging along on sales calls, it was that "you don't bullshit a bullshitter". She wished she could just talk to him on his own and let him tell Mary, but he didn't want to be the go-between. It would have to wait.

"Gotta run," she said, standing up and plucking tufts of cat hair off her sweater. Lucky patted her hand. While Lucy usually offered a light hug when leaving, her mother struggled to her feet and walked to the kitchen to avoid it. Lucy hollered, "See you later, Ma" as she slipped out the side door, her heart saddled with unfinished business.

Out in the yard, she put on her helmet and yanked her bike out of the bushes, catching a glimpse of her mother peering out from behind a curtain. Why did she do that if she didn't care about Lucy? She almost waved at her mother, except her face looked dull and full of pain. Lucy winced.

CHAPTER 8

She wished more than ever they could settle their past differences and be civil to one another. While she shared the blame with her mother for their inability to get along, they were both stubborn. Lucky pointed out they were both behaving immaturely.

The family also noticed Mary showing signs of dementia in certain conversations. Lucy knew she should take the high road in these situations. She sighed and added it to her mental to-do list: make amends with her mother. Sadly, they wouldn't settle it in one session, and not today.

Lucy turned her bike around and pedaled fast. She had more pressing matters.

Chapter 9

Max

Seated on the balcony in the morning sun, Max leapt to the kitchen counter to answer the phone in a single ring. Once he realized it wasn't a medical call, he barely listened as the plumber rambled about another delay. A part still hadn't shown up, so he halted the project. By the time it arrived, he explained, he'd be leaving for summer vacation. Although he made light of the situation as he delivered the news, Max understood that's exactly what would happen.

"Any news?" asked his wife Katarin, hovering in the foyer as she prepared to leave for work.

"Yes, the fixture for the bathroom is stuck somewhere."

"What's that now… ten weeks?"

"I may get a kidney before the damn part arrives."

"Parisian plumbers," she joked.

He walked over to her. "You're growing," he said, cupping his hands on her tiny bump.

"She's been kicking."

"A girl? You sure?"

"Trust me, I know," she said with her hand resting on her

tummy. "I think we've got a wild one."

Katarin grabbed a jacket and scarf, followed by applying a dash of crimson lipstick. She turned from the mirror and looked at her husband, "Are you OK? You seem so far away."

"I dreamed of having my kidney sorted out before the baby arrived."

"Me too. But what are you going to do?" She kissed his cheek.

Max looked in the mirror and noted the outline of beautiful red lips. "Very cheeky."

"I thought you'd like that," she said, heading out. "I have a couple of meetings today, so I'll see you at the office later."

As the door closed, Max wandered around the apartment looking for items needed for dialysis over the next four hours. Before going to the room, he surveyed the renovations in the nursery and bathroom, dreaming about what was to come with the baby. The baby's room was near completion, and it looked like something in a design magazine. Every detail, color and piece of furniture and mobile functioned together, creating a magical world for their newborn.

Max pictured how his life would change when the baby came. Even though he was excited beyond belief to become a father, he felt anxious. He wanted everything to be perfect for his child, yet his medical condition would be an enormous obstacle.

Besides work, his dialysis would consume a dozen hours per week, just to stay alive. Even though he was tired after each session, he vowed not to complain because he knew each day was a precious gift.

For a moment, he considered the worst-case scenario: not receiving a transplant and the potentially dire consequences.

He stopped himself before going into a funk because it wouldn't help. Besides, he believed if anyone could track down a relative and convince them to donate a kidney, his mother could. He focused on her tireless commitment to finding one for her son, and his heart filled with love for her.

With his laptop tucked under his arm, he entered the guest room that housed a comfy chair and the home kidney dialyzer, the size of a home computer. He could order supplies for cleaning his kidneys and store them in the closet.

He could do his dialysis at home while he worked. And the data went to his doctor. After he bought the machine, he and Katarin attended a boot camp to learn how to operate the system (she served as a backup). He could now prepare for dialysis on his own in less than twenty minutes. He recalled the trainer's key point. "What this means is freedom," she said, pointing to the machine. "You can now organize your dialysis around your schedule, not the other way around."

Max could do it during the day or overnight. It was his choice. He knew many people on dialysis would have to go to a medical center and spend several hours on the machine. Those in poor health would have to get someone to transport them and wait for them, taking time from their day.

His initial disappointment about being burdened with dialysis for the foreseeable future was replaced with gratitude for doing it from home instead of a medical clinic. Even though he was young and otherwise strong, the procedure still drained his energy for several hours afterward. He also owned an architecture business and made sure he hired people who could run the place when he wasn't there.

He checked his blog for comments, then posted an update about his dialysis. After selecting the topic for the blog, he described the nausea and light-headedness that arose because of fluctuating blood pressure. He noted how much time he spent on the machine, while acknowledging he was lucky to do it from home.

Then he shifted to his deeper concern for his pregnant wife and family. He worried about being a burden to her and the baby. Although he did not have financial worries, he sympathized with those who did. As soon as he posted the blog and photos, comments piled up. His followers topped ten thousand, and the subscribers expanded weekly as readers shared posts.

The bottom of the website linked to the "In Memoriam" page, honoring people in the community who had passed away. Max was shocked to see the growing number of names. Some had waited years for a kidney but never located one, while others received the gift, only to have their body reject it. The loss of children depressed everyone the most.

Max dedicated enormous energy to "In Memoriam" to honor each life lived, mostly because he knew many through the online community. Families added photos and videos, along with stories written by loved ones, and condolences from caring friends. Virtual candles illuminated the profile of individuals, ensuring deep respect for those who didn't make it.

After four hours, Max removed himself from the dialysis machine. He rested for a while which annoyed him enormously because it took up even more time, then got ready for work.

Chapter 10

Joanne

It had been a long time since she had traveled overseas, and she spent weeks preparing. With only five hours to go, she wanted everything to be perfect. She rechecked the flight time online, reviewed her travel checklist, and stared at an empty bag on the bedroom floor. After several practice runs and reviewing all the travel details one more time, she was ready for the final packing.

Each item was rolled and held with an elastic, or folded flat and piled like a stack of pancakes. She touched each item and checked it off the list as her grandmother taught her years ago. Placing her shoes in a row, she cast a suspicious eye on each pair that threatened to fill her suitcase. Several pairs would serve double-duty and she tossed the rest in her closet to hold space for purchases and gifts.

She test-drove a hefty suitcase with wheels that rumbled along like a rolling boulder. That wouldn't work. Next, she tried Emmaleigh's backpack, but it gave her an appearance of an aging parent disguised as a student. She settled on a high-tech convertible suitcase with wheels that folded into a

CHAPTER 10

backpack for times they'd be running toward departing trains because of Lucy's tardiness.

The thought of it grated Joanne, but when she raised her concerns during their planning sessions, Lucy insisted she never missed a flight or train. It was a whopping lie for sure, but most people didn't call her on wild assertions.

The afternoon crawled by and felt even longer because Gretchen didn't speak to her. Joanne's guilt grew, as if she were deceiving her daughter. She was nervous Gretchen might create a last-minute crisis to force her to cancel her trip. However, Gretchen would have to face the wrath of Lucy, so Joanne figured that was enough of a deterrent for her. She was a drama queen, but she understood that there were certain people she shouldn't take on. Lucy was one of them.

Now ready and in waiting mode, Joanne sat beside a precision-packed bag that looked like it was organized by a valet. At the last minute, she thought of the European diary they had written together thirty years ago. She darted to the basement, looking for a shelf of boxes marked "mail and diaries". It hadn't been out of the box in years. She flipped through and laughed at the hand-drawn sketches starting every chapter and tossed it into her carry-on bag.

She felt giddy and carefree, like the first time she traveled to Europe in 1986. They had flown in the evening on a non-stop out of Montreal, arriving at Heathrow the next morning. Joanne never slept well, so the flight resembled a typical night of patchy sleeping. But they didn't care.

They had a hostel lined up for the first night and stowed their bags in a locker so they could dive right into London town. She wondered what it would be like for them thirty years later now that there was less to prove. Given they were both married, there was no reason to obsess about meeting men. On the last trip, the thought had dominated every waking moment. Joanne wondered what would replace that obsession, but she figured they'd still have plenty to chat about.

Knowing her mother's commitment to time and schedules, Emmaleigh arrived three hours before the flight, dropping her bags to stay in her old bedroom. Joanne and Emmaleigh hugged, swinging back and forth–she could tell her daughter was genuinely excited about her trip. She was tiny, with delicate features and golden braids, contrasting against the mixed colors and patterns of her bohemian outfit. None of the clothing items matched, but they all looked great together, almost in a glow. Somehow, Emmaleigh seemed to deliver light into any room she entered.

She shouted a perky hello to her sister Gretchen, who grunted a one-syllable response. Joanne told Lucy they'd pick her up at five-thirty p.m. knowing she wouldn't be ready. They aimed for six o'clock, but Joanne knew Lucy would calculate this into her packing plans.

When Joanne and Emmaleigh arrived at Lucy's at six p.m. she was seated on the sofa, her fingers darting around the keyboard. "Oh wow, is it that time?" said Lucy, appearing shocked.

Joanne tensed lightly. She and Lucy had reverted to their old travel patterns in minutes. Except Joanne no longer wanted to be the adult in charge; she just wanted to be herself. She vowed to make Lucy take responsibility for herself on this trip. She and Emmaleigh walked into the living room, and Lucy waved them to the sofa. There was soft music on the stereo, and she could hear the muffled sounds of a group video game going on in the basement with Riley and his friends shouting in friendly combat.

"Where's your bag?" Joanne asked, searching the room.

"Uh… Upstairs. I need a few more items."

"I guess you haven't started packing." Joanne and Emmaleigh exchanged light smiles.

Lucy closed her laptop. "Jeez girl, we've got lots of time."

Joanne inhaled. She'd been to this rodeo many times. Emmaleigh smiled a "don't worry" expression to her mom as they waited. Lucy clomped around upstairs, calling Maggie on her cell to find the suitcases. She didn't know, so Lucy muttered and climbed the ladder to the attic. Minutes later she tossed down several options, which crashed to the upstairs hallway.

She called Maggie again, asking if any laundry had been done during the week, knowing that she herself, hadn't done a thing. Lucy then hollered a question down the stairwell, "Is it better to take weird but clean clothes I don't like, or dirty clothes I love?"

"Some of each," she hollered back, shrugging at Emmaleigh.

"Go with it Mom, it's less annoying." The two of them laughed and shook their heads, knowing Lucy had not changed.

At six-thirty, Joanne stomped part-way up the stairs and called out, "Time to leave, Lu."

"Uh huh." Lucy replied, seated cross-legged on the floor with her laptop open. She typed furiously, looking focused and maniacal, like a circus monkey that had been let loose on a keyboard for the first time.

"Now!"

"Yup. Wonder if I forgot anything," said Lucy arriving at the bottom of the stairs with an oversized suitcase.

"If you have your passport, money and eticket, we're good." Joanne felt like an annoying mother checking the inventory of a child headed off to camp.

"Here's the ticket, and I'll be right back," she shouted, sprinting two stairs at a time.

Joanne surveyed the jammed suitcase with items spilling out the side and they hadn't even left yet. She picked up the ticket with the itinerary for Europe. Her eyes narrowed when she read the dates for Amsterdam and Paris. They seemed to be in the wrong order. If they went with this schedule, they'd miss the Van Gogh exhibition in Amsterdam. That was her top pick for the trip, and Lucy knew that. Maybe they were the right dates. As they prepared to leave, everything felt like a jumble and she couldn't remember. She didn't have time to pull out her cell and check the Van Gogh dates.

"Everything okay, Mom?" said Emmaleigh.

"I think so," said Joanne, trying to convince herself. She had to calm her buzzing nerves and the adrenaline that circled around her body in a loop. As someone who was a nervous traveler, she prepared carefully for every trip to minimize fretting.

Yet it didn't take much to become anxious with tickets and itineraries. She needed the comfort that everything was in its place, otherwise, she'd start worrying about what else could go wrong. Then superstition kicked in and fueled the flames. What if they missed a flight? What if the plane had engine troubles? How many hours were they flying over an ocean?

It was a short bridge to worrying about bigger travel possibilities. She took several breaths. Surely this was just an admin error–it wasn't the time to create a big fuss. If the tickets were wrong, she and Lucy could afford to pay for a ticket. "No biggie," she reminded herself and smiled. "It looks like a bit of a mix-up on the travel dates in Europe, but we'll get it straightened out."

"All systems go!" said Lucy. She raced down the stairs and screeched to a halt at the bottom, close to her suitcase. "Shit, that'll be heavy for us to carry," Lucy announced.

Joanne noted the word *us* when talking about carrying *her* bag but chose not to challenge her. It was how Lucy rolled–assuming help would arrive when needed to pull her out of dramas. Someone usually did. "Is that a quilted housecoat sleeve sticking out?"

Lucy nodded, but made no attempt to remove it.

"Takes up half the suitcase," said Joanne.

"Remember those creepy French hotels where you have to walk a long hallway to the bathroom in the night?"

Joanne realized this was no time to debate packing. Sitting together on the lid, Lucy coaxed the zipper around the corners. They dragged it to the front hallway, puffing and panting. Joanne and Emmaleigh stood up to leave, the airport run now delayed.

Lucy walked over to the basement door. "Riley!" she shouted. It didn't register in the basement with the boys' noise. "Riley, hon, are you going to give your darling Mom a hug goodbye?" The hubbub continued. Lucy shrugged and said, "Whatever. I'll text him and David." The dog Pepper sulked as she left, then chased them. She scooped him up in the air and held him away from her, his feet spinning furiously, while Emmaleigh and Joanne carried the suitcase to the car.

She then pushed Pepper back inside and closed the door. Chaos continued as Pepper raced to the top of sofa, barking while they headed for the getaway car. He wasn't giving up without a fight. "Bye sweetie," she yelled to Pepper, who shot her an abandoned puppy grimace.

They raced to the airport, passing every moving vehicle like a race car driver on a closed circuit. At the airport, Em helped to unload the bags and grabbed a cart for them. Joanne hugged her and cried, with Emmaleigh promising to take care of everyone.

At Stanfield Airport, the evening travel volume was low, so they breezed through security and raced to the departure lounge. With the check-in, baggage, and security complete, Joanne eased back into the chair and relaxed. It felt briefly like life back then, except so much had changed. The innocence and energy of their youth–believing that everything in life was possible–had somehow shifted.

Life happened: marriages and children arrived, jobs came and went, family and friends faced divorce, illness and death. Joanne knew they had both racked up thirty years of living, but for the moment, she wanted to tap into that beautiful carefree feeling they had known on their first trip to Europe.

Joanne pulled out her eticket and checked it against her calendar and the website for the Van Gogh exhibition. As she suspected, the dates were switched. She wondered if she should ask Lucy about the dates for Paris and Amsterdam. Lucy had a way of acting impulsive, then begging forgiveness. That wasn't new. And mostly, things turned out to be more fun with Lucy's ways–maybe she should just go with it this time.

Yet when Joanne's family traveled, she looked after the details, so she didn't like to be in the dark about plans. In fact, she regretted letting Lucy book the tickets, even if they were free. "Hey, Lu," she said, holding the paper. "I noticed

CHAPTER 10

you changed the dates for Paris and Amsterdam."

"Oh?" said Lucy, leaning over to look at the paper with Joanne. "Guess it's what was available."

"Any reason for that?" said Joanne, trying not to sound controlling. "I ask because that would mean missing the Van Gogh exhibition, and that was the whole point of going there, right?" Lucy paused for a little too long, which concerned her.

"What if I told you I have an errand in Paris?" Lucy finally blurted. An errand? Joanne wondered what exactly Lucy meant by the word. Who has 'an errand' for a place on another continent? Errands are trips to the grocery store, picking up items at the hardware store, dropping kids somewhere. "Yes, telling me about your *errand* in Paris would be nice, for starters." She watched Lucy's micro expression shift slightly. Nobody else would notice it, but Joanne knew it from childhood.

Lucy took Joanne's hand and held it. "I will, Jo, but I may not even need to run it. I'll know soon. But for the moment, could you just trust me?"

Yikes, they hadn't even taken off and Lucy appeared to be classic Lucy. Joanne's mind raced with a case of the "what ifs". What if something was wrong? Why had Lucy taken her hand? It felt serious. Should she pursue her questioning right now? But what if it was big? Would they call off their trip? What if her friend needed help? What if Lucy had a rare condition that only could be solved in France? But then again, that was hardly an errand.

Maybe it was something positive. What if Lucy had a big surprise for her and she was just being churlish? Wouldn't that be embarrassing? She had promised herself to be more fun and spontaneous on this trip. Already she was balking.

She placed her right hand on top of Lucy's "Okay, I'll go with this. Promise me you'll tell me as soon as you know."

Lucy nodded and dug around in her handbag. "Well, shit. I forgot my toothbrush and paste," she said.

"Here we go," teased Joanne as she watched Lucy dash off to buy hygiene items in the airport store, where she would pay a fortune for them. As she walked back from the store, Lucy beamed, holding up her newly purchased toothbrush and paste. She grabbed her bag and told Joanne she'd be right back after using the washroom.

As soon as Lucy was in the washroom, the gate agent announced boarding and rhymed off the zones for loading. Joanne tapped her passport impatiently as if trying to hurry Lucy along, but she knew it was no use–she was on 'Lucy time' as Joanne sometimes called it. By the time Lucy returned, they were at the end of the line to board.

They settled into their seats; the airplane took off from Halifax against the evening ink-blue sky. They ordered a glass of wine and toasted, leaving their lives and work obligations for a few weeks. Both squealed with excitement. Joanne pulled out a tattered journal and waved it in front of Lucy.

"Is that our diary from the first trip?"

Joanne handed it to her. "I brought it for a laugh. Let's read an entry that shows how much we ate, drank and flirted back then."

"I forgot about it." Lucy laughed and shook her head as she flipped through the diary. "Oh yeah, we had a song of the day. Remember? That's a riot. And check this out," she pointed. "We drew illustrations of our adventures. And we each wrote in insults on the other's entries. I love it!"

"Is that really our handwriting?" said Joanne.

"I think we were drunk when writing our entries." Lucy pointed to a section. "See here? You always called me Slutsky when you were drinking."

"Well, you were different under the influence." Joanne could rhyme off countless times from their past escapades when Lucy behaved more provocatively in direct proportion to the amount of booze imbibed. No need to recap, Lucy wouldn't remember any.

"Still am," Lucy joked, clinking plastic cups. "London, here we come!"

Chapter 11

Lucy

The plane landed at Heathrow at sunrise and the pair started the first day in sleep deficit mode. Lucy was sporting one of those sluggish headaches that made her feel like she had brain fog and had to focus intently to comprehend every communication.

"Suggestion, Jo. Let's keep each other awake for the next twelve hours and go to bed early tonight, or we'll risk days of lingering jetlag."

"Yup, we know the drill. It's hard on the first day, but each day gets better," said Joanne.

Such an optimist, thought Lucy about her friend, as she looked around the airport humming with the chaos of people moving in all directions. Joanne had researched their transportation options before the trip, so Lucy stood back and let her run with it. All they had to do was find the express train to central London.

Dragging their suitcases in the wrong direction three times, Lucy stumbled along like a kid, not helping but not really caring. They finally found the right platform and entered a

CHAPTER 11

train packed with bleary travelers, resting on their bags.

By the time they finished the train ride, found the tube in London, then a taxi, it was already noon. "Let's drop off our bags at the hotel until check-in later in the afternoon," said Joanne, which relieved Lucy that someone was on the ball. They headed out to wander the neighborhood with Lucy complaining about how exhausted she was until they spotted fun clothing and vintage shops appearing on every corner.

Lucy knew the emails were piling up about the medical tests that she had started back home a month earlier. So far, the results were very encouraging that she would be an excellent candidate for donating a kidney. However, she had to work through additional tests right up to the last minute and tend to a lot of paperwork. To complicate matters, she lived in Canada and Max lived in France–and he knew nothing about his birth mother. Elise, who had raised him with Jacques, was the supreme puppet master in all of this, and Lucy dreaded helping her. Yet she couldn't stop thinking about the son that she didn't get to raise.

Whatever unfolded on this trip, Lucy wanted to make sure that she and Joanne would still have lots of fun. They could do both, she reminded herself over and over, so that she wouldn't feel so guilty about everything.

They wandered around street markets, zipping into stores the minute anything unusual caught their attention. Lucy's phone timer beeped. "Yay, it's time to check into the hotel," she shouted over the street traffic. They hauled the bags to their room and took turns blocking each other from lying down for a "quick cat nap".

At six o'clock, Lucy and Joanne grabbed the diary and headed to the nearest pub, The Uncouth Swan, for an early evening pint of lager. As they chatted in the corner and sipped their beer, Lucy watched Londoners on the street hustling about. She loved the action.

Suddenly, Lucy felt like she had some much-needed energy. She opened the tattered notebook from their trip and flipped through it, laughing. "Okay, here's my first entry for London in 1986… "*"Dear Dairy,"* she said, smiling at Joanne. "Yup, I was drinking. Couldn't even spell diary!" She held the book at a distance to avoid wearing reading glasses in public: *"Day One: Welcome to the Hostile Hostel. We're staying at this weird place called The Abbey. It's amazing, because it really was an abbey centuries ago, but the guy who runs it is a right crank. Geoff is his name, but we call him "Goff" because of his dumb spelling. Within seconds of meeting this horse's arse, he's soon chiding us about rules. What he doesn't get is we are twenty AND fully formed adults, damn it! Anyway, it only costs five pounds a night to stay there, so we will put up with him."*

As she was reading, Lucy looked at Joanne, who was shaking her head in recognition of their behavior. "Well, weren't we feisty?" said Lucy. "Was I that mouthy back then?"

"You still are!" said Joanne, sipping her beer. Lucy feigned hurt, then returned to the diary. "Check this out. What was the first thing we did? Go to a pub."

"Right," said Lucy. *"We came back five minutes before our curfew and Geoff leapt from behind a door. Chewed us out. When I pointed to my watch, he then asked if I saw his note taped to my bunk bed. He told me I left the room unkempt, and I asked him to describe a kempt room. He gave us the boot. I said we paid for the night and we'd damn well stay the night,"* said Lucy.

"Look at our theme song for today: Hall and Oates' "You're out of Touch" dedicated to grumpy, ancient Goff," said Joanne.

CHAPTER 11

"What's your take-away from day one?"

"I was a foul-mouthed, spikey, inebriated little twenty-year-old who used a lot of slang and didn't take shit from anyone. And those were my better points... And you?"

"Couldn't have said it any better!" Joanne shouted over the chatter of the crowd. "Your three brothers taught you well!"

Lucy closed the book, still laughing about their diary entry. She looked around and became distracted as the pub filled with groups of friends and colleagues clinging to the bar, tables for two packed with half a dozen people, and patrons pressed into corners using the windowsill as glass holders. She loved that about pubs: nobody made a fuss where they sat or stood; they just figured things out as they chatted.

Joanne leaned her tall glass of ale toward clinking glasses. "Here's to a fun day of walking the streets of London bagged and jetlagged."

"And finding the ancient abbey, but not Geoff," laughed Lucy. "Although part of me wanted to find him and ask if the place was still as kempt as when we stayed there."

"He was old then; I'd be more frightened if he was alive."

"Come to think of it, he was likely our age," said Lucy. "Everybody looks old when you are twenty." Lucy closed the diary and looked at Joanne. "Hey, isn't it great to be here?"

"Yeah, there are so many things I want to do. Do you want to see any shows in the West End? We could book something for Friday," said Joanne, her voice animated.

Lucy shifted. It was natural for Joanne to come up with ideas while in London, but Lucy had to be flexible with her plans. Depending how things unfolded with the medical clinic in Paris, she might have to do more tests, and that meant changing plans to accommodate the transplant schedule. She couldn't lock herself into any plans. "I'd rather go on the spur of the moment. OK?" She saw disappointment in Joanne's eyes.

"Sure, but it's hard to get tickets."

"Who knows where we'll be at the end of the week? Maybe fly off to Greece instead of staying in London," Lucy joked. She checked Joanne's expression to see where her idea landed.

"That's crazy talk, girl."

"Here's to crazy talk. It's how we landed knee-deep in so many adventures," said Lucy, toasting. A man, several tables over, looked directly at Lucy and smiled, tilting his glass. She smiled and returned to Joanne.

"Slutsky," said Joanne.

"Am not."

"I know that look from way back. You're firing up the old charm to see if you still got it."

Joanne and Lucy left the pub far later than expected. With only a dash to the hotel, they walked arm-in-arm fueled by laughter and several beers. "Hey Jo, what songs did we sing back then?" Lucy said, rhyming off hit songs from their first visit.

"Well, there was 'West End Girls' and 'Addicted to Love,'" said Jo. She sang lightly, but no longer at full volume like they would have done on the first trip. They abandoned songs as they forgot the lyrics but got through an entire verse of 'Sledgehammer'. Lucy looked at Joanne, who had been through a lot of strife over the past few years. She was happy to see her looking relaxed.

Lucy and Joanne arrived at the hotel and swung the front door open with great fanfare. They hustled to the elevator and waited. Soon Lucy was moving, dancing from one foot to the other.

"Hurry, I have to go," said Lucy, laughing and looking pained. They jammed in the tiny space and tapped the button impatiently until it rumbled to the seventh floor. Each grabbed their key, preparing for arrival. "Race you," shouted Lucy, practically prying open the doors. They wobbled down the hall as quickly as possible; Lucy wedged in the door first. Joanne waved her in, noticing that Lucy looked far more desperate.

In minutes they flopped into the miniature chairs tucked in the corner. "I can't wait to crawl in bed. Which one do you want, Lucy?"

"Whatever... How about by the window?" She walked toward the small chair in the corner and sat down. "I need to sit up for a minute, but you go ahead and crash. I'll check my email," said Lucy, clicking on her cell.

"Good idea," Joanne said, staring at her phone, even though she was nodding off. "Hmmm, nothing from Gretchen, or Emmaleigh."

"That's means everything is okay, right?" Lucy didn't want her friend to worry.

"I thought they might wonder if I arrived safely."

"Why should they worry?"

"I don't know. I'll send them a note anyway to say we're okay."

"Good idea," Lucy said, checking her inbox. There were dozens of emails piling up, including a number from Paris. Elise had endless questions about the clinic. This was going to take a little time to get through. Joanne had finished with her cell and her eyes were closing. "What do you want to do tomorrow?" said Lucy, dividing her focus between her friend and her inbox.

"How about a museum, a little shopping, and a curry for dinner?"

"Perfect," said Lucy.

Joanne crawled into bed and conked out. Lucy worked through her emails. She saw Joanne wake up a few times during the night, looking dazed and confused. Lucy smiled lightly and watched her fall right back to sleep. Things were unfolding quickly for the Paris trip. Her tests which started in Halifax, continued to show her as a compatible donor for her son. Why wouldn't they? She wondered how Elise explained to Max why she couldn't be a donor, but Lucy knew this woman could make it sound plausible. Exhausted, she stumbled to bed after an hour.

***

A grinding bus outside the window yanked her from a deep, unrestful dream. She lifted her eye mask in a haze of confusion. Sunlight sliced through the center of the curtains, shining in her eyes and making her wince. It took a second to remember she was in London and with Joanne. She felt like she was in a trance. The alarm clock beamed bright red numbers that told her a lot of time had passed, but it made no sense.

Lucy turned over the covers and opened one eye, as if to test the moment. Her dry tongue glued to the roof of her mouth begged for water. She gulped from the bottle by the side of her bed and then gasped for a breath.

Joanne sat up and removed the ear plugs that filtered out some noise. "Good morning," she said as a generic waking up ritual, but her expression said otherwise. She stretched each arm toward the ceiling and over each shoulder, with little cracks escaping from her body.

"Hey, Jo. What time is it?"

Joanne glanced at the alarm clock. "Ten-thirty."

"In the morning?" It surprised Lucy to see Joanne nod. "Are you kidding me?" said Lucy, raising herself on her left arm. "Then why the hell don't I feel rested?"

"We slept in spurts–a few hours here and there–but there were double-decker busses rumbling all night. Plus add in jetlag and drinking beer at the pub, which is disgusting and dehydrating."

Lucy groaned and flopped over on the bed.

"Did you stay up late, Lucy?"

"No. Not too long after you."

Joanne looked at the desk. "You sure were busy for a while. What are all these notes and phone numbers?"

Lucy glanced at the pile. She should have tidied up all her paperwork before going off to sleep, but she was too tired. "Work. Sorry, I know we agreed not to do that…"

"I didn't mean to pry. I thought you were organizing our trip."

"So, is it museum day today?" Lucy asked, changing the subject. Everything needed to sound normal for them. "We're in Bloomsbury, so do you fancy the British Museum?" she asked in a plummy English accent.

"Sure. We loved the Egyptian artifacts last time. And the Greco-Roman section."

"Can you believe we made it to Egypt on our trip? From the U.K. to the south of Egypt in two months flat. I'm exhausted thinking about it," said Lucy.

"That's why you travel Europe when you're young."

"How about we grab a shower and a bite to eat, then head

out?"

Joanne nodded. They each took showers, but both were sluggish and agreed they were in a daze. At one p.m. they were sitting in a coffee shop, sipping their second coffees. "Is it wrong to use up valuable time in London drinking cappuccinos instead of walking around the museum?"

Lucy felt like she was operating in slow motion; there was no way she could speed things up. "We need more caffeine these days. Besides, we can do whatever we want." She was still checking her texts and emails with an occasional apology to Joanne. After half an hour, they picked up their things and headed to the museum. "It's mid-afternoon. About time for a coffee break, don't you think?" Lucy joked as they checked their bags, but that was about all she felt like doing.

They wandered through the Egyptian section and searched to see if the mummy cat was still there. Joanne studied each label and artifact before moving on, while Lucy scanned everything. She couldn't believe someone would read every freaking label. Soon she was ahead and had to work her way back to meet up with Joanne. "Right," chuckled Lucy. "We have different interests in museums."

"I know, I know," said Joanne, "I'm tiring myself out. I will pick up the tempo."

After nearly an hour, Lucy had enough. Best friend or not, she couldn't read another damn exhibit text. She had seen the mummy; the rest didn't matter to her. "Listen Joanne, I'll sit in the restaurant for a bit, while I sort out this work thing. Take your time and when you're ready, come back for me."

An hour later, Lucy saw Joanne headed toward her. "How were the Greeks–still looking good?"

"Amazing, I was lost in there. How about you?"

CHAPTER 11

Lucy gathered her items and jammed them in her bag. "Your timing is perfect; I'm wrapping up now. Let's get changed at the hotel. We can head out for cocktails and a curry."

They window-shopped on the way, taking photos of outfits they'd like to try on. When they arrived at the hotel, Lucy was relieved for a chance to sit down before going out. She forgot that leaving clothing strewn everywhere in the tiny room might be annoying.

"Clothes tornado!" said Joanne, surveying from the doorway.

"I haven't heard that since we traveled together!" Lucy laughed. In one day, the space resembled a clothing drop zone. The outfits from Lucy's suitcase looked like a cannon had shot them all over the room: tops dangled off door handles, sweaters draped over chairs, jeans tossed on the floor and undies clung to the towel rack in the bathroom. She noted Joanne's bag wedged into the corner, with all items neatly folded and sorted. "Sorry, Jo."

"Do you do this at home?" Joanne asked, feigning disgust.

"Are you kidding me? David's a neat freak. Now I get to be myself traveling with you."

"I'm honored," she laughed "Lucky we aren't staying at Geoff's hostel, or he'd ban us for life."

"Fasten your seatbelt, I'm about to make more of a mess." After trying on four outfits, Lucy settled on the first one. She missed having her favorite clothes that were stuffed into a laundry bag and tucked into her suitcase, which Joanne predicted would not get washed on this trip.

They entered the Velvet Vindaloo, an Indian pub, packed with diners. Lucy's friend had told her about this restaurant, nicknamed the "Vicious Vindaloo" because of the owner's refusal to serve non-Indians his famous dish. "Too hot for you," he'd say, wagging his index finger. She loved this kind of challenge.

Lucy had begged a friendly local group to order a vindaloo curry. "Here's a small sample," said the table spokesperson. "If you finish this without squirming, guzzling beer or water, I'll smuggle a full dish to your table–and it's on me." Everyone leaned in while Lucy gave it her best shot. Two forkfuls later, her face flamed with the agony of defeat and embarrassment.

In no time, they had joined tables. Within half an hour, Lucy had scored an invitation to an Indian wedding in London on the weekend. She loved meeting new people and implicating herself and Joanne into new situations. When Lucy joked she had nothing to wear, they offered saris.

As they prepared to leave, Lucy exchanged cards with everyone at the table and promised to attend. After the meal, Lucy and Joanne sat in a pub near the hotel, Lucy still reeling from the vindaloo. "Jay-zus that hurt," Lucy said, tapping her fist on her chest, while popping antacids. She felt like her insides had been torn out. "And that was only two bites," she said, gulping the golden brew in front of her.

"I guess that's why Buddy didn't want us eating vindaloo."

Lucy wondered if this kind of outing was getting on Joanne's nerves. She loved this kind of interaction, but knew Joanne had a limit. "Yeah, but we had fun, right?"

Joanne nodded and sipped her beer. She looked around the room, her legs crossed in a relaxing pose. "I heard from Emmaleigh today," she said perking up.

"How's she doing?"

"Great. She told me Gretchen's basil plant is popping up through the soil. Emmaleigh said Gretchen and Ally-Up have been tending it for weeks at the Deep Roots greenhouse."

"Who's Ally-Up?"

"He's a nice guy who has been volunteering at the garden for a long time. He's a young Syrian refugee, about eighteen. His family started growing food and now he's helping others.

"Gretchen and a guy raising plants together, is this serious?"

Joanne looked at her cell. "Dunno, I've only met him a few times–he seems nice. However, if Emmaleigh says he's an exceptional guy, that's good enough for me. But Gretchen hasn't mentioned going to the garden, or hanging out with a guy…"

"Isn't that a child for you? She's all miserable around you, bringing you down. Next minute, she's out whooping it up with some guy. That's the one thing you wish she wouldn't keep to herself."

"Well, she made a light joke before I left. I wondered if she was happier. Maybe I feel a little…"

"The last to know?" offered Lucy.

"Something like that. I've dreamed of her being happy and eating again, but it seems so far away. When I text her, she doesn't respond. Why can't she tell me she's doing fine?"

Lucy pointed to her cell. "Look, it's nothing personal. Riley only texts me to locate the cheese dip." Lucy caught Joanne's forced smile because she knew Gretchen was programmed to be miserable all the time. "Anyway, enough complaining!" Lucy announced and then she was off to sleep.

***

The next morning, the inbox pulsed with activity. Lucy knew that Joanne was fed up with her saying she was almost finished. The best thing, she decided, would be to let Joanne wander around London while Lucy sorted a few things out.

If she could squeeze in a few more hours, it would all work out. It wasn't what she pictured for their European revisit, yet this project was crucial.

"Hey Lucy, there's a really cool looking exhibition on at the Tate Modern–would you like to go?" said Joanne.

"Sorry, Jo, I am not much fun on this visit, but give me a little more time. I swear."

"Any more updates on this big errand of yours?" said Joanne. "More specifically, what it is? Given that it's taking up a lot of our time together, maybe I should know more."

Lucy sighed. Joanne had a point, but what if all this chaos was for nothing? Why should she turn the two of them inside out when it might not even happen? Yet her friend deserved better. "Jo, if I told you it was to do with a medical situation, would that help you?"

"Oh my god, Lu, are you okay?" Joanne gasped, her eyes popping. "Did you come to Europe to cure a rare disease or something?"

Lucy stepped in it. "No, I'm healthier than I deserve to be based on my lifestyle. It's to help someone else, but it may not even happen–so I don't want to get too bogged down. Is that enough to hold you over until I can confirm details?" She noticed Joanne's face fall. "Please Jo, I'm feeling crazy pressure right now."

"Okay, I get it. How about we meet back here around six o'clock and then head out for cocktails?"

Lucy hugged her. "Thanks for being a loyal friend." She vowed to get everything sorted right away. That was always her plan. What could go wrong?

Chapter 12

Joanne

The next day, Joanne knew she was on her own in London. Not exactly what she had hoped for because Lucy was keeping her in the semi-dark about her plans; however, she was excited to do many things. She knew what she'd do without Lucy, who suffered from a short attention span. "Hey Lucy, I've got an idea for today. I'd like to see *A Midsummer Night's Dream* at the Globe Theatre."

"Okay," said Lucy, dragging out the word.

"Listen. I know Shakespeare isn't your thing, but I've always dreamed of attending a play at the Globe in London. I'm happy to enjoy the atmosphere by myself–there'll be no disinterested kids, husbands or bored girlfriends in tow."

Lucy laughed out loud. "You got me there. Seriously Jo, please go have fun. And when you come back, this stuff will be all wrapped up."

Joanne took a deep breath. She was glad that Lucy acknowledged she was throwing a wrench in their plans. "Okay, great, because we were supposed to do things together." She saw Lucy's face fall and immediately regretted saying that. "And let's have a lively evening out, tonight. Right?"

"You got it," Lucy said, spreading her arms in a dramatic gesture. "'Verily I say unto you. Go forthwith to the play, young wench and Godspeed.' Unfortunately, that's all the Shakespeare I can remember from Mr. Rand's class."

Joanne laughed. "An entire year of English class condensed into a single sentence. Pitiful. I'm convinced this is the right thing to do on my own." She agreed on a time to return to the hotel, hugged Lucy, and exited the room.

***

Joanne stepped outdoors and turned onto Southampton Row, walking toward Waterloo Bridge to get a view of the Thames. With massive clouds rolling over the horizon and only a hint of sunshine, she figured the weather was as good as it gets in London. She strolled toward the Southbank Centre, wishing Lucy would sort out her problems, so they could continue with their trip. She was receiving way more emails and texts for work than predicted.

However, as Joanne knew from experience, Lucy threw wrenches into plans. Always. She knew it was best to give her space and wait for Lucy to come around. That's how it worked.

Over lunch, goosebumps rippled across her arms as she read the brochure that described the Elizabethan performance she'd be attending. Reconstructed in the style of the original building, the Globe was a large three-story amphitheater space, with an open roof and room for three thousand people. Inside, at the base of the stage there was a "pit", as they named it back then, where, for a penny, people could attend the performance.

There were no seats, but people stood or pulled up some

straw. Remaining faithful to its roots four centuries later, the Globe offered seven hundred standing places in the Yard for only five pounds. The place was crammed.

Around the sides, the stadium seating included a roof that blocked the inevitable drizzle in London. She paid for a seat with roof cover and raced to her spot. The air buzzed with people of all ages. She could picture the place over four hundred years ago. People talked, laughed, ate, and drank beer–every inch filled with excited theatergoers.

Joanne sat down and smiled at the man next to her, who was joking with everyone within a two-seat radius. She stuffed her bag under the seat and looked around, unable to focus on anything.

"Isn't this fabulous?" Joanne blurted to the couple next to her. She wondered if she sounded too bubbly. But they agreed and began chatting with her. They were twins, Simon and Gemma, visiting from the north of England. They taught English and adored anything about Shakespeare. At intermission, Simon and Gemma invited Joanne to join them for a beer at the bar. She watched the twins lob insults at each other about *A Midsummer Night's Dream* until Simon told Gemma to "Puck off". That caused more puns about actors, with other nearby drinkers groaning. Joanne could hardly contribute, she was laughing so hard. Simon and Gemma asked her to say who was misbehaving the most. She said she was just an "innocent Lysander". They howled. The lights flashed to end intermission.

She wished the magic wouldn't end. For an afternoon, she forgot about her life, her ailing daughter, her husband, and her friend Lucy. As the play wrapped up, the twins invited Joanne to join them at a pub. It was one of those encounters she wished would continue, except she had promised Lucy she'd be back for cocktails.

She walked along the Thames, pumped about the play, yet let down without Lucy. When she popped her card in the hotel door, she could hear the shower. "I'm back," she hollered and heard Lucy reply something in the bathroom. She plopped into the nearest chair, feeling restless.

Lucy yelled something about wine. Joanne noted she had opened a bottle and placed two glasses on the table. She filled a glass and put her feet up. She still had lingering jetlag, made worse by walking all over London. And she was starving.

In Lucy's carrying bag, she spotted a tube of potato snacks formed into fake chips–each one identical. They were perfect for a ravenous person with growing hunger in a hotel room. When Joanne pulled out the tube, she noticed a half-folded sheet of paper showing an illustration for an expensive hotel. What was going on?

Did Lucy make some arrangements without discussing things? Lucy was still singing in the shower. Should she peek at the document? Maybe it was for someone else in Lucy's family, which was none of her business. She had no right to snoop. That word alone made her feel cheap.

As she placed the tube back in the bag, the paper opened further, revealing an address in France for a clinic in a château. The dates overlapped with their trip. What the hell? She heard the doorknob turn in the bathroom. Guilty, she jumped back, the paper still in her hand. Lucy wandered out of the shower, wrapped in a set of towels. "How was the Globe?" she asked, reaching for her glass of wine.

"Great," she said, looking past Lucy. Somehow all the light-hearted fun she had enjoyed that day had vaporized. She needed to broach this topic carefully to avoid a big showdown. Something was up and they both knew it. "What's this?" said Joanne, sounding sharper than she meant to. After all, what if there was a logical explanation? Then again, she figured Lucy should have explained it all by now.

"A reservation," said Lucy, her eyes darting around the room, but not locking with Joanne's.

"Objection. Weaseling," Joanne said, using a term saved for times when they called each other on bullshit. She was joking, yet it meant she still wanted an explanation.

"Okay, I'll tell you what's going on. I have a major decision to make, and I need your support," Lucy said in a quiet tone.

Joanne's body tightened. "I thought we agreed to discuss big decisions." They were back to their old ways, which meant Lucy's hidden agendas, like the time she convinced Jo to attend a summer recreational camp, so she could pursue a camp leader, Collin. She had little interest in the activities while Jo mostly sat around waiting for her. And when things soured with Collin, as Lucy's mad flings inevitably did, Lucy wanted to crash the other camp across the lake.

That was Lucy–changing her mind and zigzagging her way through life. On the one hand, Joanne knew it wasn't the end of the world to be spontaneous and change plans, yet this time it wasn't summer camp. It had better be important.

Lucy set down her glass of wine. "Seriously Jo, it's big."

Joanne's guts folded squarely in two. "Life-altering big?", she asked, noting Lucy's fair-skinned face and freckles morphing into a translucent tone. This was serious. Did something happen to her or her family? Joanne couldn't imagine what was brewing, but it explained the volume of emails and texts since their arrival. She braced for one of Lucy's curveballs.

Chapter 13

Max

In the early hours, Max walked out of his apartment and descended the spiral staircase. With the sun beaming down from a roof window, the twisting iron grillwork below the handrails cast patterns on the floors, walls, and ceilings.

As an architect, he appreciated the delicate touches that brought these old apartment buildings to life. Some buildings in Paris were hundreds of years old and had withstood endless renovations inside each apartment, yet he loved the hallways and foyers because they stayed the same.

At the bottom of the stairs, he walked across the foyer on the dark ceramic tile floor and pressed a buzzer to unlock the tall wooden entry door. Stepping outside, he noticed the soft blue morning light and walked toward the office, taking the long route along the Seine. He got up early every day and set his fitness watch to fifteen thousand steps, to make sure he met his goal before arriving at the office.

Some people loved Paris at night–the lights, the packed cafés, the beautiful people walking the streets. Not Max. He loved first light in the morning. Paris was a city that woke up

CHAPTER 13

slowly, stretching and inching its way back to life after long nights of socializing and little sleep.

The sounds were simple: workers with brooms and small machines cleaned the streets, people walked and talked to their dogs, and a few tourists strolled along to enjoy the sights before rush hour. A sprinkling of cafés gradually opened on every street with a soundtrack of coffee machines grinding espresso beans.

Max walked at a fast clip to get his heart rate up. While he felt tired often from his condition, he mostly kept it to himself. He believed it was better to focus on the positive instead of the fatigue.

Lately, his hopes had grown as he got updates from his mother. She said she had located someone, a woman in Canada, who was considering a kidney donation. Over the past few months, she had taken many tests and each one was encouraging, as his mother explained.

Although his mother had turned up more potential donors than he thought possible within his extended family, most fizzled out. Either they weren't a blood match, or they were eliminated because of health conditions. Every time his mother uncovered another distant relative, she acted like that person would "absolutely be the one". While he appreciated her team spirit, he learned to adopt a wait-and-see attitude to reduce his disappointment when it didn't work out.

Yet, there was one woman who remained "on the books" as his mother described it in her all-business way. It moved Max to think a distant relative in Canada might consider it. Why? He would ask his mother.

As his blog followers grew, he learned a lot about the generosity of people. Often there was some connection between the person in need and the donor. That made sense to Max. Why else would someone put themselves at risk to help another?

He was always curious to find out their story and what motivated them. He invited donors and recipients to tell their story on his blog, including those who donated to anyone. He was so moved by the humanity of that act. Most people were more likely to receive a kidney from someone who died. With a waiting list of over 16,000 people in France, Max used his blog as a platform to encourage donations from every source.

Although most donor prospects did not work out, this mystery relative in Canada was looking good. His only concern was that the process dragged. His mother told him not to worry; they were "this close" she'd say, holding her finger and thumb together. And there were documents to sign. Max took her at her word because he knew few people said no to her. Still, it wasn't a done deal.

While waiting, Max pressed his mother for details. He so wanted to meet his potential donor, or at least find out about her and invite her to be a guest on his blog. Each time he asked his mother how they were related, she would tell him she couldn't say how.

He wondered why she wouldn't ask as part of getting to know the donor. His mother also said the woman insisted on remaining anonymous throughout the process, in case it didn't work out. Max accepted he wouldn't meet her before the operation but asked about after. His mother shrugged and said she'd do her best, but ultimately, they had to respect the donor's wishes.

Max knew that some donors didn't want to meet the recipient because they didn't want them to feel obliged to

CHAPTER 13

them. Also, he knew if the kidney were rejected, it would be a terrible blow for everyone.

Max had heard it all before, but this situation felt different because it was him. As he thought about receiving a live organ from someone else, his body felt a wave of energy flowing through him. Max dreamed of expressing his gratitude and he felt an incredible connection to this woman whom he had never met. He didn't even know her name! That felt wrong.

He pestered his mother, who wouldn't budge from her position. She warned him to be prepared in case the donor didn't want to meet him. Max stopped asking about it when she raised the topic. However, what his mother forgot was that he had inherited her iron will.

Chapter 14

Lucy

Her right eye twitched, which annoyed her because it revealed weakness. No matter how bad a situation, she was infamous for revealing nothing through her body language or speech. Lucy took acting lessons and played poker when she was studying law to learn the art of controlling facial expressions.

Joanne had demanded a full account of what was happening, and Lucy told her she had a life-altering decision to make. She wanted to be better prepared before explaining things to Joanne, yet she also knew the trip was in jeopardy if she didn't tell her exactly what was going on.

"Is this about your son, Daniel?" said Joanne.

Lucy jumped. It amazed her that with no hints, Joanne zeroed in on the source of the story. "How did you know?"

"He lives in Paris. Two plus two equals duh," said Joanne.

Lucy motioned her to sit down. Stress pulsed through her body in a figure eight. She had kept this terrible burden to herself. Surely Joanne would think she'd totally lost it for not being able to talk about her son and his situation. It felt so messy and complicated. "I'm not even sure where to start."

"How about the beginning," said Joanne, her voice calm "Since it's been holding your attention since we got here."

Lucy swelled with embarrassment for withholding something major from her best friend, who judged her the least of anybody she knew. "He needs a kidney transplant," she blurted.

"Oh my god, Lucy. Our baby!" gasped Joanne.

Lucy understood how much Joanne loved him. The three of them shared an apartment in Montreal while they were at university. It was there that Lucy became pregnant after a "stupid" weekend fling, as she described it. Joanne had helped her to figure out the implications of having a baby and going to university, and she encouraged her to finish her degree for the sake of her future. Together, they created a little nursery in the corner of Lucy's room. They shopped at second-hand stores to buy baby goods and supplies, which meant looking up all the words in French when asking for specific items. Joanne had taken a part-time job in a bar where she could earn maximum tips to contribute extra.

While a newborn was the last thing on their minds at university (they were dreaming about being career women), when the baby came home from the hospital, both changed. They adored Daniel Max Morin–who was given his father's last name–and fawned endlessly, marveling over his tiny, wrinkled feet.

He was a happy little boy with olive skin, arms and legs waving wildly, as if trying to make them laugh. It worked. He sported a large tuft of long black hair that folded on the top of his head like a cheap toupee when they messed it, or the wind caught it. The more they messed it, the harder he'd laugh. With his cute hair, beaming smile and adorable dimples, they called him Mr. Mop and Glow.

They both looked after him, even though Lucy reminded Joanne he wasn't her responsibility, and she should be out partying. Yet, Lucy welcomed the help because her mother had denounced the pregnancy and said there was no way she was traveling to Montreal to help her daughter. She was mortified by Lucy's behavior and informed her that God would punish her for her sins, as if He had updated her mother directly about his plans.

Lucy had expected her mother's dark response, but she still felt lonely and shunned. She knew she was leaning too much on her friend, but Joanne insisted she was doing it because she wanted to, and everything would be okay with Daniel.

If it wasn't for Joanne, Lucy wondered if she would have made it. Joanne was always there for her and the baby, no matter how crazy things got–and it got crazy. She also grieved almost as much as Lucy when the Morins took him away. Joanne knew more about the situation than anybody else on the planet, and that's why she deserved to know the truth about her son. "Yes, it's serious, Jo. Without it, he'll likely die."

"How do you know?"

"Elise got in touch."

"Jacques' wife?"

"Says she's desperate for 'her son' to survive," Lucy said, adding air quotes.

Joanne's eyes widened. "And?"

"She talked to me about Max," Lucy gulped.

"Max?"

"He now goes by his middle name. He sounds amazing. She told me a bit about him. He's only twenty-nine, already an architect, and married."

CHAPTER 14

"Incredible."

"What about Jacques? Why won't he help his son?"

"He's dead."

"When?"

"A few years ago."

"From?"

"Maybe bad karma?" Lucy said. Although she was joking, they both knew the hell that he put Lucy through to gain custody of the baby. Lucy could tell the news shook Joanne and was running scenarios through her mind. Their European vacation was shifting as if they were dancing on quicksand. It was all her fault, again. She refilled the wine glasses. "I'm so sorry to add this to our lives."

"So, if I understand, saving his life all comes down to you?"

Lucy gulped. She felt her responsibility growing. "I did several tests over the past couple of months. Things like blood, tissues, health conditions, among others. It's looking good for me to be the donor."

"How about Jacques' family? Couldn't anybody donate a kidney?"

"Elise contacted all of them. A few did tests, and they didn't work out. Most said no."

"She must be desperate," added Joanne.

"No kidding. I'm the last person she wants to beg."

"Did she grovel?"

Lucy smiled. "Not yet, but I want to see some before this is over."

"How do you finally confirm you are a suitable match?"

"There'll be a few more tests."

"When?"

Lucy gauged the look on Joanne's face. She had been

noticing sympathy up to this point, but now Lucy had to level with her. "Umm. That's why I booked the tickets to Paris." She saw Joanne's eyes had darkened and her face flushed from white to pink, then red. "Sorry to spring that on you."

"SORRY? Is that it? Was this why you invited me to Europe?"

Lucy shifted in her seat. Jo's glacial tone unnerved her. She sounded so upset and calm, it scared her. "Jo, I... I..."

"And why didn't you tell me?"

Lucy knew it was a simple question that deserved a brilliant answer, yet she came up short. Her lips stiffened around her mouth. "I don't know and I'm so sorry, Jo. Really."

"Well, it's not the first time you've pulled this nonsense, Lucy McGee," said Joanne. "Quitting university in the first year. Your father's heart attack. Don't get me started. I don't know why you live in such a secret world."

Lucy took the verbal blows without arguing. "Joanne, you are so right. I don't know," Lucy said, sounding just as perplexed. She could see Joanne had hit the boiling point and was slowly returning to a simmer. "I am sorry, Jo."

"Well, shit. Never mind about that right now. Is Max okay?"

"Yes, he's okay now. But he won't be in the future."

Chapter 15

Joanne

Even though Joanne was concerned about Max's health because she was part of his life for the first two years, Lucy's actions frustrated her. She had promised herself that things would be different on this trip and she'd be part of the decisions. And she no longer wanted to be the friend who just responded to Lucy's agenda.

Joanne knew serious things were in the works, and they had to figure this out together. Taking an angry stance against Lucy was counterproductive, she decided. "Okay Lucy, help me understand what you were thinking when you planned this trip."

"Honestly, I wanted to get away. When I thought about Europe and the fun we had in 1986, it just made sense."

"You haven't thought about me very often in the past few years."

"I was busy. When I didn't return a couple of messages, I felt stupid when too much time had passed."

Joanne's high spirits were vaporizing with every passing minute. She dreamed of a vacation from her own life, and it sounded so exciting and out of the blue. Now it was going sideways with Lucy at the helm. "Guess I'm a slow learner with you," she said, but soon regretted it. That wasn't her normal response to anybody, let alone her friend. But she couldn't disguise her hurt with the scenario unfolding.

Lucy took a breath. "Nobody else knows what happened back in Montreal."

"What happens if something goes wrong with the kidney transplant?" Joanne pleaded as extreme scenarios played out in her head.

"That's why I want you with me. Please, Jo, I need you beside me to get through this."

Joanne shifted in the chair. "Well, shit." She could see that for once, Lucy showed a rare side of herself: vulnerability. Joanne found it a relief from her usual tough exterior. Lucy's problem was that she either had to be in control of a situation or be the victim. Both stances were annoying.

"I realize it's not ideal. You of all people deserve better," added Lucy.

"You probably faked running into me at the Farmers' Market. Am I right?"

Lucy blushed. "I had to. Dave and the kids aren't aware of this chapter in my life. Will you help me?"

Joanne stared out the window to gather her resolve. She wanted to show Lucy she was no longer a doormat. She had boundaries. Lucy needed to grow up. Yet she knew Lucy was telling the truth about her as a travel mate. They were like sisters. She turned the wine glass by the stem, staring at the bowl to avoid eye contact.

"Please, Jo," Lucy whispered.

Joanne glanced at Lucy who, under pressure, normally

resembled a fenced-in bull, ready to bust out of the pen. She looked panicked. Joanne realized that she'd been holding her breath for the past minute and let the air escape. "Well, what are the next steps in this crazy Lucy escapade?"

"You mean you'll help me through this?"

Joanne nodded. Lucy jumped up and hugged her longer than she had ever done before. Lucy finally pulled herself together and leaned back. "Thank you so much, my friend. I love you. I owe you big time."

"Jeez, don't get too soft on me, girl. It's not like you," joked Joanne, even though her heart filled with warmth and love for little Max, who was now an adult. In fact, the thought of seeing Max again excited her.

Although Lucy was the natural mother, Joanne had forged a solid bond with him as a baby. Back in Montreal, when Lucy gave up custody, Joanne remembered in painful detail the day the authorities took him away to be raised in France. Lucy curled up on the sofa for days, gripped by grief.

Now the whole painful past was resurfacing. For Joanne, something seismic shifted when Lucy explained the new turn of events. She wondered what might unfold over the next few weeks, yet she sensed it was a chance for Lucy to do right from her past.

She wanted Lucy to finally meet her son again and establish a relationship with Max as an adult. Also, Joanne knew it was time for Lucy to tell her husband and family about a secret she had carried for twenty-nine years. She felt it was the right thing to support Lucy; however, she wondered what would happen with their vacation. She decided it was secondary.

"Okay, what happens now, Lu?" Joanne asked, signaling that she was agreeing to the complete plan.

Lucy shifted into official mode. "Well, it starts with me doing a live donation at a private clinic in Paris. And Max gets the kidney right away. Healthy donors are usually up and about within two to four days."

"A few days? That's it?" Joanne said.

"Yes. It's done with a procedure–laparoscopy–the cuts are tiny and there's minimal disruption. So as long as everything unfolds as it should, no problem."

"Wow. Then what?"

"Here's the fun part," said Lucy. "You would join me at this clinic, which looks more like a stunning château. You'll enjoy a week to ten-day spa experience, while I convalesce in style."

"So," Joanne said, trying to imagine all the things that Lucy might have skipped. "If I say yes, Lu what are the next steps?"

"Easy, peasy," said Lucy. "We take the Chunnel from St. Pancras in London. In less than three hours, we'll be sipping café au lait in a Parisian bistro. I'll do a couple of last-minute tests to be sure I'm okay. Then I prepare for the operation."

Joanne recognized Lucy's expression. They were either in for a wild and fun time, or just a wild time. "What's that going to cost me, Lu?"

"Not a cent and we're talking thousands of euros a day," added Lucy.

"What about Max, do I get to see him again?" said Joanne. Suddenly she was gripped with joy about seeing him.

"I'm not sure if we can see Max after the operation. But you know I want to!"

"Who's behind this? Elise? And what do we have to do?" Joanne groaned, she knew the answer by the soured look on Lucy's face.

"Yes. Worse, we have to meet her. It won't be pretty."

Chapter 16

Lucy

Dragging herself around the room, trying on a few more outfits, Lucy couldn't get herself to hurry. She watched Joanne as she kept busy checking her watch, gathering her carrying bag and putting her shoes on. The afternoon loomed in her face, yet all she wanted to do was curl up for a nap.

"We need to leave soon to meet Elise," said Joanne.

The two of them walked quickly, double the speed of most strolling Parisians, arriving at the café ahead of their meeting. She scanned the room to see if Elise Vincent Morin had arrived. Lucy was familiar with Jacques' wife from Max's Facebook page–the type of woman who wore chic clothes and never had a bad hair day. It was hard enough talking to her on the phone, and she dreaded seeing her in person.

Lucy ordered cappuccinos, and the two friends chatted in spurts, ready to stop anytime. Lucy fidgeted, but kept talking about nothing. Fifteen minutes past the arranged time, a woman walked in. Heads turned.

"Looks like Madame has arrived," said Joanne, nodding toward the front.

Lucy swiveled her head around and returned it quickly, doing her best to appear disinterested. Lucy knew from the woman's dress style she believed she was the most important person in the room.

Elise wore a black suit with gold buttons and a delicate trim around the edge of the jacket. The skirt, an inch above her knees, led the eye down her slender legs to designer pumps. Her hair, nestled behind her ears, revealed tiny earrings. A raincoat with the tie wrapped in back, and an expensive leather bag signaled wealth.

She tugged each finger out of her leather gloves, like a magician building tension to dazzle the audience. Lucy hadn't even met her and already didn't like her. "Ah yes, the aging French woman who looks perfect. She must be a size two."

"More like minus two." Joanne mused. "How do they achieve that simple, yet exquisite vibe?"

"Who knows? I wore my expensive outfit, new lipstick, and fussed with my curls for an hour to make it appear messy. How come I don't look like that?"

"You're trying too hard to act like you aren't trying…. if you know what I mean."

"Sadly, I do," Lucy said. "And if I tucked my hair behind my ears, you'd accuse me of not washing my hair."

"True that," said Joanne, continuing to sneak glances.

Elise stood at the door, as if waiting for the world to come to her. She checked the room, nodding at a couple as she made her way to the back. Lucy could see there was no smile or expression on her face, only a practiced look of Parisian exquisiteness.

"We must look like tourists," said Joanne.

Lucy tightened up. She was ready for Elise. "Well, too bad

for her. I've got the spare kidney, and therefore the upper hand."

"Do you want me to leave?"

"Don't move, my friend." Lucy smiled at her friend, yet she was distracted by Elise arriving at the table. She looked at Joanne, then Lucy. Joanne rose, as if responding to the woman's superiority. Lucy remained welded to the seat.

"Lu-ceee," she said, extending her hand to Lucy in a strict adherence to manners. Lucy paused before shaking hands and caught a wink of support from Joanne. With her two-second delay, Lucy assumed control of the meeting. Although she sensed Elise wouldn't back down without a fight.

"Elise. This is my best friend Joanne."

"Enchanté," Joanne said, blushing slightly.

Lucy realized her friend's formal and awkward response, which made her sound enchanted to meet Elise, was straight out of their high school French class.

"Allô," Elise said, ignoring her. A cloud of tension hung over the table.

"How's Max?" said Lucy. For the first time, she could see Elise had lost her cool. Her facial expression, as if painted gradient shades of red, looked ready to burst.

"I'll get right to the point," said Elise. "He has end stage renal disease. The dialysis is only enough to keep ahead of the game. Although he's young and strong, there will be complications as it progresses."

"Uh huh," said Lucy.

"A new kidney is the only solution. He is on a waiting list, but it could take years. He also has a rare blood type."

"AB positive by chance?

Elise exhaled. "Yes."

"Same as me," said Lucy, watching Elise squirm as she scored the first point for being the birth mother. "If he doesn't get a transplant?"

"He could die. The doctor said a live family donor gives him the best chance of surviving. In fact, he could lead a normal life."

Lucy stared at her, emotion pumping through her body. She wanted to throttle the woman who caused her so much pain. "If, and that's a big if... tell me about the medical care."

"As you are aware, France has the best health care system in the world."

"Go on," said Lucy. She was unaware of that fact but would not admit it to Elise.

"Once you do the last tests to make sure everything is okay, the transplant from you to Max will unfold precisely and quickly," said Elise, her words struggling to keep up with her thoughts. "I will provide a nurse concierge for the entire time at the clinic. She will manage your stay, navigate the system, translate if needed, and ensure you do not have a single worry."

Elise slowed down slightly to take a breath. "You can take all the time you need to convalesce. I have arranged for two top-rated nephrology specialists to look after you exclusively while you are there. Benedicht is also a family friend."

"Of course," said Lucy. She figured Elise had likely befriended him once Max's condition was diagnosed, just in case she needed him later on.

"I personally guarantee you will have the best care in the world. You'll be on your feet within one week to ten days," said Elise. "Then you can return home to Nova Scotia."

Lucy stared at Elise with no expression. She knew Elise was aiming to impress her with the luxury of it all. She was entertained by Elise's sales pitch to grab the kidney and send her home in days, as if she couldn't wait to get rid of her. Lucy wasn't letting her off the hook that quickly. "And what about Joanne?"

"Who?" said Elise, looking around without noticing the woman to her left.

"My best friend," said Lucy, gesturing to Joanne. "I want her with me after the operation at this Six Star medical spa."

Elise waved her hand lightly, as if whisking away a buzzing mosquito. "My concierge will book a private room for her and take care of everything." Elise smiled for the first time. "Does this mean you'll do it?"

Lucy inhaled deeply and looked Elise in the eye. "I need to weigh all the factors." She wanted Elise to feel the helplessness she felt back in Montreal when she and Jacques took Max from her.

"He's your son," Elise hissed. "What do you want? Money? Name your price."

She fumed that Elise fixated on money, as if it could solve every problem. Health was the great leveler. Lucy knew someone could have all the money in the world, but without health, nothing else mattered. "I don't care about your money." Lucy took a deep breath. "I want to meet Max."

"Absolutely not. I can't."

"Can't or won't?" Lucy shot back. She could see Joanne scorekeeping a fierce game of tennis. Forty-Love for Lucy. Clearly, Elise was used to issuing orders, not taking them.

Elise stared at her coffee before looking up. "This is no time to be stubborn."

"Glad to hear you say that, so let's tell him about me, shall we?"

"I won't put my son under more strain before a life-saving operation."

Lucy drew a breath. She sensed a thought bubble from Joanne, that Elise had made a good point. While Lucy didn't like to admit when she was wrong, she understood the art of negotiation: everybody needs to win something. She paused for effect. "Okay. How about after?"

"Why must you make such demands?"

She wanted to inflict pain on Elise and make her see she didn't get to control every detail. "Don't you get it? I want to see my baby now that he's grown up. I want to hug my son and mostly, I want him to know who I am."

"Status quo is what he needs now. That's the best way forward," said Elise, crossing her arms. Lucy could tell Elise's negotiation style was bludgeoning people into submission. "I have my needs too," said Lucy, not caring that customers were noticing her tone.

"This is not what he needs at this stage of his life and health condition. We were exemplary parents. We gave him everything. Promise me you will give this further thought."

"You too. See if you can come to your senses."

"*Au revoir*," said Elise, sounding barely civil as she left the restaurant.

"Wow," said Joanne.

"Double wow. Can you believe her arrogance? I'll show her."

"Why do you insist on getting back at her?" said Joanne.

Lucy sat rigid in her chair, anger snaking around her every thought. After a minute of silence, she looked at Joanne. "Why are you asking me this?"

"I want to understand your motivation. Do you want Max

to know who you are? Or do you want to be the hero who swoops in and saves the day—"

"What are you trying to say?" Lucy fumed.

"Why continue the battle with Elise? You both have a common goal here, saving Max's life. I guess do it for the right reason, to save his life. And really, get on with it."

Lucy sighed. She wished she had a fraction of Joanne's wisdom and integrity. It wasn't what she wanted to hear right after the heated conversation with Elise.

She picked up the tiny spoon and scraped the foam in her cup. "I heard what you said." Lucy's tone softened, but she fixed her gaze across the restaurant to avoid looking Joanne in the eye. "I still need time to nail down details with Elise. But yes, let's do this."

Chapter 17

Max

Max arrived and kissed his mother on both cheeks. They sat on a formal, creamy white sofa that looked like it had never received a visitor or dealt with the daily drudgery of mucky kids. There were no empty glasses on the coffee table, minor spills, or messy clues revealing that anyone lived there.

The elegant living space could receive an architectural magazine editor dropping by with no tidying. Expensive furniture in the Louis XIV style rounded out the room. While Max appreciated his mother's taste, he viewed her place as a triumph of style over comfort.

A massive apartment in the sixteenth *arrondissement* served as her Paris home. The principal room entertained friends and clients of the family vineyard when they were in the city. Max had spent most of his time here in his youth, yet still felt like everything was so distant and not like a home. Someday, he would inherit this apartment in his family for generations. Yet he couldn't imagine living in a rambling formal space with three people, when it could hold ten. As an architect specializing in tiny spaces, he was more excited to figure out how to repurpose it to reduce its environmental footprint and house a small village.

Without brothers and sisters, he recalled the dull evenings seated at the dining table with visiting adults who discussed business with his parents. He couldn't wait to be excused from the guests so he could return to his passion: building a town out of Lego.

He smiled at her; she returned a preoccupied smile. Max knew something was in the works. After his father died, his mother surprised everyone with her business acumen. She and her lawyers had negotiated a buy-out with the law firm that her husband had founded, showing an uncanny ability to beat them at their own game.

Buoyed by that victory, she then took control of her family's winery, sagging under the incompetence of her brother's ownership. After implementing tough changes that everyone fought, she revived the family fortune within five years.

Success carried pain, such as cutting back on expenses and eliminating employees and unprofitable products. Yet she led the company back to prosperous times. When she won several business awards for her feats, she was interviewed about her achievements. She claimed there was no secret–only common sense and hard work–a comment aimed squarely at her oldest brother.

Max applauded his mother's talents. While he was growing up, she busied herself with activities such as charity events, shopping and lunching. She never appeared enthusiastic about any activities, even though her fundraisers were legendary for their astronomical results.

Every charity dreamed of her chairing their event. As she started learning the wine industry from her father and uncle,

Max observed her incredible success in the new role. He knew it was not about money; she was protecting the family vineyard that had begun five generations earlier. Over time, she proved she should have been the successor to the wine business, not her brother, who stayed on the payroll without "getting in the way" as she described it.

She slid a fluted glass toward Max and lifted hers by the stem to avoid warming the glass. *"Kir Royale?"* he asked, noting the red blackberries and bubbly champagne dancing up and down. She nodded, proposing a toast.

Max raised the glass and went along with the ritual because he knew she preferred not to drink alone. He no longer drank at all; instead, he focused on staying healthy. However, during each visit around cocktail hour, she still served him, and he pretended to share a cocktail.

"I met with your relative," said Elise.

"How did it go?" said Max, trying not to sound obsessed.

"We're nearly there. She's a strong-willed woman."

"Guess we get that from both sides of the family," said Max, teasing her.

"She has minor concerns."

"Such as?"

"Things such as timing, legal and practical questions. But don't worry, it will work out," said Elise.

Max believed her, yet it didn't sound like they were nearly there in his mind. "Are you sure? Anything can happen."

"One hundred percent. Perhaps the lure of recovering in a luxury clinic, along with her friend, will sweeten the arrangement. She could never afford this."

"Is money an issue for her?"

"Non. She has a home, career, family and annual travel–you

know, the usual. Modest by our standards." Max winced at his mother's description. He never liked the "us and them" description for other people; in fact, it was the opposite philosophy of how he ran his business. Yet, it was a long-entrenched attitude in his family. He loved her and didn't feel it was his place to change her. "Sounds like she and her family have a decent life."

"Yes, although I sense she has a taste for luxury well above her station. My offerings will help clinch the deal."

"How is she related to us?"

"I can't say exactly, but she's connected to your father's side. I dug around, and one thing led to another. *Et voilà!*"

Max glanced at his mother. Something didn't sound quite right. "Oh, really? I don't remember him mentioning relatives in Canada."

"Your father wasn't close to his extended family."

"Or immediate family," he joked, knowing his father hadn't connected beyond their household. Max thought about his own relationship with his father, which was barely a relationship. His legal practice demanded long hours, plus with his business travel, Elise's family and their social calendar, he spent little time with Max.

Eventually, Max joked he was just a family prop to complete the expectations of upper bourgeois society. As proof, there were few family photos, because there were few events they did together. The friendships that Max forged at university became his family.

"I didn't want to pry about family connections, so I was careful to tread lightly," she added.

"Understood."

"Honestly, it doesn't matter how she is related. As long as

she donates a kidney."

"Why do you think she might do it? Dozens of relatives have said no."

Elise slipped her delicate fingers around the stem and took a sip. "She offered no explanation, and I didn't wish to push—"

"Of course not," said Max, not wanting to pry. His mother asked him to entrust it to her, and she delivered on her promise. It amazed him how far she searched to find him a kidney–and that she never lost her motivation despite all the negative responses she received. "I wish I knew her. What's her name?"

"As I said, she wants to remain anonymous."

"I will respect that, yet I'm deeply moved by her generosity–assuming she says yes."

"Don't worry."

Max glanced at his mother, full of hope at the thought of getting a new lease on life. With that, he could care for his wife and child, have a career, and follow his dream of helping others.

Inside, he felt much love for his unknown cousin, but mostly for his mother, who wouldn't quit until she found a match. He gave her a hug. A tear hovered in her eye, yet she stared straight ahead. He released her but stayed nearby. "Thank you so much, *maman*. I love you and I can never, ever—"

"Ssshh," she said, squeezing his hand. "It's what any mother would do for her child."

Chapter 18

Joanne

She opened her tablet at the hotel and checked her inbox. Nothing from Gretchen, which didn't surprise her, even though she asked for an update. Damn. Her husband Peter avoided email where possible. The silence from Emmaleigh puzzled her; she was the daughter who loved to stay in touch.

There was an urgent message from her cousin Bev. Through a rambling note, she revisited the possibility of selling the shop. She wished Bev wouldn't drink and email. Joanne would contact her when she got back. What she wanted was news of her family.

She called Gretchen; it went to voicemail. She sent a text and waited five minutes. Gretchen was never far from her cell, even in the shower. Concerned, she rang Emmaleigh, who picked up right away. A wave of relief swept through her.

"*Bonjour, Maman,*" she sang in her best French accent. Joanne glowed. No matter how things unfolded in her family, she could always count on Emmaleigh to bring positivity to the situation. "How are you, darling?" Joanne settled in to get the news.

"Perfect. And you?"

"Better now that I've heard your voice. I contacted everyone and didn't get a single reply. I wanted to make sure everything is fine."

"It's all good, Mom. We were trying to let you have a fun vacation. How is it?"

Joanne hesitated before responding. She thought about the complications surfacing by the minute, thanks to Lucy. Although Emmaleigh would understand if she explained, she didn't want to reveal anything that might cause worry. She felt annoyed with Lucy for pulling her into something that she felt she couldn't reveal. That wasn't the way she functioned with her family, and she vowed to let them know as soon as she understood what was happening. For now, it was a vacation report to her daughter. "Awesome. We had a great stay in London. I went to Shakespeare's Globe and saw *A Midsummer Night's Dream*."

"Cool. Wish I could be there with you!"

Suddenly she felt homesick and missed her family, wishing she could have shared that experience. And she wouldn't be in the thick of Lucy's mess. "Let's do this sometime, Em. The entire family."

"You bet," said Emmaleigh, pausing. "I thought you were going to Amsterdam after London."

"Anything can happen with Lucy McGee." She heard Emmaleigh erupt with a hearty laugh. Joanne loved that she never judged others, yet she understood the flying circus that was Lucy. "How are you and Gretchen doing?"

"Great, she's been coming out to the garden lots every day."

Joanne winced. She wished she could better understand Gretchen. At home, Joanne tried to get her into the fresh air

CHAPTER 18

and sun. Gretchen turned down requests with one syllable that made Joanne feel stupid for even asking. But she never gave up, likely due to Gretchen's irritation. "Wow, what's your secret?" she asked, feeling inadequate whenever someone had a breakthrough with Gretchen.

"I can't take credit, Mom. Ally-Up is more of a motivator. He's going places, I can tell you. He's already applied to study at the chef school."

Joanne laughed. "Well, maybe he'll motivate Gretchen to eat."

"In all seriousness, Mom, it wouldn't surprise me," said Emmaleigh. "There's something about him that is so uplifting, it rubs off on her."

While Joanne wished she had been the one to help her daughter deal with her issues, she was happy at least someone could reach her. "I guess I shouldn't worry, right Em?"

"Not at all. She's progressing. You have yourself a wonderful time and don't fret about a thing."

"Love you. And send my love to Gretchen. If you can fit in a hug, even better."

Emmaleigh chuckled. "Right! The sister with a no-hug zone around her. Love you, Mom."

She hung up, torn between feeling elated and inadequate as a mother. Why couldn't she and Gretchen have fun with each other? "I spoke to Emmaleigh," she said to Lucy, her mood lifting with news of her family.

Lucy almost looked up from her work. "All good?"

Joanne nodded. "She said Gretchen leaves the house now."

"Uh huh," said Lucy, but Joanne could tell that she was preoccupied.

"Seems like Gretchen is crushing on—"

Lucy was busy typing texts and pinging back and forth. "Go on—"

"That guy, Ally-Up," said Joanne.

"Hmm." Lucy finally muttered, letting Joanne down with her lack of interest. Whenever Lucy raised a topic, Jo was always keen to hear. Now that something was happening with her daughter, Lucy's mind was far away. It didn't bother her when they were younger, but on this trip, it was annoying her. But she also understood that Lucy was in a tough position–all her own doing but still problematic.

"Oh, and Bev sent me an email and said she'd sell the business for a hundred thousand dollars."

Lucy howled while still typing. "For what? She doesn't even own the building. She should pay you a hundred grand."

"I know. Maybe I'll offer her ten grand when I get back." Lucy didn't respond. Whatever, Joanne thought, she wouldn't worry about Lucy's opinion. Maybe Bev's shop wasn't even the answer. She'd still have to renovate so much it wouldn't be worth it. But she loved the thought of working with her friend Holly at the café. She chose to focus on the present and let things at home unfold as they should.

"Well, Lu, you are deep in thought. What's up?"

Lucy looked surprised. "Okay, before I make the final decision about the kidney, there's something I have to do. And I'd like you to be part of it."

"Does this involve breaking the law?"

Lucy ignored her comment. "How do you feel about moving to a hotel in St. Germain? This is positive and fail-proof."

"Fail-proof? I'm not concerned about the hotel, it's your plans once we get there."

"Well, I didn't raise Max, so he still seems so... distant to me," said Lucy. "I have to see him, make sure he's real, so to speak, before I do this. The last time I saw him–hell, *we* saw him–was twenty-seven years ago. He was a toddler, for heaven's sake." She continued, "I've missed all the milestones–every birthday, school graduation, and university. The list is endless. And I don't care what anyone says: when a mother loses a child, whether it's by adoption or custody, she never stops thinking about them. Never. We push it down deep, but honestly, that feeling still simmers in the background. It's a hurt that won't let up."

Joanne almost gasped to hear her talk about Max. Lucy had never acknowledged her lifelong pain to Joanne, and possibly not even to herself.

Joanne was the one who shared that time in Montreal with Lucy and little Max. And over the years, Lucy said little, even when she asked questions. Suddenly, Joanne felt tenderness. "I get it, Lucy. I'm not his mother, but I sure loved the little guy. I can't even imagine what he looks like as a young man."

"That's why I wanted you here with me."

"Fair enough," said Joanne. "So, why move to St. Germain?"

Lucy's eyes lit up. "The hotel is on the same street as Max's architectural firm. On his blog, he mentions walking there every day. The place opens at eight in the morning. My plan is to be out for a stroll as he arrives, to get a glimpse of him. Then I can truly get my head around this operation. What do you think, Jo?" Lucy belted out.

"Whoa, slow down, Lu!" Joanne wondered what else Lucy had planned. But that was Lucy. Lucy looked disappointed that Joanne was even hesitating. Images of young Max flooded her memory. "Let's do it!" she said.

Lucy picked up her empty suitcase and pointed to Joanne's,

indicating next steps. She beamed like a carefree kid. In fifteen minutes, suitcases bulging, they were ready to leave. Joanne joked she had now seen Lucy pack quickly when she put her mind to it–and she'd be expecting more of it in the future.

Joanne had to do one last check of the room, with Lucy arguing, until Jo found her curling iron. She handed it to Lucy with a told-you-so look. Lucy laughed and shoved it into her bag, then whisked them both out the door.

Chapter 19

Lucy

While they were waiting to get into their room, they visited a café next door. Lucy pulled out the diary, flipping through until she found a section that amused her. "Remember Serge?"

"Of course! Lucy, you were wild back then."

"Maybe yes, but I swear we had more fun than anybody else backpacking through Europe." She returned to the diary. "Blah, blah, blah," she said, turning the pages. She looked at Joanne over her glasses, then went back to read: "Serge owns the trendiest club in Paris, *Salle Tight Squeeze*. Impossible to get in. And he tells us some incredibly famous woman that we never heard of got her start there. I want in!"

"Yeah, you begged him to give us guest passes, Lu. It's what you offered in return," said Joanne.

Lucy laughed. "Right, this is when I made up the *Lulu and JoJo Show*. I promised him we'd perform a dance that was better than Josephine Baker. Jeez, I was arrogant!"

Joanne shook her head. "All I remember is that Serge called you Venus on the half shell dressed by Madonna."

"And called you Heidi, making you wear that wholesome

outfit."

"Lu, to this day, I still don't know what you did out there on the stage."

Lucy sipped her coffee and shook her head. "It's a blur. I recall peeling off a tank top and a t-shirt, with many more layers. Good thing it was the eighties."

"I refused to dance, so you made me catch things."

"Shit, you folded the clothes neatly and placed them on a chair," Lucy mimed her friend's careful folding. "Brought the house down. I yelled, '*Elle est canadienne!*' as if that explained your desire to perform domestic laundry chores instead of dancing. They thought it was part of the act and cheered you on!"

Joanne blushed. "Oh my god. I didn't know what to do. All I remember was you, Lulu, half drunk, swaying and shouting over the music to me, 'Wave the hair, girl, wave the hair!'. And then we ran off backstage and escaped with that crazy woman from wardrobe chasing us. Honestly, I don't know how we got outside."

Lucy said. "Me either, but we sure got nice outfits out of the deal. Here's the zinger," she said, reading the last sentence: *"Our theme song for today: Tina Turner's "Private Dancer" (mais oui!)."*

Lucy slapped the diary closed. "Admit it JoJo, *that* was a night to remember."

Joanne flicked the little packet of sugar on the side of her latte. "True, but you could have gotten us into a lot of shit with Serge."

Lucy shrugged. "I took us to the brink, and you saved us with your antics." Lucy tossed back the rest of her coffee, her face looking more serious. "We have something bigger and more important to achieve on this trip." She checked her watch. "Look at that. We can now officially check into the hotel."

***

"It's great to be back in St. Germain," said Lucy as they stepped off the elevator. They pushed their way down a cramped hallway. She opened a narrow door which hinted at the room's square footage. Lucy surveyed the pint-sized space. She couldn't imagine it for herself, never mind sharing it with Joanne.

There were two single beds pushed together in the middle, skirted by a one-foot path around the beds. "Wow, given what we are paying, I can't imagine what it would cost to have enough space to walk around." She walked into the bathroom and hooted. Things were getting smaller. "Check this out. You have to curl into a fetal position to get in the shower. Then you get this little nozzle. How the hell do you take a shower?"

Joanne walked to the door, unable to squeeze in fully with Lucy. Laughing, she backed out of the room to let Lucy out. "I'm getting claustrophobia. How many nights did you say?"

"I didn't," she said as they edged into the room and plopped on the bed. She was in the perfect location for Max-spotting and nothing was going to move her. "Glass of wine?" Lucy asked without waiting for an answer.

She pulled two tumblers out of paper wrappings and a bottle out of her bag. She slid a glass towards Joanne. "Funny, if we served wine in a scratched tumbler at home, we'd be crass, but in France it looks cool," observed Lucy. They clinked. "I like the small size though–you can refill them more often."

"Now wait a minute, let's not get too carried away with the

drinking. We've got a big assignment tomorrow," said Joanne.

"Yes. Mom." She had no intention of going overboard with the wine and didn't need her friend dousing a tiny flame with a firehose. She noted hurt on Joanne's face and knew it was just her way. "I get it, Jo. But let's just have a drink and a few laughs."

Once they settled in, Joanne asked. "So, what's the big clandestine plan to see Max?"

Lucy stood up and eased around the room to the open window, waving her friend over. Excited, she leaned over the iron grill work, surveying the scene below.

On the street, there were three lanes of cars merging into two, and munchkin-sized scooters on the sidewalks parked so tight you couldn't slide a euro between them. Lucy pointed. "See that building down the street? The one with three large windows?"

"Yup."

Lucy's heart thumped with excitement and pride. "That's Max Morin's architectural firm."

"Really? *Super chic*," said Joanne.

"Yes. He works there with his wife."

"You know this because….?"

"Facebook and his blogs," said Lucy.

Joanne sighed. "Are you going to ambush him?"

"Of course not. I promised not to reach out before the operation since he'll be under enough stress. I just need a view of him."

"Does this mean we will have to hang out the window like goof balls?"

"Not at all. I don't want to draw attention to myself."

"That'd be a first," said Joanne.

CHAPTER 19

Lucy sent her a wry smile. "Tomorrow morning, we'll go for a walk around seven forty-five, until he arrives at eight. That's when they open."

"How will we know it's them?" said Joanne. "There are endless beautiful young couples in Paris."

Lucy opened Facebook on her laptop and brought up Max's profile page. The posts were mostly about architecture that he loved and his wife Katarin, who looked stunning. They both gushed over the gorgeous couple.

"So how did you friend him on Facebook?" said Joanne.

"He's a public figure. I sent a friend request."

"Using your name?"

"I used an alias: Jane Dough. As in D.O.U.G.H."

"Oh my god, that is so you!" laughed Joanne.

"Now that our plan is in place for tomorrow, let's go out for a carafe of wine," said Lucy.

On the way back to the hotel, Joanne bought a large bottle of water to help counter the wine and they drank in turns. When the alarm rattled the room at seven the next morning, both growled and turned over until the third snooze alarm, which sounded more insistent. "Shit," said Lucy.

"What?"

"We barely drank and I'm so hungover."

"Not fair," whined Joanne, searching for her bottle of water and gulping it. She handed it to Lucy.

Lucy sat up and took a big swig. Her head felt foggy, yet she was charged with energy and ready to roll. "Life's not fair. But it's seven-fifteen and we need to get ready for Max."

"Uh huh," said Joanne, slipping back into a snooze.

"Seriously, Jo. I want a glimpse of him." Lucy felt like Joanne wasn't quite getting the importance of this morning's mission.

Joanne swung her legs to the side of the bed. She paused briefly.

"What?"

"I'm still trying to wrap up a dream," Joanne yawned. "Why do we want to finish a dream that has no beginning, middle or end?"

"You think too much, girl," said Lucy, tossing a sweater at her. They needed to keep a pace on, or she'd blow her entire plan.

"Caffeine. I need a lot."

"Max first, then coffee," said Lucy. They pulled on their clothes and stepped outside, looking like they had forgotten there was a mirror in their room. Joanne pulled a comb through her hair and handed it to Lucy.

They shuffled along the other side of the street, groggy and deep in thought. No sign of Max. While Lucy had a plan, there was no telling whether he would show up that day. He had to–she was officially willing him to do it. They walked up and back, appearing suspicious with each turnaround. They stood around, trying to fill time without becoming too distracted. Joanne stared at a small poster in a shop window. She chuckled.

"*What?*" said Lucy.

"Look, a lost pet poster, Parisian style. Check this out: '*Perdu*' and it has photos of a pooch."

Lucy chucked at the pink polka dot rain outfit with matching paw covers. "And it's a studio shot, with little umbrellas in the backdrop."

Joanne loosely translated. "Last seen in this area four days ago. Reward of five hundred euros–holy moly. Get this, it goes by the name of 'Madame Bovary'."

CHAPTER 19

"You sure that's not the owner?" This was exactly what she needed for a light distraction.

"No, she's Madame Laurent and here's her phone number." Joanne snapped a photo of the poster.

"Seriously?" laughed Lucy, her head wincing.

"That's a well-heeled Parisian dog."

"Can you imagine calling for this dog back home in Point Pleasant Park? *'Venez, venez Madame Bovary!'*" Lucy joked. "It would get a double ass kicking: once for wearing a froufrou outfit and twice for the name."

Lucy turned her head, and her heart jumped. She nudged Jo. Max and his wife appeared at the corner, clasping hands and chatting. The morning sun beamed a light around him like a halo–he was more beautiful than she could have imagined.

A tall man with shiny dark hair, he looked far beyond his years. His outfit was sophisticated and stylish, as if he had walked out of a photo shoot with French *Vogue*. His petite wife, with long straight hair, looked like an updated model from the 1960s. A perfect baby bump was barely noticeable through a designer t-shirt.

Lucy and Joanne snapped into action as if a film director had yelled "Action", linking arms, and suddenly walking and talking. Lucy couldn't stop staring. The couple joked, and he wrapped his arm around her and kissed her forehead.

"She's wafer thin!" Joanne gasped. "Oh my god, they're too cute!"

Lucy crossed the street. She needed to get closer, just a little closer. She felt Joanne holding her arm to prevent her from doing something stupid, but she didn't want her friend's help. A silent push-pull struggle unfolded.

Adrenaline surged through her body like an electrical

current, and instinctively she crossed the street. He was her baby, yet he looked nothing like a person from her world, with zero resemblance to her two children back home. He looked very French and oh so beautiful. As Lucy and Joanne neared the other side of the street, Max and his wife halted to share a laugh over a text. The four nearly collided.

"*Pardon*," he said. Lucy noted his impeccable manners as he side-stepped to let Lucy and Joanne pass. Lucy's arm brushed Max's sleeve and their eyes connected for a blink. A little further along, the couple turned into the architectural firm. Max glanced back briefly at the two women while holding the door for his wife. Lucy felt like her body had been created out of twisted wire.

Joanne reached out to hug her. "He's perfect, eh?"

Lucy choked up. "I remember the rush of emotion from when he was a boy and I was losing him."

"I know." Joanne said. "Me too." They walked in silence toward the hotel. "Does that help, Lu? I mean, to see him?"

"Yes and no," she mumbled. There was little to say; it would all sound clichéd. And yet she felt so torn up. She walked further, then stopped and stared at Joanne. "So, why should I put myself at medical risk, give them a kidney and politely disappear from their lives? Elise gets her damn son, a grandchild, and her life continues as it always does for people of wealth and power."

"As you'd say, 'Asked and answered, your Honor.'"

"It's not fair."

"Let me ask you something: what do you want out of this?"

Lucy hesitated. "I want to know my son Max."

"Okay, but I think it goes much deeper and I believe it's central to a happier future."

Lucy wondered what on earth Joanne was getting at. Even though she made excellent points, it sometimes took a while for her to get there. Lucy threw up her hands. "I'm lost."

"Okay, describe your life as you want it to be. Not just this trip, or Max. Everything."

Lucy raised her eyebrows at Joanne. "Well… let me think… My two beautiful children in Halifax happy and flourishing in their lives. My husband loving me despite my endless flaws. And Max, holding him and being part of his life–even in a tiny way. We've moved on from the past and now have a relationship."

"Anything else?"

"No more lying, or withholding the truth–to you, my family, my parents and friends. I would connect all the family dots as a unit."

"What do you think would happen then?"

Lucy thought about her question. Her friend sure had a way of drilling down to painful places. "I guess I wouldn't feel so alone. Sometimes I wake up from a dream and I'm sad. Then I think about everything."

"You mean that dream about the island? With the package that the rowing team keeps tossing back to you on shore."

"Ah shit, do you think the package represents Max?"

"Who knows?"

Lucy had never thought about analyzing her dream, but perhaps there was something to it. "Maybe the rowers are my family–and I've never allowed them to connect."

"Hey, I'm not a shrink. But you've had that dream for a long time."

"I can only remember wisps."

"Interesting, Lucy. Is there anything else?"

"I guess being accepted and loved for who I am. That would be the ultimate."

"Awesome."

"How do I get there?"

"Have you ever thought about forgiving?"

Lucy's face fell. She churned inside with the pain of Jacques and Elise. "Are you kidding? Those people who hurt me? It was shameful what they did. Jacques got me pregnant, then refused to have anything to do with me when I decided to keep the baby. He refused to give financial support because I wouldn't do what he wanted. And then his wife finds out about Max. She can't have children, so she decides she wants his child to raise. He only agrees to seek custody to save his marriage," said Lucy. By now words were pouring out; she couldn't hold back on the anger. "Joanne, he didn't even want to have children. He said that when I told him I was pregnant."

"I remember, and that's tough," said Joanne.

Lucy felt annoyed with Joanne for being sensible. "Does that explain why I don't want to forgive them? I want Elise to pay for the pain they caused. Otherwise, they get off scot-free."

"Forgiveness isn't about letting them off the hook. It's about letting go of an immense weight on your shoulders."

"And I should do that because—?"

"It will help you move on in life."

"I want an apology," fumed Lucy. Why wouldn't this be obvious to her friend?

"Jacques is dead."

"Elise isn't."

"I don't see Elise apologizing. Not her style."

Lucy looked defeated. "Well then, what's in it for me?"

"Letting go of the anger you've held for decades," said Joanne.

CHAPTER 19

A noisy car raced by, honking at a pedestrian who completely ignored him. Joanne waited until it passed. "Lu, I hope I didn't hurt you—"

"It's okay, Jo. Go get some coffee," said Lucy. "I need time to think on my own."

"You sure?"

Lucy nodded. "See you soon."

"I'll be at breakfast, ingesting as much caffeine as possible."

Lucy sat on the steps of a closed shop. She couldn't remember a time when she was more miserable. She knew she shouldn't punish Max. Yet she also realized that donating a kidney would mean telling her family the story of her and Jacques and the custody ambush long before her family was in the picture.

She thought about Max. He looked so happy with his pregnant wife. Lucy was healthy and almost fit. The risks for her donating her kidney were minimal, according to her research. She could give him and his family a beautiful life.

Noise from down the street rattled like a conga drum in her head. She stood up from the curb and waited for the stars dancing in front of her eyes to settle. As usual, Joanne had been the voice of reason and Lucy had lashed out at her. To Lucy, forgiving had always seemed like a sign of defeat or weakness.

She wondered how her friend could be so different from her. How did they even get along? Yet she loved Joanne. She imparted wisdom to Lucy (who sorely needed it) without being pushy. It just took a while before Lucy could understand the wisdom and admit it was true.

She walked back to the hotel restaurant. Joanne was gone; Lucy winced. She dragged herself up to the room and found a note from Joanne, saying she was off to the Luxembourg Gardens. Joanne suggested texting when Lucy was ready to talk.

A wave of relief swept over Lucy. She was lucky to have such a friend and wanted to reconnect immediately. She grabbed her jacket and headed out the door toward the gardens. First, though, she needed to address her urgent need: coffee.

Chapter 20

Joanne

After walking around the city and visiting museums all day, she stepped out of the Metro in St. Germain on the Left Bank. Even though she was tired, Joanne strolled through the narrow streets, glimpsing into art galleries, cafés and churches.

A honey-colored building invited her to turn onto Rue Jacob, which led to Place Furstemburg and a courtyard with graceful trees and Parisian lampposts. It cast a romantic hue in the darkening streets. That's what she loved about Paris: spontaneous visits on side streets revealed all kinds of beautiful places.

She returned to the hotel and settled into a chair to wait for Lucy. Strolling around a beautiful city on her own made her feel lonely–Paris was best enjoyed with friends or lovers. She visited the Louvre, knowing that Lucy would say she wanted to go, but would not end up doing it.

All day, Joanne's thoughts distracted her from taking in the masterpieces, even though she was in a museum with some of the best art in the world. With her love of art, she should have been more excited, yet she kept thinking about Gretchen, who hadn't texted. Although Gretchen didn't stay in touch like her sister, she'd usually respond with a syllable to her mother's texts, signaling everything was okay.

When she spotted the gallery that housed the Mona Lisa, she recalled the paper Gretchen had written for her art class in high school. It was one of the few proud moments that Gretchen shared with her family.

As Joanne entered the *Salle des États*, she gasped. A throng of people blocked the view of the painting for everyone except the pushiest viewers. Those who maneuvered through the crowds only got close enough to see the masterpiece, the size of a modest poster, behind glass. She noticed half the visitors standing with their backs turned, more interested in getting selfies with the painting in the background. Joanne remembered their visit in the 1980s with a handful of enthusiasts in the room studying the work of art, and one bored guard on a chair in the corner.

As she stared into the chaos surrounding Mona Lisa, she recalled the fun project she shared with her daughter. Gretchen had left it to the last minute, unable to find a topic that moved her enough to write a paper. Joanne had just read a story that highlighted theories around Mona Lisa's smile.

She showed the piece to Gretchen and encouraged her to come up with an alternative theory. For unknown reasons, the idea intrigued her. Joanne took her to the library, where a librarian showed Gretchen how to research the topic while Joanne added color photocopies to make her paper look better.

Gretchen proposed a theory about Mona Lisa's smile, or "lack of a smile which was hiding something" as she described it. The librarian said it was a brilliant topic. She worked feverishly on it most of the weekend, without complaint, and even handed it in on time. The paper received A+ from the hard-to-please art teacher, who asked her to present it to the class. Joanne and Gretchen celebrated with a giant smoothie, and they would sometimes joke about Gretchen's grimace as a Mona Lisa smile.

Joanne inched her way toward the painting and took a few shots, which was mostly of the back of people's heads and their outstretched arms and hands holding cell phones. After checking the photos, she wandered to the gift shop where she could take a better photo on a book cover. She popped off a teaser text that said 'smile', hoping for a fun reply. She waited five minutes. Joanne dialed Gretchen's number.

"Hullo," said Gretchen, her voice a metallic gray tone.

"Gretchen? What's wrong?" Joanne's heart pounded.

"Nothing." She dreaded these one-word conversations with her daughter. Something sounded odd, but it would be a major challenge to figure out what was going on in her daughter's head. Each episode with Gretchen chipped away at her confidence, and she wondered how it ever got this way. She had done her best to be a good mother, yet Gretchen steered the emotional agenda in most interactions. Even after years of asking, Joanne did not have a clue what she wanted. She thought about her friends with daughters running off to spas, more like best buds. Joanne didn't expect the two of them to be best friends, but why were they at loggerheads so often?

Joanne reviewed the photo of the Mona Lisa, ready for some fun. "Guess what I did today?"

"No."

"What do you mean, no?"

"Guessing stuff is stupid. Tell me."

Joanne ignored her rising irritation. "I saw the original Mona Lisa," she beamed.

"Uh huh."

"You don't sound good."

"I just woke up."

Joanne checked her watch; it was three in the afternoon back home. It seemed odd that an eighteen-year-old needed a nap. However, asking might trigger an outburst. "How are things?"

"Fine."

"So, what have you been up to?" Joanne's tone teetered between breezy and nosy.

"School, homework. The usual."

"Emmaleigh said you've spent some time at the Deep Roots garden."

"She had no right to tell you that."

"Honey, I wanted to find out if you're okay." An insistent beep looped in the background every two seconds. "Gretchen? What's that beeping?"

"What beeping?"

"Are you in the hospital?"

"Stop snooping," she said, hanging up.

Joanne stared at the phone, as if it might explain her daughter's reaction. Normally she took the high road, but today she dialed again, bracing for a snark-fest.

It rang four times. "What?"

Joanne recounted her life coaching session to help her communicate with her daughter. "Gretchen, I feel hurt when you speak to me that way," she said, her voice trembling.

Silence crept in, filling the air with deadweight. Joanne

would usually fill the quiet gaps, but this time she stayed silent.

"Sorry," Gretchen sulked in her best grumpy tone.

"I accept your apology. Honey, I have feelings. And I love you so much that when I think you are in trouble or—"

"Broke my leg," she blurted. There was no context setting. It was more of an info tease, likely to rattle her mother.

"Oh my god. How?"

Gretchen paused. "Dancing," she said, as if a single word explained everything.

Joanne gasped. Her mind spun like a roller coaster that reached its peak and was now plunging downward. "I don't know what to say," Joanne said, picturing Gretchen's mean-spirited grin whenever she delivered another blow to her mother.

"Then don't say anything. It just is. Hang on a sec—" Gretchen turned away from the phone to engage with people trying to move her. She yelped in pain and cursed at the person helping her.

Joanne panicked. "GRETCHEN... GRETCHEN, what's going on?"

She heard Gretchen in a heated conversation with someone. Then she caught Emmaleigh's voice in the distance. Joanne hung up and dialed Emmaleigh, her fingers shaking so much she had to correct each number she pressed.

"Hi Mom," Em said, sounding too normal.

"Em, what is going on? What's wrong with Gretchen?" her vocal cords straining.

"Hang on, I'm heading out to the hallway," she whispered as Gretchen wailed in the background. "Now I can talk. Gretchen is okay, she broke her leg–they're putting a brace on her, so she can go home."

"She said from dancing. Is that true?" Joanne needed to hear it from Emmaleigh before she would believe it.

Em paused as if choosing her words. "Yes... and several gashes that needed stitching."

"Where did it happen?"

"A rave at an abandoned barn on the South Shore."

The word "rave" fired up Joanne's anxiety. It wouldn't have been a "social dance"–what the hell was she thinking? That could only mean one thing. "Was she doing drugs?" Joanne asked, the stress ratcheting up to another level. Gretchen seemed hell-bent on continually shocking her mother. Maybe that wasn't fair, but that's what it felt like on the receiving end.

"You should ask Gretchen."

"She won't tell me. Please Em, I'm in Europe and I want news about my baby girl," her voice whispered pain.

"Gretchen danced nonstop for hours, then stepped into a rotting hole in the barn floor and fell. But maybe it was a blessing because she was dehydrated. She didn't realize she broke her leg until she tried to walk on it. The doctors set it and say it will heal."

Joanne filled with relief and fear. "Was she doing Ecstasy?" she asked Emmaleigh. Keywords like "dancing for hours" and "dehydration" raised the red flag. She couldn't for a minute imagine her daughter would do that, but Gretchen was full of surprises.

"I really don't know Mom, I'm sorry. She had a rough night, but she's doing better."

"What about Ally-Up? I didn't think he'd be doing that—"

"He refused to go asked her not to. She decided she was going anyway with a group of friends from school. Gretchen mumbled something about them splitting up over it, but she was miserable, so I didn't want to get her to repeat it."

"Oh jeez, Em, this is terrible. If she was walking on a broken leg, she may suffer from complications for the rest of her life. I'm coming back."

After a pause, Emmaleigh delivered the final blow. "Ah… Gretchen said not to come home. Sorry, but you realize what she's like. Dad came by right away and she sent him off. And she's barely tolerating me."

"Can I talk to her a moment?"

Emmaleigh said she'd return to Gretchen's bed. She told Gretchen their mother was on the line and Gretchen sounded peeved. She took the phone. "Look, I don't know what Em said, but it was a clean break that will heal. I'm in pain, so I need to sleep."

"But I need to find out what happened."

"I'm sure Miss Perfect told you every detail."

"Gretchen, I want to come home—"

"Mom. DO NOT come home. Finish your damn vacation with Lucy," she snarled, her voice a mix of anger and pain. Joanne froze with despair but didn't reply. She heard Gretchen take a breath. "Look, I'm not going anywhere with this broken leg, so don't rush."

"Did you do drugs, Gretchen?"

"Enough stupid questions for one day," she said and hung up the phone.

Based on her defensive tone, Joanne knew the answer. Now her daughter had another problem to add to her growing health woes. How did this happen? Joanne studied the photo of Mona Lisa on her phone. She recalled Gretchen being unimpressed by the painting and art world hype.

In the school paper, Gretchen suggested Mona Lisa expressed more of a "fuck you" smile–a calm, in-control smirk as if she had the goods on whoever was looking at her. And further, she was waiting for the right occasion to throw it in their face. Who better to figure that out than Gretchen? In fact, that was likely the expression she had only a moment ago, when she told her mother the news of her leg break. Joanne deleted the image.

She drew in a breath and pictured the biggest bouquet of colorful gerbera daisies to divert her emotions. She'd save crying for later when she was alone.

Chapter 21

Lucy

Lucy closed the door behind her in the hotel room. She saw Joanne sprawled across the bed, sniffling. It was unnerving to see her upset; it was as if they had switched roles. Lucy sat down on the edge of the bed and put her hand on Joanne's.

"Sorry I missed you at the Luxembourg Gardens this morning," said Lucy. She heard Joanne mumble something about not being a big deal. Lucy could tell she wasn't used to being comforted. "Gretchen?"

Joanne turned toward Lucy, her eyes red and patchy. "How d'you know?"

"She causes the most stress," said Lucy, wondering if she should probe, or just let her be. Yet as she read the sadness on Joanne's face, she decided it was no time to sit back. "Do you want to talk about it, Jo?"

"She went to a rave in the middle of nowhere, did some Ecstasy and danced until she fell and broke her leg."

"Shit." Lucy adjusted her seating to get more comfortable. She didn't understand that girl at all. From her observation, Gretchen seemed hell-bent on upsetting her mother. "What was she thinking?"

"She wasn't."

"Are you sure she was doing drugs?"

"She wouldn't say. I got bits from Em until I figured out which friends she went with. Then I texted Solange's mother. She confirmed everything."

"What about that guy she was hanging out with.…. what's his name?"

"Ally-Up."

"Em said he refused to go and asked her not to. It sounds like they split over it."

"Sorry, Jo. It just seems like she doesn't want to be happy in life."

"I dunno," Joanne mumbled.

Lucy knew this wasn't a good frame of mind for Joanne while traveling. She didn't want Joanne to slip into a deep funk. "You're in a state. Tell me what you are thinking."

"Why is this happening to me?" Joanne said, half-moaning and half-wailing.

"What do you mean, why you? Why not you?" said Lucy.

"Not nice."

"Sorry, but I don't get it when people say that. Is bad luck supposed to dog everybody else, except you?"

"I did everything for her."

"Yes, you sure did. You are an excellent mother–maybe too excellent. Things happen in families. Look at me. I got more than my fair share of tough luck."

"Well, you made choices…"

"What you mean is stupid choices," said Lucy, feeling prickly because her friend had just delivered a judgment. It wasn't like her, but she knew Jo was in pain and people lash out when they hurt. She should know, she did it all the time.

"Sorry, I—"

"Look, shit happens to everybody—it's not about whether you deserve it," said Lucy. "If that was the case, I'd have more misery thrown my way than you."

"Could be."

"Funny how different we are. I stumble through life assuming everything will work out and often it doesn't. You're always anxious and focusing on the one nit-picking detail that could bring you down. And it goes well," said Lucy.

"Right. There's Gretchen, and now problems with Peter."

"Okay, fair enough." Lucy realized she was generalizing about Jo, when in fact, she had been through a lot in the past couple of years. And yet, Joanne's life had really been a model of having her act together. Lucy envied how her friend sailed through her life doing apparently well, while she stumbled from one hiccup to the next—at least that's how she felt. "I guess I was thinking about all the great things that happened in your life. You had a positive childhood, good parents, and you looked after yourself. And then when you got married, everything was smooth for the first sixteen years," said Lucy, taking in a breath. "I meant it as a compliment compared to me." Lucy placed her hands together in a yoga pose, releasing a deep breath. "Sorry."

Joanne smiled between a sniffle. "Me too. Pity party is officially over." Lucy extended her hand and helped her friend to sit up. With that moment settled, Lucy wondered if she was going to lose her rock—the only person she wanted by her side for the operation. "Are… you going home?"

"Yes… No… I don't know." Joanne brought her knees up and wrapped her arms around them. "Gretchen insisted she didn't want me there. But I'd like to be with her. And now she's added drugs into the picture."

"She'll grow out of it, Jo. Remember the stupidity we got into? Well… I got us into. It would have freaked out our parents–if only they'd known."

"We didn't take Ecstasy."

"We did other things that were just as dumb," Lucy said. She wanted her friend to see that sometimes kids got into trouble, no matter how hard parents tried to control things.

"I realize that, but we seemed more streetwise. Don't you think?"

Lucy shrugged. While she was streetwise from growing up in the North End of Halifax, Lucy learned more about holding her own against her raucous brothers. While they were petty law benders, they weren't criminals.

Yet they had given her a sense of false bravado and ready-to-brawl confidence, which in hindsight, helped her out in many of life's situations. Joanne never gave off that vibe. Instead, she drew on her ability to stay calm and think clearly in situations. Lucy lifted the wine bottle and pointed to the empty tumblers with a question mark expression.

"We agreed we would not drink anymore before the operation."

"That was before you got the news. Besides, there is still one last test two days in advance before the final go ahead, so we can work it out in the spa."

"A sip then."

Lucy poured two glasses, sliding one to Joanne.

"Aren't we a pair?" Lucy said, putting her arm around Joanne.

"Yeah."

CHAPTER 21

Lucy was relieved to see her friend looking less burdened by her problems. She had stopped crying and her eyes bulged a bit from the sobs, but overall, things were looking up. "Don't worry, my friend, this is just an MFH."

"Which is?"

"Massive Family Hairball. It's big and gross, but it will pass. Trust me."

"How did this trip turn into such a shit show?" sniffed Joanne. "It's almost like she waited until I left on vacation to stir up a big drama."

"Almost?" said Lucy, wondering when her friend would realize that Gretchen had her own passive-aggressive manipulation game on the go.

Joanne sighed. "You're probably right, Lu. I get it."

Lucy took a sip and stared out the window. She was questioning her own life lately and didn't know why. "I don't know a lot in this life, but I think I've cracked the code about why we feel so at odds with our loved ones." She checked Joanne's expression. "Do you want to hear what I think is the problem?"

"Of course," said Joanne.

Lucy leaned toward her. "It's the difference between what we want to do with our lives and what everybody else thinks we should do. Case in point: Growing up, my mother thought I should embrace her religion, do nightly homework, behave like a little suck-up, never question her or authority, then find a boring job and settle," said Lucy. Things were becoming clearer by the second. "I was the opposite of every expectation, and she took great pains to let me know I was a failure in her eyes. But those were her dreams, not mine."

"Good point," mused Joanne. "It's also funny how everybody

thinks they can see exactly what you need, when obviously you can't. So, they feel it's their role to tell you."

Lucy nodded. "What I'd like to know: How is it that everything in life can roll along reasonably well until your forties? Then somehow you spin the karma wheel of misfortune, and next thing, you lose a job, split up with your spouse, or have a health scare. And then somebody dies: a parent, a colleague, or a friend from high school. One thing finishes, and something else takes its place," said Lucy.

"I have several friends going through it as we speak."

Lucy knew they could both rhyme off a bunch of people in their lives in the same situation. "Makes me wonder. I mean, you work hard and the minute you settle into life's cruise control, the arse comes right out of her. Is this what it's all about?"

"Damned if I know."

Lucy picked a hanging thread from the duvet cover on the bed. She tugged on it until it snapped, then realized the whole thing was unraveling. She glanced at Joanne. "You're obviously deep in thought."

"What I don't understand is how Gretchen can hate me so—"

Lucy shook her head. "She doesn't. Honestly? She's angry because she messed up. Trust me, I know from experience."

"I tried to make her happy—"

"News flash, Jo: There's no proportional return on happiness based on how much love you give your children."

Joanne raised her eyebrows. "Hmm. Did you just make that up?"

"I guess I've always known it."

"Okay, Soul Truth moment," said Lucy. "Is Gretchen driving

you nuts at this very moment?"

Joanne stared at her. "This is not the best day to be asking me."

"Come on. We promised to be honest."

"Look, she has a mental illness. Even though she causes me emotional pain beyond belief, I love her to bits. Isn't that unconditional love?"

"I guess so," said Lucy.

"How about you? What have you decided about the kidney?"

"Well… I'm of two minds… maybe three."

"Speaking of Soul Truth. If you could go back, would you still have had your fling with Jacques? I mean, especially if you had known what would happen because of your actions?"

"Hmm, should have known that was coming." Lucy thought for a moment, choosing her words. "I need to break this into two parts. Max is an exceptional young man, and I'm glad he made it through all the hoops. Honestly, I wasn't ashamed about getting pregnant and being single–that was more about society's judgment and my mother who turned it into such a flaming fiasco."

Lucy's voice cracked slightly. "It's funny, but the mother who hangs in there to look after the child gets saddled with the hated 'single mother' label. Anyway, while the timing sucked for university, the minute I saw Max's adorable face, I had no doubts. I loved him and would do anything for him."

"And my question about Jacques—"

"Now that I am almost grown up, I can see I was intoxicated with Jacques, wasn't I?"

"You still are."

"No way," said Lucy. She didn't like it when Joanne made these definitive statements about her history with Jacques.

"Give me one example."

"That sunflower painting and the amazing metaphor that it literally hangs over your head in the office."

Lucy shifted. She hadn't thought of that painting until Joanne mentioned it when she visited back before the trip.

"Why is it still there after all these years?" Joanne continued, "In fact, you can't get *Jacques-ass* out of your head."

"Come on," Lucy gasped, annoyance building. How could she describe her feelings to someone like Joanne, who was never a "hot mess" when it came to relationships in her past? There were no torrid flings or heartbreaks. Nor did she end a relationship by throwing a guy's clothes over the balcony, hurling either insults or saucers at him as he walked away.

While dating, Jo had limited but quality relationships. If they didn't work out, they would be put to rest politely. Both parties would move on. Then she married Peter and life was rock steady for years. "It's hard to describe, Jo. I admit Jacques was a supreme scoundrel. But during that tiny window when he was into me, I never felt so special."

"Right. Special, as in the lawyers he hired to dig up stuff from your past and humiliate you into giving up your child."

Lucy shivered as she recalled the lawyer, Mr. Lortie, and his dog-with-a-bone attitude, dredging up sludge from her teenage years. She was already distressed and nervous leading up to the court date. He invited her and her legal aid lawyer, Marie, to meet him, beforehand "to work things out," as he described it.

When she entered the room and sat at a table across from him, she could sense him twitching, ready to pounce. After a brief introduction, he slid a piece of paper toward Lucy and Marie–they both laughed as they scanned it. The sheet was signed by her Girl Guide leader that Lucy had failed all her badges to do with domesticity: Child Care, First Aid, Home Defense and Life Saver. "That's ridiculous," said Lucy, remembering the uptight Guide leader, Mrs. Hunt, who irritated Lucy to no end, so she quit. "I didn't fail, I just didn't finish them." Mr. Lortie didn't respond, but simply pushed the next sheet which described her babysitting debacle whereby she had given one of her neighbor's little miscreant children an evening-long time out–allegedly causing him undue stress.

"The little shit tried to garrote me with invisible fishing line across the door jamb into the kitchen, for a laugh," Lucy retorted, but Marie touched her hand to keep quiet. Just as Marie rolled her eyes and announced he'd better come up with something more substantive, he delivered the one-two punch.

It was a hand-written suicide note from sixteen-year-old Lucy, sent to her boyfriend Gerard, who had just ditched her for the most popular girl in the school. Lucy reeled; she couldn't remember the exact words but recalled aiming for high impact in the note. She exchanged glances with Marie, who sent daggers for not informing her about it.

Lucy had totally forgotten her drunken antic. She wondered how on earth they got the note, until she remembered stumbling to Gerard's home and stuffing it in the mailbox on a Saturday night. She hid and watched in horror when his mother opened the door and looked around, then pulled out the envelope.

She opened the note addressed to Gerard, and promptly called the police. The cops found Lucy sleeping off her stupor at the local ballpark and took her home where she faced months of detention. "First, I'm here, so obviously, I didn't do it. I can explain," said Lucy, trying to sound unfazed. "I only said things to hurt him, for hurting me. Honestly, I had no plans to kill myself." She looked at his blank face.

Mr. Lortie said, "And what about the fact that you were pregnant?"

Lucy gulped. Had she written that whopper? Oh my god, she thought, why, why, why on earth had she written something so stupid? "That wasn't true," she gasped. "I just said that for dramatic effect. I blame teenage hormones and alcohol for that note." She could tell Mr. Lortie didn't believe her, and by Marie's expression, neither did her own lawyer.

Then Mr. Lortie presented a list of all the calls she had made to Jacques' office, copies of letters sent, and then calls to his wife Elise at home. Marie asked for some time with her client. Lucy knew what was coming: a "Hallway Arrangement" as they described settling a case at the last minute to avoid going to court.

Her head pounded. Marie was blunt: she reviewed everything he presented and said that was just a warm-up for shredding her in court. She recommended that Lucy not put herself through the humiliation because she didn't have hope. After all, she was a single mother with no income, a terrible track record as a grounded person, and a series of damning evidence against her. She pointed out that maybe it wouldn't be so bad for his father to raise the child, since money wasn't an issue and Elise would be a stay-at-home mother.

She reminded Lucy that she could also complete university and make something of herself. Defeated, Lucy signed the papers to give Jacques custody of Daniel Max Morin. The rest was a blur.

"Lucy?" Joanne said, gently touching Lucy's sleeve.

CHAPTER 21

Lucy jumped; she was still thinking about that point in time that was just as raw now as it was then. "That was the worst day of my life... the day they took Max out of my arms," she observed. She recalled the terrible regret for a situation that could not be reversed. She thought of the shoving and yelling at the person waving the papers at her and promptly removing the boy.

Worst of all, she remembered in vivid detail the look on Max's face as if an artist had captured every nuance of the pain he expressed. Even though he wasn't old enough to understand what was happening, somehow *he knew*. The look of shock on his tiny face–that his own mother had deceived him–still haunted her. She whispered, "I don't know what I would have done if you hadn't helped me, Jo."

"I know. It's so tough to revisit that scenario," said Joanne. "I remember well."

"Giving Max a kidney is a way to make up for the mess I made of his life so long ago. At least he had an amazing childhood. They gave him the best education money could buy and looked after him properly."

Joanne looked at her. "So, will you do it?"

Lucy knew she needed to buck up and adopt a positive attitude if this was to succeed. "I have two kidneys, so what the hell? Glad it's not a gallbladder or heart."

"Or your liver," deadpanned Joanne. They both chuckled. "Did you let Elise know?"

Lucy nodded. "She almost thanked me."

"Remember, this is an emotional time for everyone."

Lucy pushed a small cracker in her mouth and chewed quickly. "True, but could you stop sounding so magnanimous for a minute," she said, then shifted into a serious tone. "She still refuses to tell Max who I am."

"Can you live with that?"

"I guess it makes sense," said Lucy.

"I'm proud of you. You're growing up."

Lucy waved her away. "Don't make me a hero. I heaped all this shit upon myself." She was afraid to ask. "So… are you going home?"

"Can I confirm with you tomorrow? I'd like to call Gretchen again. And Emmaleigh."

That was not the answer Lucy was hoping for. The old Joanne would have stuck by her no matter what. "Whatever you decide is okay," said Lucy. "I kind of got you here under false pretenses."

"Kind of?" said Joanne.

"Touché!" Lucy replied, nudging her friend's shoulder as if to say, 'get out of here', but she knew Joanne was behaving like a different person. If only she could connect with Gretchen and help her, Lucy believed Jo could enjoy a more peaceful life.

Chapter 22

Joanne

The next day she called Gretchen, who had softened since they spoke. Joanne normally tensed up when Gretchen answered, but this time her voice sounded almost calm.

"Mom, I thought about it, and what I was trying to say is that I want you to continue with your trip," said Gretchen.

After being commanded by her daughter to stay away from home, Joanne felt a shift. This time Gretchen's perspective had changed, and she was thinking about her mother rather than herself. Joanne couldn't remember the last time Gretchen had given much thought to others around her. "You sure darling?" Joanne asked, almost as if she hadn't heard correctly and dared not get her hopes up.

"Yes, Mom, I'm sure."

Joanne's heart swelled. That was the tiniest sign needed to confirm her daughter's change in attitude from the last call. She leapt into her motherly role. "So, tell me about these large gashes. And how many staples did you get?" she asked, trying to fuss over her daughter thousands of miles away.

"I didn't count or anything. Too gross," said Gretchen.

There was a pause. "So, was the Mona Lisa smile as irritating as I described?" she said, with a snide little giggle.

"To be honest, you can't get near it–it is behind glass and there's too many people thronging around it," said Joanne. "Remember how you stayed up until midnight the night before it was due and got the theme just as you were finishing?"

"Yup, then we had to go back and fix everything," said Gretchen. "That's me. Everything ass-backwards."

"I wouldn't say that Gretchen. You were just getting up to speed by then," she laughed. It surprised her to hear Gretchen laugh and she savored the moment like it was the most exquisite croissant ever served.

"I have to go, Mom," said Gretchen.

As much as Joanne wanted this conversation to go on for hours, she understood stopping while she was ahead with her daughter. As they wrapped up, Gretchen said she wanted her to finish up the vacation she deserved because things hadn't been easy for her. Joanne gulped.

It was the closest her daughter had come to owning her mental illness and acknowledging that her health problems hurt the family. Joanne agreed to stay on and thanked her daughter, for what she wasn't sure, but she couldn't stop herself. "Darling, can I ask one more favor?"

"What?"

Joanne sensed that tone of rising irritation, but it was too late. "Darling, the only way I can stay relaxed is knowing you are safe. Please keep in touch, even if it's only to respond to my texts with an emoji?"

"Okay Mom. But you know the rules: no texts longer than five words and no multiple texts in a row on one topic. That is not the point of a text."

CHAPTER 22

"Tough cookie," said Joanne. "But I will respect it." Who was she to make up all the rules about communication between them? Yet it was better than nothing. At least Gretchen was showing some concern for her mother.

Joanne hung up, feeling better about her daughter than she had in a long time. She wished things could have worked out differently between them and wondered if she had been a helicopter parent. She recalled the bond she had with Emmaleigh, her firstborn. Em thrived with her mother's attention, and keeping each other in the loop felt natural. She said 'I love you Mom' daily. Things just flowed with Em and her life was unfolding in the same peaceful way.

Joanne assumed since the approach worked so well for Emmaleigh, it would work for her next girl. When she reflected on Gretchen's upbringing, Joanne realized she hovered near her like a shadow, one step ahead of every little move she made. She was always organizing activities, preempting problems, or advocating on her behalf, and not once did Gretchen appear interested or grateful for her mother's interventions. The opposite. As a result, in her brief life of eighteen years, Gretchen had faced nothing scary, difficult, or uncomfortable because her mother had looked after it all. Now it was coming back to haunt her because her child rejected her upbringing. Worse, she harmed herself with a medical condition destructive to her and the family.

While Joanne raised her child with incredible love in her heart and good intentions, she understood Gretchen resented the family and was miserable as a kid. Where Emmaleigh took the high road, Gretchen took the hard road. The more Emmaleigh shone as the golden child, the further Gretchen distanced herself from the family. The harder Joanne tried to be the perfect Mom, the more her daughter rebelled, until it all imploded.

Joanne thought about her own upbringing with her brother. While they were well looked after, her parents didn't attach themselves like Velcro to every movement of their kids' lives. She also faced adversity on her own, in school and community activities.

As a teen, her life became a trial-and-error game–sometimes she won, many times she lost. There were many triumphs and disappointments, but that's how she figured out life. She and Lucy also got up to all kinds of shenanigans, and her parents had not had a clue. But it all worked out.

She knew those were different times, and the next generation experienced something hugely different. She saw it in her daily work in HR: parents who had written their child's résumé (and lied), and those who called to demand the status of their child's job application. Some even accompanied their children to interviews, insisting on sitting in and haranguing her if their child didn't get an offer. She wondered: is this what she was like with Gretchen?

She called her husband and shared the shock about Gretchen's situation. Together they tried to figure out what was going on with Gretchen and how best to support her. He said he had no clue how to help his daughter. All he knew is that he loved her more than anything and would do whatever he could to help. After much discussion with everyone in her family, she felt officially comfortable continuing her trip with Lucy. Lucy hugged her for several minutes and declared a beautiful "soul sister" moment.

Chapter 23

Lucy

Her inbox pulsed with action, each subject line vying for attention. She skimmed for important messages, but after reading three, she realized nothing registered.

Even though she didn't enjoy being alone, Lucy encouraged Joanne to do what she cherished most: peruse the neighborhood for French hors d'oeuvres. In her natural habitat, she browsed beautiful specialty shops where she could sniff out ripe cheeses and appetizers.

Each day, while Lucy organized the logistics of the operation, requiring calls, emails and tests, Joanne would shop for hours. She'd arrive back at the hotel, juggling beautiful boxes of gourmet items to share with her friend. Lucy wasn't into treasure hunts for food, yet she loved eating what Joanne found. It was a friendship made in heaven.

As she stared at the bottle of wine they kept in reserve, she thought about how her life was about to get weird. She figured a little sip would be okay before heading to the clinic, and besides, she still had a few days before the operation.

For the first time, she thought about what it would feel

like to have a kidney removed. She understood the risk was minimal–and for Max, there was so much to gain. She opened the briefing package for the clinic that Elise's people had delivered as she called them ("My people will drive you to the clinic" or "My concierge will arrange that for you"). It sounded like she owned them, which she probably did.

Even though Jacques was behind most of Lucy's grief, his wife came a close second for her part in taking Max from her. Lucy's body tightened at the thought of being connected to someone who offended her on so many levels.

Yet it was the brochure for the *Clinique Allard* that caught her attention. It resembled a château hotel from one of those TV shows she called "Lifestyles of the Rich and Fatuous", programs created to show viewers places they don't have a hope of ever owning or visiting. Every detail of the clinic whispered luxury–traditional architecture, sweeping foyers, fresh-cut flowers (exotic and proper, not from the corner store). Discreet and tucked out of view was the latest medical equipment. Plus, everyone in the pamphlet was beautiful, and she wondered if they were staff or brochure stock photos.

She read the biography on the Swiss specialist and family friend (and why did the word Swiss automatically mean the best?), who would continue medical care for her at the clinic. He sounded more like a saint than a kidney specialist.

Lucy and Joanne would be driven to the clinic by a chauffeur and accompanied by the concierge who would be on call for any requests. It sounded nice and impersonal–exactly what she wanted. She also learned that Elise wouldn't be there, which was a relief.

Who was Elise Vincent Morin, anyway? She wondered what sins the Vincent family committed to be that rich? Lucy had researched several business interests in Elise's family and learned there was a château, estate, and vineyard, among other things.

Her thoughts darkened like a tornado brewing as she considered the mess she had gotten herself into. Suddenly, she wanted to tell her family in Halifax how much she loved them before the operation. But it wasn't the right time to reveal the truth through a phone call.

She was tired of managing her stories to control who knew what with her family and friends, and she felt weary about keeping it filed away in the back of her head.

***

When Joanne returned to the hotel with her gastro treasures, she arranged them on a cardboard plate with a fancy napkin underneath. "These look fabulous, Jo," Lucy said, eyeing the selection. "Glass of wine with these smart little snacks?"

"I thought we agreed we would take a break from the wine until after the operation."

Lucy stared at the glass, still nearly full. She tilted it and paused briefly. "I guess you are right, Jo." She felt embarrassed about breaking the commitment and having it pointed out. "Shame to waste it though, right?"

Joanne reached over and picked it up. "It's not like it's the last bottle of wine in Paris, eh?" She held the glass in the air. "Do I have your permission to throw out this glass of wine?"

Lucy sighed. How could she refuse her friend who was just doing what came naturally: behaving herself. She nodded and watched Jo toss it in the sink with a quick flick of the wrist. Her friend was so disciplined, she didn't even hesitate. It felt a little weird, not having a drink to relax before such a major event.

Unfortunately, Joanne made a good point. To show she was part of the solution, Lucy twisted the cork back inside the bottle that was nearly full. "Let's leave this for the cleaner; it's barely started." They avoided discussing the clinic and what was coming the next day.

Joanne brought out her tablet for an impromptu karaoke session. "I thought we could continue with the diary stories and sing our favorites from back then," she suggested.

Lucy wasn't in the mood, but she couldn't imagine how else to pass the time and her friend was trying to help. "Good idea, Jo!" she said, trying to convince herself.

Joanne opened the karaoke app while Lucy looked for songs. "How about Linda Ronstadt's 'You're No Good'? Remember how hard we worked on our harmonies until we got it perfect?"

"The idea of perfection depended on who was listening," said Jo. They began singing and sounded shaky the first few times, but eventually nailed a few lines in decent harmony. There were several taps on the wall between rooms. They paused their singing. "Do you think that was a knock of delight, or horror?" said Joanne, giggling. They lowered the voices for a few minutes, then forgot and eased back to full volume.

After repeating several songs, Lucy's voice became hoarse. "Remember when this used to happen at bars?"

"I certainly do," said Jo. While Lucy had a decent voice for someone without training, she didn't know how to control it and would get hoarse quickly. "By the end of the evening, it sounded like your vocal cords were paved with gravel and whiskey. You played it up and had all the guys falling for you. Remember the 'Raspy Hour'?"

CHAPTER 23

Lucy smiled, thinking about all the great times they had back then. Even though she was a big show-off at the bars, there was a certain innocence about the era. "My two favorites were 'It's a Heartache' and 'Bette Davis Eyes.'"

Since there was no booze involved, they wrapped up the evening early to get a good night's sleep. Before heading off to bed, Lucy's thoughts turned to the clinic. "Listen Jo, since you are kind enough to accompany me on this unplanned part of the trip, you can choose any service once we check in at the clinic."

"Unplanned? That's a nice euphemism," joked Joanne.

"Got me," said Lucy. "Seriously, what would you love to have done at the spa?" They started a medical 'misery list' for each since top European health care professionals were at their disposal. "Now we're ready for the place. And thanks for the evening of singing, Jo, even if we were sober."

As they climbed into bed, Lucy felt tense and totally wired, despite popping a sleeping pill. She waited half an hour. Nothing happened. Since she was a poor sleeper Lucy felt the dread of insomnia as she listened to Joanne slip into a light snore. She looked at the wine bottle on the dresser and reached for her eye mask to help her forget. Lucy reminded herself she could do this–she had the strongest will of anyone she knew.

At three in the morning, she sat up. She lifted her mask and glanced at the bottle. Maybe a small glass of wine, like a shot glass full, might help. She checked Joanne, who was mumbling and fitful, but sleeping.

Lucy poured a small tumbler of wine and stared out the window, watching people wander by, laughing and enjoying themselves. Thirty minutes later she was still wide awake and poured another tumbler. As the early morning sun peeked through the curtain, Lucy slipped into a begrudging but deep sleep. So deep she couldn't rouse herself to address the insistent rapping on the door which morphed into pounding, becoming part of a dream in which a French S.W.A.T. team was kicking down the door.

Chapter 24

Joanne

A ruckus at their door made her sit up in bed. Joanne felt like she hadn't slept longer than ten minutes. Lucy was snoring at full decibel, her eyes closed and twitching as she dreamed. She checked her cell alarm clock. The alarm had gone off, but somehow, she had dismissed it.

What the hell? She wondered if Lucy had done that. Even though Joanne didn't drink the night before, she felt like she was emerging from under a steamroller. A terrible night's sleep felt almost as bad as a hangover which, in her mind, wasn't fair.

Although she desperately wanted more sleep, the insistent knock continued. She dropped her feet to the floor from the bed, as if built out of lead. Stumbling to the door, her bloodshot eye hovered over the peephole. Based on the startled look on the young lady's face and a jump backward, Joanne realized it resembled a scary eyeball in a horror film. She spied a well-polished young woman with a professional smile.

"*Oui?*" she muttered.

"Madame Lucy McGee Baxter?" she asked in a polite tone while pounding on the door.

"No. Madame Cambridge."

"Hello, I am Nicole Simon, your concierge. Are you ready to go to the clinic?" She sounded way too perky, which gave her that sinking feeling as she considered the implications of missing the alarm clock. "Almost," she replied, glancing at Lucy, who looked like a seal splayed on a rock in the afternoon sun. "Give us five-ish minutes," she said, knowing they couldn't deliver on that promise.

"Okay, *merci*. Your car is downstairs waiting for you." Joanne was relieved the knocking had stopped. She surveyed the room. The bottle of wine on the dresser was nearly empty. She worried about Lucy drinking last night (on her own, no less) and the need for a glass in the middle of the night. While she enjoyed wine, Joanne had found it hard to keep up with Lucy on this trip.

Her friend looked terrible in her sleep, as if she'd alternated between drinking and crying. Joanne didn't judge her–she had a major operation coming up. Who wouldn't be frightened? Yet Joanne dreaded getting Lucy out of a massive stupor. She wrestled her shoulder. No response. She rolled her back and forth, barking, "LUCY, LUCY. WAKE UP!"

"Go away," gasped Lucy.

To get her attention, she pushed Lucy's cheeks together into a big pout. Lucy uttered a growl and exhaled through her squeezed lips, sounding like a demented elf whistling a merry tune. Joanne rocked Lucy by the shoulders, trying to rouse her–which led to nasty retorts.

She got up and jammed items into bags while shaking Lucy's feet, which annoyed the hell out of her but didn't result in any action. Joanne finally yanked the blanket off her and tossed it on the chair, so she had to get up to retrieve it.

"What the hell are you doing, girl?"

"Time to go," said Joanne, sounding like her mother when she meant business.

"Where?" Lucy asked, running her fingers through her red curls, and messing it into worse shape. She raised her elbows as if to get up, then dropped back down again.

"To the clinic."

"Already?" Lucy said, looking confused. "I wonder when the concierge is coming."

"Fifteen minutes ago."

"Huh?"

"She's waiting in the car. I said we'd be there in ten."

"I'm tired," said Lucy, somehow stumbling to her feet.

"Me too," she said, letting her friend know she wasn't the only one suffering. "And look what happened overnight, Lu. The wine evaporated in the bottle." Lucy shot her a bloodshot look.

"I need a shower," announced Lucy, heading to the bathroom.

"You can have one later at the clinic. The more pressing emergency is your breath," said Jo, holding a bottle in her hand. She filled her own cheeks and passed it to Lucy. Together, they wedged into the bathroom, spitting out the minty green liquid into the doll-sized sink. They gasped as they caught themselves in the mirror under the fluorescent lights.

"Where is this clinic, anyway?" said Joanne. She noticed Lucy's face cloud over with confusion.

"Uh… somewhere outside Paris," Lucy said, distracted as she stared at the mess in the room. "And it's some quaint village with a name that's way too long, very French, and unpronounceable," she added, returning to the job at hand of half-heartedly picking up the rest of her clothes.

Joanne scanned the room for remaining items, shoving them into carrying bags. They dragged the suitcases to the door and glanced back in case they had left anything behind. "Wait." Joanne pulled out her cell phone, taking a selfie. "You got to be kidding me," groaned Lucy.

"It's a historic moment," Joanne protested and continued with the shot. Lucy shrugged, looking too tired to care. Joanne clicked multiple times, hoping for a decent shot. They reviewed the photos, groaning. Lucy's eyes looked like a pair of soft poached eggs and her hair sprung in all directions. While Joanne looked marginally better, they laughed at a deep crease running the length of her face where it had folded during her sleep. "Maybe we should add plastic surgery to our list at the clinic."

For once, Lucy had no comeback, witty or otherwise. She looked ready for nothing other than a long sleep. "Let's go," she said, slamming the door.

Chapter 25

Lucy

Lucy and Joanne stepped out onto the sidewalk, wincing with the sudden burst of morning sun. Both the driver and the concierge emerged from the shiny limo which smelled new, even from the outside. Lucy watched as they opened the back doors at the same time (did they practice that?) and invited the ladies into the car. The driver picked up Lucy's suitcase, but didn't miss a beat, concealing his shock at the weight as he hefted it into the trunk.

"Hello Madame Baxter and Madame Cambridge. I am Nicole Simon," she said. "I am a nurse and your concierge for this trip. It will be my pleasure to look after your every need."

Lucy gasped, "There's enough work for you to make a career out of being a concierge?"

"I work exclusively for the Vincent family," she replied.

"That so?" Lucy shook her head in surprise.

"And this is Victor," she added with a flourish of her hand toward the driver.

Dressed in a dark marine suit, white shirt and stylish tie, Victor's handsome demeanor looked more diplomat than limo driver.

Lucy thought of the usual North American dress code for business leaders that consisted of chinos, stone-washed shirts, clashing ties, and scuffed brown shoes that doubled for hiking boots on the weekends. Only in France, she noted.

The car sped up with a whoosh. They maneuvered through the traffic as if they were in a video game. Victor drove fast enough for Joanne to cling to the armrest. She leaned over and whispered to Lucy, "This is like those old New Wave French movies from the 1960s. Get ready for a good-old-fashioned-Parisian-careening."

Lucy let herself sink deeper into the plush seats, surrendering to Victor, who had likely started life as a race car driver. Despite the pain in her head, she felt like she was plunged into a big adventure. She said to Joanne, "Yeah, it's like we found ourselves in a crazy spy assignment in France."

Lucy guzzled from her bottle of water. Tired, hungover and dry as an old raisin, she felt ashamed for drinking wine (alone, no less) the night before. Staring out the window, the scenery shot by so fast she felt woozy. Jo was bursting with energy, and Lucy worried she might talk the entire trip.

"So, this is kidney donation in Europe," mused Joanne. "Imagine if we were back in Nova Scotia? We'd be picked up by Uncle Joe in a truck and dropped in the entryway to the hospital. He'd tell you that his doctor up in Cape Breton removed the kidney from him last night and asked if he could deliver it to Halifax since he was coming anyway–save the courier costs. Then he'd hand you one of those red and white organ containers and say, 'Buddy told me to give it to the transplant doc on Floor 9.'"

Lucy whimpered a minor chuckle. Normally she would

have belly-laughed because of Joanne's description but needed to minimize head movement. Once they got onto roads with fewer curves, Lucy succumbed to the smooth fluid motion of the luxury car.

***

"Lucy… Lucy… we're almost there," said Joanne, tapping Lucy's shoulder.

Lucy figured she had just drifted off to sleep and wondered why Joanne was bothering her. "I thought it was hours to get there," she sputtered, her eyelids drooping.

"It's been almost two," said Jo. "You'd swear we drove to Switzerland, but Victor assured me we're still in France." Victor arrived at the turnoff to the estate with a driveway that meandered as if in no hurry to arrive at the estate. "Look at these amazing botanical plants and flowers. It's like being in an exotic garden," gasped Joanne.

Lucy looked but didn't respond to any comments. A deep dread gripped her as they edged closer to the place. Joanne was heading to a luxury spa and had every reason to be excited. For her, it seemed like her world was spiraling out of control. The clinic appeared like a mirage in the misty forest setting. Manicured gardens, landscaping and stonework guided them toward the château where Lucy's life was about to change.

The limo eased through the roundabout driveway and stopped at the front door, where a pleasant man in a suit was waiting. Joanne squeezed Lucy's terrified hand. "We're here."

Lucy felt like a concrete sculpture that would have to be moved by a large crane. She sensed she was stuck in this car forever, and maybe that's where she wanted to be to avoid all the stress.

"Talk to me, Lucy," said Joanne, her voice taut.

Lucy didn't know what to say. She thought about being at the epicenter of everything and the pressure on her: Elise's demands, clinic staff, limo drivers, Joanne–and mostly her son Max, desperately awaiting a life-saving kidney. It was too much.

Lucy thought of her husband Dave who, when he noticed she got stressed, would shout, "Hon, you blew a circuit breaker!" She loved his funny electrical terms to describe her state of mind and behavior; it always made her laugh. A wave of guilt washed over her for not telling Dave. Of all the people she should have told, it was her husband.

She looked at Joanne, her expression a mishmash of hope, fear and expectation. Lucy searched for words, but nothing happened. She finally sputtered out to Joanne, "I can't do this."

Chapter 26

Joanne

"Too late," announced Joanne. The welcome committee swung open car doors. Staff members appeared elegant even though they were in uniform. Excited, Joanne nodded to them as she stepped out of the car into the peaceful grounds. The scent of delicate flowers permeated the air. She saw Lucy slumped in the back seat, looking about as lively and pale as a celebrity statue in a wax museum. "Coming?" said Joanne.

Lucy gazed at a focal point with no fixed address. "I said... I can't do this."

Joanne looked around the grounds as the team gathered, preparing for the big day. "You realize they've already spent thousands of euros on this."

"That's pocket change for the Morin family. Fuck 'em."

She knew this wasn't the time to make Lucy feel guilty about anything–she would only become angrier. "Understood. Mind if I ask, what's the problem, Lu?"

Lucy paused, her eyes darting as she searched for the words. "Why is it always me who has to make the compromises, take the high road, so somebody else can have their way?"

The description almost made Joanne giggle, except the timing was wrong. "No offense, but I don't recall you being overburdened with compromise throughout your life."

"I am now," Lucy said, scowling.

Joanne nodded in sympathy, even if she didn't buy Lucy's life theory. Still, she needed to shift her into a more positive frame of mind. "I'm listening. Tell me more."

"Why should I do this for Elise, after what she did to me?" said Lucy, her voice climbing the ladder of hysteria.

Joanne's fatigue slowed her down, but she could see Lucy was freaked out. "Can I ask you to see the big picture here? This isn't about Elise; it's about helping your son–who was innocent in all of this."

"Will Max even know or care? Or is he going to grab the kidney and say, 'Thanks madame, have a nice day.'"

Joanne knew her friend was missing the point and worse, could live to regret not taking the right action. "Lucy, this is a turning point in your life."

"You think?" Lucy shot her a look for stating the obvious.

Undeterred, Joanne returned the glare. "You have a choice here: Is this a decision made by the old Lucy, the one who can be petty and vindictive? Or is it the new Lucy, her heart stirred by a beautiful young man–your son, I might add–who deserves a normal life?"

"Anything else?"

"Since you asked: is this the new Lucy doing it because it's the right thing, even if she doesn't get full hero status?" Wearing a neutral expression, Joanne leaned into the car and held out her hand to Lucy. Nothing happened. Joanne softened. "Look, there's still time to back out if you so choose. But you should at least give it a chance."

CHAPTER 26

"Remind me, why?"

"You dragged me all this way to Europe under false pretenses, so at least let me stay one night at France's most exclusive clinic!" Joanne said.

Lucy picked up her cell phone and clicked on her keypad. Joanne stood at the car door, sweat trickling down her forehead. She glanced at the entry area and smiled at the calm, yet puzzled team, who probably had more pressing issues than to wait for a neurotic client to emerge from the limo.

Her voice fluttered. "What are you reading, Lu?"

Lucy turned the cell to face Joanne. "Max's blog," she said, handing it to Joanne.

Joanne scanned it. "What a story! Tells you all you need to know, right Lu? Now will you come inside?" She held her breath, watching one of the most stubborn and changeable people she knew inching across the leather seats to the car door. All eyes were on her. The staff looked ready to embrace the drama, as if watching an intoxicated client on a high wire, knowing it was their job to move the net and catch her. Joanne figured they had probably seen all kinds of crazies in their time and appeared ready to wait there all day if need be.

Joanne leaned down to the car door level and sent Lucy one of her "are you coming?" looks, hoping to god it would work. All was quiet. Lucy lowered her sunglasses from the top of her head. She swung her two legs out of the back, toes pointed together as they settled on the ground. The beaming concierge offered his hand as if to request a dance.

She accepted, and he eased her from the backseat to a standing position in a single motion. Joanne figured this must be one of his job competencies–to make a woman appear elegant when exiting a limousine.

Joanne gasped. "Lu, you look like a movie star. Did you practice that or something?" For the first time, Lucy's lip almost formed a half smile. The staff, out of earshot, smiled generically, not understanding what had just happened. They welcomed the nutty entourage with impeccable English.

Lucy and Joanne walked toward the entry, Joanne whispering to Lucy, "I think both of us have our mouths gaping open." Their steps activated the fifteen-foot doors to whoosh open, revealing a foyer with impeccable marble floors, skylights and sparkling chandeliers that bounced light patterns everywhere. Massive vases of flowers guided them to the front desk.

"I'm Isabelle, the manager," she said warmly, shaking both of their hands. Joanne felt like they were international ambassadors or something. "Please, may I guide you to your room," she asked, beaming with a full smile. She briefed them along the way in a place that rivaled a luxury hotel. Chic muted colors dominated the walls, all tied together with accents and furniture in each room. Every staff member walked with a purpose, but they never appeared rushed. Isabelle introduced them to the team members, who stopped to chat as if they were strolling around the gardens with nothing better to do.

"Here we are," said Isabelle, landing at a cream-colored door with intricately carved details. "You may wish to take a rest after your trip." Joanne figured she based how awful they both looked on not enough sleep and Lucy's hangover. Yet Isabelle showed no sign of judgment. "Feel free to read about all the wonderful spa services, organic meals and health treatments for both of you," she said, swiping her card at the door, then disappearing.

CHAPTER 26

"Wow. Look at this," Lucy said, examining everything. "The medical equipment is stowed out of sight, yet ready if needed."

"Check out the garden view," Joanne gasped. She noted how the two enormous Roman windows, with delicate panes in a rounded section at the top, filled an entire wall. The afternoon sun flooded the beveled glass, highlighting the outdoor flower garden. "It looks like a Renoir painting," she sighed, putting her hands up to the window and looking out.

The courtyard beckoned, with a wrought-iron bistro table and chairs by a fountain decorated with cherubs aiming water into the pool below. Walking paths, dotted with flagstone and densely packed brown and green moss, looked centuries old.

"Jo, look at this," said Lucy. Joanne turned and walked back. A massive vase of wildflowers filled the room with subtle fragrances. There was an antique desk, set with vellum writing paper, a gold pen, and an area with a hidden electrical bar for computer plug-ins.

A French linen duvet graced the king-sized bed, accented with bright cushions. Large armchairs and a sofa invited conversation. A series of custom-made cabinets hid everyday items such as a television, refrigerator, blanket holders, and a generous closet sporting two plush housecoats. There were telephones everywhere–by the bed, on the desk, in the bathroom–just in case anybody had a thought worth sharing any time of the night or day.

"Enough about the rooms," said Joanne, yet they kept noticing things. They walked back and forth between rooms, exclaiming about the design and the amenities.

"In an hour, we're meeting the attending doctors, so let's have some refreshments," said Lucy, picking out the most beautiful tray of cheese and crackers. "Guess what would go well with these smart little snacks?" said Lucy.

"Let's not talk about wine."

"I was joking. But you go ahead, Jo. You aren't having an operation."

"Nah. This is my chance for a time-out from drinking wine for at least a week. I've been meaning to do it for years."

"Me too," said Lucy, staring out the window. They chatted quietly until it was time to meet with the doctors. They walked down the corridor to the consultation room that was beautifully lit without a fluorescent bulb in sight. "Jeez, I guess they invested heavily in beautiful, well-lit rooms so we can read the endless contracts we're about to sign."

Chapter 27

Lucy

At the office, the two doctors wearing white lab coats arrived and shook hands with them. Lucy glanced at the specialists who were responsible for her life. Somehow, even in lab coats, they appeared wealthy.

Maybe it was the fine leather shoes on the man and the designer pumps on the woman. Lucy arrived not wanting to like them but couldn't identify why. Most likely, it was because of Elise's hand in the project. Still, they had an air of confidence that made her feel better. They were a perfect age for the operation: young enough to be energetic and resilient, yet experienced. Lucy relaxed.

"I am Dr. Benedicht Haberling, and this is my colleague, Dr. Zoe Stettler. We're your surgeons, and we'll be with you the whole time."

"Are you on staff here?"

"*Non*, Madame Vincent Morin brought us here from Switzerland," said Dr. Stettler.

"We work out of the highest-rated clinic in Europe. You are in expert hands," added Dr. Haberling.

"So I hear," said Lucy with an edge to her voice as she thought about Elise, who had orchestrated this expensive project. Joanne shot her a grimace.

"First, thank you so much for your generous gift to this young man. There are over 16,000 people waiting for a kidney in France. He is otherwise healthy, so we're confident he will enjoy a long life," she said.

"Great. And I've read a lot, but I want to hear from you how it will work for me."

"We're getting there," said Dr. Stettler, asserting authority over the meeting. "We reviewed your health history, and the tests you did earlier. Lucy, everything looks excellent."

"Now we'd like to discuss some details about how the operation will unfold," said Dr. Haberling. "For a live transplant, we do this laparoscopically. We place a camera into the bellybutton and examine the organs within the belly. We make two more tiny incisions and install long instruments we control from the outside while they do the movement on the inside. It's all captured on a monitor. With three minor cuts, we'll prepare to remove the kidney."

"So far, so good," said Lucy, barely taking in what they said. "Then what?"

"We have to remove it whole, so we can transplant it to the recipient. When we are ready, we make about a five-centimeter incision at the lowest part of the belly–the bikini line area–and remove the kidney. For a healthy person, we find that one day after the operation, most are already up and walking—"

"Are you aware that the recipient is my son?" Lucy interrupted. The two doctors exchanged glances. "Yes, of course, Madame Baxter. That information is important to know when reviewing your test results. After the operation—"

Lucy jumped in again. "Can I see my son?" Suddenly the urge to see Max welled up inside her as she thought about it.

"I'm sorry, that's not our area of responsibility," said Dr. Haberling checking his chart. "Now, after the operation, you may not feel hungry, but you can eat food. Most people leave around two days after the operation and come back for a check-up about a week later. Since you traveled so far, it will be more convenient to keep you here longer. You may feel a low energy sensation, but you'll be able to do light activities such as gentle walking. As you'll discover, there are beautiful places to explore here."

"Let's assume this goes swimmingly, Doc, and I can leave after a week to ten days. Then what?"

"For the first six weeks after the operation, you can't lift anything heavier than three or four kilos. After that six-week period, life returns to normal," said Dr. Haberling.

"Yes, that's the usual outcome," added Dr. Stettler.

"What's not usual?"

"There are potential complications. Sometimes, blood pressure may rise after the donation process," said Dr. Stettler, glancing at her partner.

"Tell me everything, good and bad," blurted Lucy. She knew what to expect because she had researched everything leading up to the operation. But she wanted to make sure they were up front about it, and she wanted Joanne to understand potential problems.

Dr. Stettler straightened up. "According to your tests, the match is near perfect, so we don't foresee a problem. In rare cases, a few donors lose their kidney function and require dialysis. The chances are extremely low. However, it is important for you to be aware of all risks, even tiny ones. We have carried out a thorough screening. Your blood pressure is normal, your kidneys are functioning well, there are no medical deficiencies showing up. We believe you are an optimal donor."

Lucy glanced at Joanne, who held a neutral expression, yet appeared freaked out. Lucy figured she was creating an inventory of all the scary things that might happen.

"We will let you think about it before we ask you to sign these forms. It's important that you do not feel pressured," said Dr. Haberling. "Do you have other questions?" Lucy drummed her fingers on the table. "Will I lose weight with this operation?"

"Your kidney will weigh around a hundred and fifty grams. Picture a deck of cards," said Dr. Stettler.

"That's it?"

"Your appetite may not be robust as usual, so you might lose a little. But I wouldn't count on that as a weight loss strategy."

"Damn," said Lucy, winking at Joanne.

"Other questions?" said Dr. Stettler.

"Is a kidney recipient better off getting a live transplant versus getting one from a dead person?"

"Studies show that those receiving a live transplant, on average, double their life expectancy. You, madame, are extending your son's life by decades, perhaps," said Dr. Stettler, beaming.

Lucy smiled. "Those are all my questions." With that, the doctors shook hands and left. Joanne and Lucy walked back to their rooms. Lucy sensed Joanne had a million questions floating in her head but was too polite to ask. As Lucy scribbled her signature on the forms, her stomach buckled.

CHAPTER 27

Done deal and she hoped to god it was the right thing. She remembered the same feeling when she signed Max's adoption papers. She looked at Joanne and said, "This is for Max Daniel Morin and his family. For the beautiful son I did not raise."

"What an incredible gift, Lucy," said Joanne, hugging her.

But Lucy wasn't finished yet. "I'd like you to do one more favor for me. While I'm in the operation, can you respond to my family's texts for me?"

"Impersonate you?" Joanne gasped. "No fricking way."

"Come on, personal assistants do it all the time."

"Jeez Lucy."

"It will raise suspicion if I don't respond."

"What will they ask?"

Lucy knew that somehow she had to make it all sound normal for Joanne to get her head around it. "Look, it's just a bunch of standard 'where's this and that?' questions at home. I'll jot down most answers on a notepad."

"I still don't like it."

Lucy refused to get into a long discussion. "I only need your help for twenty-four hours. Besides, if there's anything you can't answer, just say you don't know."

"As you would say, what could go wrong?" said Joanne. "I take it I have no say in the matter."

It relieved Lucy that Jo was coming around. "Well, I wouldn't put it that way. But what I would say is that it's not a big deal."

"You're right. No biggie."

"Oh, and one more thing."

Joanne shook her head. "That's two things."

Lucy now realized this was a much bigger request that merely asking her friend to pose as a personal assistant. Yet she didn't want to freak her out. "This popped into my head. Before I go under the anesthesiologist's magic spell, I want to make sure someone understands my wishes. And… since you are the only one who knows about the operation—."

Joanne faltered. "You mean… a life decision?"

"Yup, as in when to pull the plug."

"Well, that would be David's decision."

This was all standard procedure in Lucy's mind, and she had no intention of dying. "Yes, technically, except they don't know my wishes," said Lucy. "Don't worry. I filled out the clinic forms, but sometimes things can get complicated."

"When you're involved."

Lucy's ire rose, but her friend had a point. "Fair point, but enough out of you."

"What then?"

"If I go into a coma and I'm too slow to respond, turn it off."

Joanne gasped. "Shit! What do you consider too slow? A month, six weeks, six months?"

Lucy honestly didn't know how to answer that because this was new to her. "What's reasonable in this situation, Jo?"

"How the hell do I know?"

Lucy didn't want to drill down too far because she believed everything would work out. Yet she couldn't leave Joanne in a mess in case the unthinkable happened. All she needed was a general plan. "Three weeks maybe?"

"That doesn't seem long."

"I should be able to do more than drool by that point. But I suppose I could rally. Okay, a month."

"What if you were to come back in thirty-two days? I'd never forgive myself."

"No offence, but I'd be dead, so like, how would you know?"

CHAPTER 27

Lucy said, hoping to release tension.

"Touché. But you're stressing me. I don't know what to expect."

"The doctors will say things like: 'At this stage, she'll never come out of the coma', or 'We've poked her for eons with no response', whatever. You have my permission to make any choice."

Joanne teared up. "You sure?"

This wasn't what Lucy wanted, circling around fear, but she needed Joanne to feel comfortable. "I'm sure, Jo. I love you and trust you more than anybody, including myself."

"Have you considered any other situations not included here? This is serious, so don't blurt out the first thing that pops into your head," said Joanne.

Lucy had already signed the directives with the clinic. There was nothing to worry about. She paused. "Now that I think about it…. If I'm unresponsive, leave me plugged in for two years, so I can run Elise's clinic bill sky-high!"

They hugged each other, laughing and crying. Yet as she let go of Joanne, everything they had discussed flashed through her head. Suddenly, it sounded real. Before, it was just blah, blah, blah nonsense paperwork for her. Yet she suddenly felt a jolt of mortality. She realized she hadn't considered how she might feel about the operation. Up to that point, it was all stats and logistics. Maybe she focused on those things to avoid thinking about how she really felt. A weird sensation floated through her head, and she ignored it. She had just calmed Joanne down, so this was no time to mention her own fear. It would pass. She needed to hold it together so that Jo wouldn't implode. At least that's what she told herself to get through the moment.

Chapter 28

Joanne

Joanne wandered into the gardens without her usual intense focus on the plants and flowers surrounding her. Normally, she would have been entering everything on her plant app. She thought about Lucy who was resting on her own all day to prepare for the operation.

Joanne obsessed about the weight of responsibility she now carried. She had no reason to expect anything to fail because most operations went well for the donor, and Lucy was under the best care. It relieved her that Lucy finally agreed to donate a kidney. They both knew the biggest risk wasn't with giving up a kidney–it was the effect of telling her family about it. Lucy made choices about not revealing her earlier life to her family, but Joanne understood that at that age, Lucy was full of fire, not wisdom.

She remembered how crushed Lucy was by the last two years at university. First, becoming a mother at twenty-one, coming to terms with it and loving Max as she had never loved a human being before. Joanne thought about the anger that first gripped Lucy, followed by depression. Although Joanne thought her friend would never pull out of it, she finally did.

That era in Montreal bonded them together forever. And when Lucy finally crawled back from the murky darkness to engage in life again, Joanne understood why Lucy blocked out that era of her life. Lucy always credited Joanne with saving her life, which Jo waved off as an exaggerated claim. She now realized she had helped Lucy more than she imagined back then. And she loved Lucy, no matter how much of a pain she could be.

She also understood why Lucy wanted to go with her to Europe. It wasn't about revisiting their youth; she needed her best friend by her side for this big decision because Joanne knew everything. Joanne would be full of unconditional love, paired with her sense of responsibility.

A text from Lucy's phone pulled her from her deep thoughts. Dave asked a simple question, and she cursed Lucy as she texted. She thought about Lucy's children, Riley and Maggie, and worried because they didn't even know about their mother's previous life.

And Dave? Not fair, but Lucy was Lucy. She shuddered, hoping she wouldn't have to contact them with bad news if Lucy's operation went south. This pain wasn't something she could share with Lucy, but it weighed on her. After a few minutes of deep breathing in the garden, she pictured everything going smoothly and felt better.

She wandered back to her room and sat in a soft chair. The urge to talk to her own family welled up inside her. She wondered how Emmaleigh and Gretchen were doing. Joanne missed Peter, and wished their lives hadn't become so complicated. They had faced no major problems in their marriage until now.

Sure, a few incidents cropped up, but they were calm people who didn't get into the blame game. Gretchen's anorexia knocked him sideways. At first, he questioned if it was even an illness. Once the reality set in, he hoped it would pass in a few weeks or months, once she came to her senses. His initial concern morphed into frustration after a year.

When Joanne tried to learn more about the disease by reading, attending lectures and talking to counselors, he invented excuses not to attend. Joanne's sense of abandonment increased the tension between them, yet she had to help her daughter overcome anorexia. Every attempt from Joanne to first get her daughter help, then her husband, seemed to hit a brick wall.

In addition, she found herself at life's crossroad with everything up in the air. Nothing seemed right anymore. Her successful career in HR no longer excited her. After thirty years, it was more of the same. She kept asking herself, "Is this it?" and "Why am I not doing something more meaningful with my life?" Should she go on a volunteer vacation and help people in need somewhere? Why not help closer to home? There were so many things she had planned to do: learn Spanish, paint flowers, take over the family flower shop, study yoga.

It was one thing to stumble along in her twenties and thirties, taking sudden career detours as she pleased. In her forties, she continued with her work because that's what you did, yet still had that nagging voice in her head. Now in her early fifties, that nitpicking little chatter grew louder, more insistent, and lately more demanding, complete with a soundtrack of a ticking clock.

She didn't know what she should do. It was as if she had set out on a journey without a destination or a map–and now she was lost. How embarrassing was that? An HR professional with no plan.

Yet what bothered her more deeply, she hadn't discovered her purpose in life and that kind of question wouldn't solve itself easily. She was proud of what she had done: raised a family, pursued a successful career, and volunteered in the community. Still, she needed to do something creative or spiritual with meaning for her. She had dreamed about her own flower shop but wondered if that was just to keep her from feeling discouraged.

She thought about her father, who needed more help. While she adored and wanted to look after him, she recognized it would become an all-consuming stage in life. Her daughters were young adults, and soon they wouldn't need her anymore. The end of an era loomed in front of her.

A light tap on the door pulled her from her daydream. The concierge reminded her about an appointment with the massage therapist and meditation leader. Within an hour, Joanne relaxed and prepared to help Lucy the next day. The naturopath had given her an herbal sleep supplement, and she crawled in bed at nine.

She tried to read a page in her book, it fell on her face three times. Giving up, she sent a "love you" text to Emmaleigh, Gretchen and Peter. Em pinged five-hearts. Gretchen sent a yellow face with a straight line for a smile (how did that kid find a neutral emoticon?). Two out of three wasn't bad.

After easing onto the pillow, she woke up nine hours later with a clear head and no brain fog. She bounced out of bed, hurrying to Lucy's room for what she would call a "large" day.

Chapter 29

Lucy

Joanne entered Lucy's room and sat down by her bed. Lucy looked up from her tablet and did a double take. "You look like a million euros."

Joanne smiled. "I slept through the night. It's been a long time."

Lucy looked around. She felt good for getting ready to hand over a body organ. "Got to love this place, eh?"

Joanne nodded. "You should donate some other organs, so I can get caught up on sleep."

Lucy beamed. She loved it when Joanne slipped in a funny comment at her expense. "I'll take that under advisement. NOT," she joked back. "Seriously, Jo, to what do you attribute this restorative night?"

"Well, there was an awesome massage and herbal sleep supplements, but sadly, staying off the wine for a few days probably helped."

"Why are fun things so bad for you?" said Lucy. "Another of life's mysteries." She shuffled the bedding and fluffed her pillows. "Any texts last night?"

CHAPTER 29

"A few simple questions, like you said. No biggie."

Joanne peered over Lucy's tablet. "What's up with Max?"

Lucy tilted the tablet toward Joanne. "Max is documenting his transplant journey in both English and French. He's a talented writer in both languages."

"Way cool."

"It irks me. He says the donor insists on remaining anonymous." Lucy knew it wasn't Max's fault–it was his mother who told him that story. She understood this wouldn't have been the time to reveal everything to Max before an operation. Yet it irritated her.

"How about instead, visualizing a perfect transplant that will make him healthy?"

"You're so sensible," said Lucy.

Joanne shrugged and checked her watch. "Are you ready for this?"

"With any luck, I'll also enjoy a few hours of pure sleep." Lucy said, putting away her tablet and phone. Now settled, she felt pensive.

"You okay?"

Lucy nodded, but she wasn't.

"What's up, Lucy McGee? This is not the time to hold back on something you want to tell me."

Lucy paused. She wondered if she should introduce the topic. It would be a big surprise for Joanne because Lucy had always maintained a hard line about religion and spiritual matters. Yet she spent part of the night thinking about her life. She looked over at Joanne, who was holding her eyebrows in a certain way when she was expecting an answer. What the hell, Lucy thought. "I have a request–and a strange one coming from me."

"Nothing would surprise me," Jo said. "What can I do for you?"

"Would you pray for me?" Lucy whispered, as if people might be eavesdropping, even though they were alone. It surprised Lucy to hear it escape from her lips.

"I've been doing it for days. You can pray too. It all helps."

Lucy's face flushed. "I feel like a hypocrite… All my life, I've denounced my family, especially Ma's obsession with religion and the Catholic Church."

"Look, Christians don't own prayers. It's practiced by many religions, and by those who are not religious."

"I'm surprised to hear that you pray."

"How do you suppose I got through the past couple of years with Gretchen?"

Lucy was impressed with her friend, who showed so much maturity. "I figured you'd stumble through it like me, hoping for a miracle."

"Sure." Joanne interjected. "And I've got a group of friends who help with spiritual matters which includes praying."

Lucy paused. "I can't explain why Jo, but suddenly I'm interested. Except I feel like a supreme cliché. You know… I denounce religion until the going gets tough."

Joanne smiled. "Whenever we face extreme situations or even death, it's natural to turn to spirituality. Tells me you are human. That's why I joined a group called 'The Unchurch'."

"Unchurch?"

"We call it spirituality for people who aren't really religious. It's about finding the spirit within yourself, not having some organization telling you what to think."

"So far, so good," said Lucy.

"It's about seeking deeper meaning in life without restrictions. We respect all beliefs, and we avoid negativity of certain faiths."

"Right. The three pillars of my mother's faith: wrath, shame and guilt. And a constant reminder I was going to hell. Wouldn't you think positivity and inspiration would be better to focus on?"

"That's a discussion for later," said Joanne. "For now, let's agree it's okay to pray for you, and I'll email my group."

Lucy hesitated. "Can we use first name only, and Lucille instead of Lucy?"

"I guess you wouldn't want the word getting out!"

Lucy squeezed Joanne's hand. "You know me too well."

A few minutes later the medical team arrived looking a little too chirpy, Lucy thought. But then again, what did she want? She needed to embrace the moment. They eased her to a gurney and explained the next steps. She could see Joanne's hand trembling, unsure what to do. Lucy's eyes pleaded with her, but for what, she didn't know. She summoned a weary smile for Jo. The enormity of the situation hit her–Lucy's life was about to change.

If everything unfolded as planned, she'd be in and out of surgery and recovering by the following day. Yet if something went wrong, she worried that Jo would have to inform Lucy's family who didn't know about the operation, or that she gave birth to a son taken from her decades ago. What a terrible thing to burden her with. But it was too late, and Lucy realized she needed to buck up. "Will you stay with me until I go into the operating room?" Lucy asked Joanne. She felt the deep comfort of Joanne holding her hand as she walked alongside the gurney. Lucy was frightened about dying without seeing her family again. What on earth was she thinking? Yet there was no going back. She was officially rolling down the corridor of no return.

Over the past few days, Lucy had pictured her and Joanne laughing and exchanging dark humor (delivered with great zeal by Lucy) as they strolled toward the operating room. Instead, Lucy held out her hand to Joanne, who appeared more focused on trying to keep up with the rolling gurney. They didn't exchange a word.

***

Lucy opened her eyes, emerging from a deep place. She was horizontal and her body had no intention of moving. Staring at the white ceiling, she tried to remember what had happened. There were wisps of dreams, but nothing added up. There was something bigger going on, but the memory danced in front of her, just slightly out of reach.

All around her, she sensed something living, like a calm, radiating energy. Lucy inched her head sideways and blinked a few times. Light filled the room, casting an otherworldly glow. Was she dead? She felt no alarm over it. She touched her leg and her arm and decided she was still alive: so far so good. Had she traveled to another dimension? Was she back? And if so, where the hell was she? Why couldn't she move?

Lucy flickered her eyes, trying to figure things out. When she opened them again, she tilted her head toward the fog-filled room. In seconds, after lifting her head off the pillow, she dropped back, happy the pillow received her.

The tapestry of gold, brown and white filaments of light dancing in front of her, intrigued her. With effort, she concentrated on the items near her and noted items coming into focus. Bright flowers filled the room. Dozens of vases blossoming with asters, daisies, and giant pink hydrangea. She basked in the beautiful energy. Gradually Joanne came into focus at her side and the puzzle pieces started moving into place.

"You're back," Joanne whispered.

Relief rippled through Lucy as she remembered the situation. "How'd the operation go?"

"Enormous success."

"For me, or for Max?"

"Both. Like clockwork. The first few days are critical, and Max is monitored constantly. Everything is unfolding as planned."

"Wish I could celebrate," said Lucy. She looked around. "Did you send the flowers?"

Joanne picked up the card on the stand. "They're from Max and Katarin. It says, *'Dear Cousin. Words can never express our deep gratitude for giving me a life. So, please consider the love and warmth in each flower as a reminder of our appreciation. With this major dream now granted, our only other wish is to thank you in person someday. Love, Max and Katarin.'*" She walked back to the chair by Lucy's bed.

"Wow," said Lucy. "I'm not sure what to say."

"The note says it all," said Joanne. "You gave him the biggest gift, Lucy." She looked around the room.

"Please, take some."

"No need. Max sent me a gorgeous bouquet of exotic flowers like bird of paradise, ginger, and others I can't identify. And the fragrance is divine. He also sent me a thank you note for accompanying you. Amazing, he is."

"He sure is," said Lucy, beaming with pride for the son she barely knew. She clung to any scrap of information about him. "And thanks, Jo. I couldn't have done this without you." They sat quietly for a few minutes–there was no need to talk at full speed like they usually did. Lucy stared at her feet for some time. "Wish I had told my family about the plan before traveling."

"Me too!" Joanne said. "But we got through it. I'm so relieved you didn't give up the ghost.

"Sorry to put you through all of that. You didn't need that hassle."

Joanne shrugged. "When will you tell them?"

"Any suggestions?"

"Soon. I mean… not to get too far into the weeds, but won't David notice your scars?"

"They'll be tiny. Besides, we're a grope-a-dope-in-the-dark type of couple."

"Let's not focus on that image too long," said Joanne. "Anyway, it'll be hard to keep it secret when you see everybody."

A ball of tension rose in Lucy's stomach whenever she thought about it and the big hurdle ahead. "Yeah, and no matter how you try to ignore it, it's still lurking in the back of your head. I was thinking the other day about how much energy it takes to manage varying stories for the people in my life."

"I don't know how you do it, Lucy."

Lucy nodded. "Especially with my memory getting a little foggy with menopause. Maybe I should ask Riley to develop an app for keeping stories straight," Lucy joked, sliding back under the covers.

She eased into another deep sleep. Each time she woke up, Joanne was by her side. Doctors and nurses breezed in and out, declaring that Lucy was doing very well. After she stayed awake for ten minutes, she asked for an update on Max. Joanne pulled out her tablet. "Katarin has taken over the social media posting. She says he's groggy but doing great."

"She's been busy posting." Joanne looked at the tablet and handed it to Lucy. "You're called the 'Great Canadian Mystery Donor', with kudos from Max, Katarin and their friends. Emoticons are piling up."

Lucy read through the posts, showing each to Joanne as she scrolled through. The thrill of how this was all unfolding conflicted with a rising sense of dread about her family. Somehow, she had to tell everyone the story, including Max. First, she needed to recover enough to crawl out of bed. The next day Lucy eased out of bed with some help and stood up. Exhausted, but triumphant, she showed excellent signs of recovery. On the second day, Lucy ambled around the clinic, with Joanne accompanying her little jaunts.

"You know Lu, I hadn't realized how tired I was from everything, and I needed a break," said Joanne, slipping her arm through Lucy's as they strolled the gardens. "Although it wasn't the European vacation I expected, I have to admit it's been an amazing spa experience."

Lucy patted Joanne's interlocked arm. "That's great, Jo. Maybe the Universe delivered what you needed instead of wanted–a rest at an expensive spa–instead of a romp around Europe."

"Well, let's not go too far with your self-serving rationalization," she joked to Lucy. "I wanted to see that Van Gogh exhibition and you owe me one for that, by the way. But I was exhausted, so who knows?"

"Fair enough," said Lucy. "I owe you another trip to Europe," she added, and she meant it. There would never be another adventure like the first trip together, but that was okay. People grew up, things changed, and life evolved. She'd travel anywhere with Joanne and knew they'd enjoy it somehow. "Any other flashes of inspiration while you were here?" said Lucy.

Joanne smiled. "I did so much thinking about my life, my family and my career. I figure some things are working well, and, I now understand something big has to change."

Chapter 30

Joanne

She walked into Lucy's room without knocking and plopped herself on the bed, smoothing the perfectly ironed comforter. "What's going on?" Joanne asked, noting Lucy's intensity with reading her tablet.

"Check this out," said Lucy, pointing to Max's string of posts. "He's describing his initial struggle with sitting upright after the operation. Says he was scared and tired, yet excited about what unfolded. Each step was a milestone for him. Amazing!" Lucy said, showing Joanne all the comments piling up under his blog.

Joanne leaned closer. "Can we watch the video he posted about first steps out of his bed?"

Lucy pressed play and turned it toward Joanne. "Get this," Lucy continued. "He thanked his mother, saying he wouldn't have received a kidney without her determination. For two years, she scoured the world for potential matches. Blah-de-dah," she said, her tone growing more annoyed. "Then Max says he'd love to meet the unnamed relative from Canada. He marvels at her generosity in one of his video posts. He admits she had become an obsession for him. If she was willing, he stated publicly, he wanted to thank her in person." Lucy beamed, "That's me! His mama."

Joanne watched Lucy becoming more animated and hoped nothing scary was brewing. "Look at this Lu, he says he's going to post a daily gratitude, sharing something that he was now enjoying because of the transplant. And he also pledges to help others in a big way once he's recovered. Isn't that something, eh?" Joanne added.

Lucy sat up, as if ready to spring out of bed. "Now he's inviting her to get in touch with him for a proper *merci*," said Lucy. Suddenly, Lucy typed in a frenzy and hit send. "Oh my god," she said to Joanne.

Joanne squinted to read her text in the comments section. "OMG is right," said Joanne leaning back, in shock. "You just revealed you are the donor." They both stared at each other.

"I just couldn't stop myself," said Lucy, looking both scared and exhilarated, like a kid in the school hallway who just couldn't resist pulling the fire alarm when the teacher was out of sight. "I used my code name 'Jane Dough' along with my cartoon photo," she added, back-peddling.

"Holy shit, Lu. Look at the comments arriving by the second," said Joanne as she watched Max's followers shower Jane with love. "I've never seen so many emoticons."

"Wow, wow, wow," Lucy gushed. The two of them sat staring at the love being shown to Jane Dough. A ringing phone jolted her back to reality. She checked the call-display, pulsing with anger. "Well, that was fast." She let it ring a few more times, then took a breath and clicked the speaker button. "Yes, Elise," Lucy said as slowly as possible.

"What the hell?" said Elise, her voice echoing around the

CHAPTER 30

room.

"Relax, I didn't use my real name."

"I don't care. We had a deal!"

For the first time in decades, Joanne could see a shift in Lucy. Elise's reign of power was dwindling, and she owed Elise nothing. Joanne leaned back to watch the fireworks.

"I only promised not to reveal I was the donor before the operation," said Lucy, her body buoyed by an emotional slam dunk.

"You weren't to communicate with him. Ever. I should send you the medical bill."

Lucy twirled a fiery red curl around her finger. "Sure. I'll give you my credit card and the clinic can have a good laugh," she said, winking at Joanne.

"There are other ways."

"Whatever," uttered Lucy, her expression showing delight for messing with the master plan.

"Don't do this." Elise said. Raging silence swept the room.

"I've got an idea," Lucy shot back. "Let's focus on the positive: as in my son… your son… our son has a new kidney. I mean, that's all that matters, right?"

"How dare you!"

"Look, I am convalescing here, and I need sleep," Lucy said, short-circuiting the conversation. She hung up and high-fived Joanne, recounting the conversation like an excited sportscaster doing an instant replay.

***

By week's end, Lucy walked the full length of the corridors with Joanne gradually easing up on helping her. Lucy's doctors arrived in the hall and invited them back to Lucy's room for a briefing.

"Lucy, I discussed this with my colleague. We're delighted with your progress," said Dr. Haberling. "You are healing extremely well."

"Does this mean I can go home?" said Lucy.

"By Friday, as long as nothing changes," he said.

"Can you believe this? We can go home within the ten-day mark," said Lucy.

"Way to go. You are amazing." Joanne set out crystal tumblers and poured sparkling water into each glass and tossed in a couple of lime pieces. She handed one to Lucy, who glowed with excitement.

"I could get used to this," said Lucy, clinking her glass with Joanne's. "Yet, I'm missing my kids way too much. And Dave, the big lug I happen to love."

"Me too," said Joanne. "Seems like forever ago that we flew to Europe. So much has happened."

"No kidding! I'm down a kidney, my estranged son has mine, and I've pissed off Elise to the limit. My work here is done."

Joanne pulled out the lime and squeezed it into the glass. "It's going to be weird to see Gretchen. I'm dying to see how she's recovering from her accident. And how she handles life."

"What do you think will happen with her?"

Joanne shrugged. "Often it's the opposite of what I think."

"I know, but pace yourself, my friend. As a recovering rebellious teenager, I know how tough it is for the child and parent. Give her a chance to change, Jo."

Joanne knew what Lucy meant, but she wasn't expecting miracles just because she'd been away for a few weeks. "Things will improve, then go backward for a while. I know the drill. And I'll be there for her, no matter what."

"I know you. Anorexia is a winding road, but it will work out. Let me know how I can help," said Lucy.

"Thanks," said Joanne, slightly surprised since Lucy's track record for support was patchy. She wanted to give Lucy a chance to change. But for now, all she wanted was to go home.

***

When Lucy got the official release from the clinic and approval to fly home the next morning, they returned to their rooms to pack. To bed early and up early, Joanne had finished her packing hours earlier and left the room spotless, so she had nothing to do but join Lucy.

She couldn't bear to see Lucy twisting to nab pieces of clothing from every surface and stuffing them in her suitcase. There was no folding, just bunching and tossing, as if she had been told to leave within ten minutes and left it to the last thirty seconds. "Here Lu, I'll help. But you sure went to great lengths to avoid packing this time!" said Joanne, winking at her.

"La plus ça change, eh?"

Joanne remembered practicing that phrase in French class. "The more things change, the more they stay the same, right?"

"Something like that. Amazing, I only wore about one-third of what I brought. And I only got the dirty clothes in the bag washed because the clinic does it for you."

Joanne checked her watch. "Let's get a move on, the limo is coming soon."

"Think it will be Nicole and Victor picking us up?" said Lucy.

"Hope so. I could use one more exciting car chase on the way to the airport." Joanne couldn't wait to leave, she had so many things she wanted to do when she got home. She thought Lucy looked amazing for donating a kidney but noted that she moved gingerly.

Those were doctors' orders to make sure she didn't undo the work. Joanne knew Lucy took the instructions seriously. While she was as sturdy as a brick wall (and sometimes as strong), she knew Lucy understood the need to look after herself. While Lucy talked excitedly about going home, Joanne detected worry on her friend's face. She had an enormous challenge ahead of her. She did too: Gretchen. Joanne knew they each carried a low-level anxiety about the next phase about to unfold in their lives.

At precisely ten in the morning, Nicole and Victor arrived at the front door. The staff scurried around, delivering suitcases to the car. Joanne watched Lucy kiss and hug everyone, as if wrapping up a family reunion. Lucy swore they would stay in touch and waved endlessly as they pulled out of the clinic.

***

Ten hours later, Lucy leaned over Joanne's seat, joining her as they squished their faces into the pint-sized airplane window approaching Halifax Stanfield Airport.

"It looks like nobody lives here," said Lucy. "Look, it's mostly trees, forest and lakes, with only a sprinkling of houses."

"That's what I love about home, there's lots of outdoor space for everyone," said Joanne, watching the plane prepare to land on the large runway. As she stared out the window, she gasped at the autumn colors in Nova Scotia–the sun illuminating the yellow, orange and red leaves. Fall was her favorite time of year, except it heralded the coming of winter, which started

CHAPTER 30

in December and hung on until March, like a visiting relative who didn't take the hint to leave. Soon there would be short days, darkness at four in the afternoon, occasional dumps of snow, rain and ice. And when people couldn't take anymore, there would be a few more storms for good measure before winter eased.

After disembarking from the plane, they stumbled like zombies through the long line of travelers waiting for customs.

"I love traveling," said Joanne. "But it's always a relief to come back home."

"I'm thinking about what I'll say to Buddy at Canadian customs," said Lucy. "When he asks if I have anything to declare, I'll say 'I left a kidney behind in France'."

After customs, they stood in the luggage area under the fluorescent lights, pacing as they waited for their bags.

"Whoa, did you see our reflection in that glass?" Lucy said, pointing to a shiny panel.

"I glanced at it, but had to look away," said Joanne. "No offence, but we aren't a pretty sight." She was tired, but she could tell Lucy was even more worn out from the long-haul flight.

Ten minutes later a loud buzz, sharp clang and flashing red light announced the suitcases' arrival from the plane. It was as if some magic force behind the contraption drop-kicked every suitcase down the chute. Jammed-packed bags emerged from the automated belt, somersaulting to the bottom, followed by a lengthy carousel ride.

Bleary-eyed travelers stared at the identical black nylon cases, with rolling wheels and pull-out handles. The only way to tell them apart was the odd sticker, ribbon, or tie that held the bag intact. A few suitcases later, Joanne spotted Lucy's bag, which they nicknamed the millstone. "I'll get this, Lu," she shouted over the noise. Lucy smiled and waved.

Joanne recognized the tartan ribbon and took a breath. She leaned over to latch onto the oncoming bag that presented more like a tank than a suitcase and hoped it wouldn't pull her into the carousel. She kept her hand on it and walked a few steps, looking foolish, but couldn't yank it off the moving belt. Her hand let it go.

Two young men further along grabbed it for her before it went around again. They rolled it back to her and eased it onto the cart, feigning injury from the weight of it. She smiled and thanked them for not having to lift Lucy's bag. It was nice to be home.

Joanne had a travel rule: she only carried suitcases she could manage. Lucy gave no thought to packing according to her carrying ability. Joanne reached for her own bag and tossed it on the cart. "Let's go find a taxi." They walked outside to the stand and were quiet for a minute in the cool autumn air. "That was some journey, Lucy Lu. How are you, anyway?"

"Tired from being in transit forever, but excellent otherwise. Although I'm desperate to see my family and I'm freaking out. I have to tell them."

Joanne almost jumped into her usual supportive friend role but caught herself. "Yes you do, and I'm glad to hear you say that. You want to know why it's so important?"

"Do I have a choice?"

Joanne knew that was code for Lucy saying she didn't want to talk about it. "It's a fib here, a tweak there and withholding of information occasionally. Then it becomes a story repeated until it sounds like the truth."

"I will tell them." Lucy paused, then waved at a taxi.

CHAPTER 30

The taxi pulled up in the loading zone, and the driver popped the trunk, waiting in the car. Joanne loaded the suitcases and felt the reality check after the European spa experience. There was no limo awaiting them, no efficient concierges, only a worn-out looking driver trying to make it through the shift. They climbed into the back of the dank sedan, wrinkling their noses at the stale air. They gave him the first address and settled in.

Lucy looked at her friend. "Jo, I want us to be close again. You're like a sister to me. You put up with all my drama. Good thing you have your act together."

Joanne's heart sank. "You forget my challenges."

"I didn't forget. When I look at you, I see someone who always knows how to deal with things. And whenever someone asks how things are, you insist they are perfect." Lucy turned to her. "I now see that's not the case. Tell me, what can I do for you?"

Joanne realized everything she said was true. All her life, she had functioned with a default "everything's fine" expression tattooed on her forehead. No wonder people didn't ask what was wrong or how to help, because she didn't appear to need it. Could she really blame Lucy for not reading her mind?

"Sometimes when I tell you about Gretchen, it seems likes it barely registers, or if it does, I feel you judge her…"

Lucy glanced out the window. "Fair enough. I could be a better listener. But you need to understand I wasn't judging her. Mostly I was thinking about my behavior at that age to figure her out. Does that make sense?"

Joanne nodded, but she wondered if Lucy was sincere or just busy arguing her way out of a corner she backed into often.

"I'm not much of a friend, am I?" Lucy said, an air of defeat circling her.

"Sorry, I didn't mean to get into an extensive discussion."

Lucy flashed a smile but stayed quiet as they cruised down the Circumferential Highway and headed across the bridge to Halifax. When they pulled up to Lucy's house, Joanne said, "Let's start over. Promise we'll both stay in touch. And I'll tell you when I need help with Gretchen."

Lucy squeezed Joanne's hand. "Thanks. Now, would you mind schlepping my bag to the door?" Lucy joked.

Joanne laughed as she got out of the car and wheeled the suitcase from the trunk up the walkway. "I love how we can call each other out and still be best friends!"

"We're soul-sisters," said Lucy, walking in small steps. The lights inside the house flashed like a disco hall. Maggie burst out of the house and raced toward her mother, with Dave several feet behind her. Lucy raised her hands. "Whoa, girl. Your dear mama pulled a muscle hefting this enormous suitcase," Lucy said, winking at Joanne.

"I'll get that, darling," Dave shouted. "But first I have to kiss my wife!" He wrapped his gorilla paws around Lucy, who looked horrified, but relaxed as he handled her like a goofy Labrador. They plied her with endless questions about the trip. He picked up the suitcase. "Wow, this must be heavy because it's over-laden with gifts," he joked to Lucy as he struggled past her.

"Where's my boy?" she said. On cue, Riley bounced out of the house. "Mom, we missed you. The kitchen fell apart, and the cupboards emptied but didn't refill by magic." He hugged her, resting his head briefly on her shoulder, then returned to the basement.

CHAPTER 30

Relieved that she had delivered Lucy back home in one piece (well, technically alive), Joanne said goodbye. She exchanged knowing glances with Lucy–there was so much to say. Another time. She returned to the taxi and headed to her house.

Ten minutes later, the car turned into Joanne's driveway. The house looked desolate with only a hall light on. She wondered if Gretchen was home.

When she pushed open the door, she hollered into the quiet hallway. A note from Peter explained that Em had gone back home because of a burst pipe in her apartment, and he had to travel to a conference for several days. Given that they couldn't give them much notice about when they were coming home, she wasn't surprised. Yet she was disappointed that life went on without her. She tossed her keys into the bowl.

Gretchen appeared at the upstairs banister and stayed put, pointing to her leg brace. Her heart pounding, Joanne ran up the stairs and took her in her arms. They rocked for ages, without exchanging a word. "You look beautiful," said Joanne. Gretchen nestled into her mother's embrace and Joanne felt high.

All the pain from the past few years melted. It was never there. Joanne held her at the shoulders and stepped back to take her in. "How are you?" Gretchen pointed downward. "Well, I'm sick of this broken leg, and I gained almost a pound. But I guess I'm okay." Joanne hugged her again, and Gretchen didn't fight it. Joanne wanted to ask about her eating but didn't want to ruin the moment. Instead, she wanted to hold her daughter forever.

While the European trip was an unusual event, she was bursting with excitement to be home, even though Gretchen's drug-induced injury was not what she was expecting. Yet the needle on the stress meter nudged lower ever so slightly. Was Gretchen placing less emphasis on the anorexia? Maybe, maybe not.

Her daughter had an incredible ability to whip the rug out from under her the minute she relaxed. Joanne flopped into bed, exhausted and jet-lagged. Thoughts swirled in her head, like an impatient eddy racing down a fast-moving river. She wished Peter were home to hold her.

As she slid into a dream, Gretchen limped into the room and crawled in beside her. They giggled as her leg brace caused havoc for them. Joanne placed her arm around her daughter, and whispered, "Everything is going to be all right." Gretchen snuggled closer to her mother without saying a word.

At that moment, everything felt perfect with the world.

Chapter 31

Lucy

She paced back and forth in her office, awaiting her first video chat with Max. Time crawled, a concept she wasn't used to. Mostly she was trying to catch up on lost time with her son.

Lucy mulled over the idea of telling Max who she was, Elise be damned. And she was halfway there already under an assumed name. But she still wanted to tell her family before springing this on Max. Right now, she was over the moon at the thought of talking to him. Everything at the right time.

Since her return home, she had become obsessed with Max's social media posts and cheered with his followers as he described his progress, rereading all of them for any additional clues about who he was. He reported daily improvements, and the doctors declared it an excellent match.

Since Lucy revealed herself to be the donor with the name Jane Dough on social media, Max had messaged her, requesting a conversation. At first, she said she was too busy, but eventually agreed–the desire to talk to him was too great.

Sometimes, she found it hard to believe that he was her son. She had two years of joy watching him crawl, walk and get into things, as toddlers did.

His curiosity showed up early and he asked funny but increasingly complex questions. For the past twenty-seven years, she battled an endless longing to see him, touch him, hold him. Apologize for not protecting him. She had thought about him every day of his life. On his birthday and at Christmas, she wondered what he'd look like that year, and how tall was he when he was twelve? How did he dress? What were his interests? While she drew comfort knowing he was looked after while growing up, nothing could match her love.

They finally agreed to talk and picked a day. That morning, she tried on three outfits and settled on a navy shirt with tiny roses on it. She sat in the office where the natural light was best for video and waited impatiently, checking emails to pass the time.

At the appointed time, she opened the video, and a happy young man appeared on the screen. She wondered if she could spit out any words. He didn't know their history, so she had to pull herself together and appear as casual as possible.

"Hello Jane!"

How she wanted to blurt out that her name was Lucy McGee Baxter. She sipped her water. "Hi Max. *Comment ça va?*" Her heart raced. This felt so huge, she didn't know what to say.

"*Bien, merci,*" he said, pausing. "And I thank you deeply for giving me a new life with your kidney. It's hard to express my gratitude," he said, his voice cracking slightly.

Lucy smiled and waved her hand. "Oh jeez, Max, I am so happy that it worked out. But no gushing," she joked.

Max nodded. "Okay, but I just had to say that up front," he said, taking a breath. "Nice accent. You live in Montreal, *non?*"

CHAPTER 31

"A long time ago. I studied law at McGill but left after I graduated."

"My father was a lawyer too, but you knew that," said Max. "Did you know him well?"

"Not really," replied Lucy, which was technically true, but not in a good way.

"Did you meet up when he was a visiting scholar in Montreal in the eighties?"

"A few times," she shifted in her seat.

"Hey… we share something in common."

"Oh?" In minutes, Lucy realized that every point, observation and question felt like a potential landmine. One false phrase and the house of cards would fall. To get to the truth with Max, she needed to bring him up to speed, a few facts at a time. After all, he was raised by Elise and Jacques, with a privileged life that was beyond her, so she was begrudgingly grateful to the Morins. But this wasn't the time to burst his childhood bubble. Her strategy for this phone call: The more he talked, the less chance she had of blurting out something.

"I was born in Montreal."

"That so?" Lucy squeaked, her guts churning.

"My mother visited my father because he was away for an academic term. While she was there, she went into labor. And *voof*," he described, waving his hands as if he was a magician. "I was a 'preemie' as you call it."

Lucy tensed up, thinking about how Elise explained his Canadian citizenship. She could make up any story and nobody would be the wiser. "Is that why you are fluent in English?" she asked in her best neutral tone.

"I attended the International School of Paris, studying in English and French, so I switch back and forth. Isn't that helpful for us?"

"Yes, for sure. How are you feeling, Max?"

"Perfect…. As a twenty-nine-year-old should feel. How about you?"

"Hundred percent. I didn't miss a beat."

"That's wonderful news. It's more successful if both people are healthy, right?"

"Excellent point," said Lucy. While she had never characterized herself as at the peak of fitness, she'd obviously done well enough. "So, how are you now after the operation?"

"First, when I wake up, I pinch myself to make sure I'm not dreaming. The last few years, I worried a lot because my life revolved around waiting for a transplant phone call."

"I can't imagine."

"I'm getting stronger every day. And I have you to thank for all this. I am so grateful, and my wife Katarin sends her love too."

Lucy's body sparkled with endorphins. "Katarin, that's a lovely name." She could see this young man had an incredible life ahead of him, which filled her with joy.

"Yes, thank you. She's my soul mate. But please, tell me everything about your life…"

"We live in Halifax, Nova Scotia. And I'm married to a big, lovable guy, Dave," she said. She could see Max hung onto every word. She focused carefully, worrying the wrong words might slip out. "Dave and I have two children who are young adults. Riley is twenty-one and Maggie is nineteen." It was weird for her to know about Max, but he didn't know about her. "That's the high level. I'll tell you more sometime. But I should probably rest up… you know the drill," she joked.

"Of course," he said, smiling at the screen. "I would like to stay in touch. Is that okay?"

Lucy could have melted; he was so adorable. "Of course, Max."

"Jane? May I ask you something?" his voice dropped to a whisper.

Lucy's heart fluttered like a bird trapped in a cage. What if it was a tough question? "Sure," she said, rocking in a chair that didn't rock.

"Could we set a regular meeting time–maybe even bi-weekly? I'd like to know you better."

"Absolutely," she said, releasing her held breath.

"I sense an incredible connection to you. I hope it doesn't sound too weird."

"Not at all," she whispered.

"Who knew receiving a kidney from someone would establish such a bond with them?"

"Truly," she said, but wanted to change the subject. "Funny, I read that organ recipients sometimes get cravings for things they never liked before."

"Really? Such as…. "

Lucy smiled as she imagined the horror on Elise's face in a fancy restaurant with Max ordering food based on Lucy's tastes. "Well, let's just say if you suddenly get a craving for nachos with extra cheese and a taste for house wine, that could be from me." He tilted his head back and laughed hard. While nothing in his looks even hinted at him being her child, she recognized her laugh: hearty, spontaneous and erupting from deep down. It certainly wasn't from Jacques or Elise, because neither of them had a sense of humor.

"That's amazing. I am going to put that in a blog to see if anyone else has experienced it. I'll keep you posted."

"Sounds perfect, Max."

"How about we talk a few weeks from today, same time?"

"Sure."

"Thanks for being there. I'm looking forward to chatting soon!"

"Me too," said Lucy, closing the app. He was a million times more beautiful than she imagined. His dark hazel eyes danced like shimmering jewels, and his black hair was so shiny it could blind a person.

A rush of maternal love infused every cell in her body. Exhilarated and exhausted, she slumped into a heap on her sofa and thought about her son. She couldn't wait to speak to him again. Two weeks was an eternity.

Chapter 32

Joanne

"What's up?" said Joanne, the phone cradled to her ear as she slipped her laptop into her briefcase and tidied her desk.

"Plenty. But first, how's Gretchen?"

She was happy that Lucy followed through on her promise to stay in touch. "She's working with a mental health counsellor and there's a lot to tackle–mostly getting more nutrition into her."

"Is she still refusing to eat?"

"Actually," Joanne said, feeling buoyant. "She's eating a bit more. The problem is she's been living on very little for a few years, so she has to introduce more food incrementally. And she needs more nourishment."

"I imagine her body isn't in great physical shape."

She wondered if Lucy was genuinely interested or just living up to her commitment, but Joanne sensed she had taken their conversation to heart. "Her body is not working well. She has malnutrition. Let's not forget the 'Ecstasy evening'. I'm trying to figure out if it was a one-off or if this is another mental health issue."

"Amazing what our kids will put us through, eh?"

"No kidding. I swear Gretchen has a Reverse Bucket List–it's as if she's picked the top ten actions to shock me." She heard Lucy chuckle. "Anyway, I was just leaving work, and you called with something important," said Joanne.

"How dare you? I was calling to catch up," she said, with mock hurt in her voice.

"Cool. And how's Max?"

"I talked to him," Lucy squealed. "And he's the most amazing kid…. or young man, I should say. Very French, and so polite and caring."

"Hmm, must have gotten that from your side of the family." She shared a giggle with Lucy. "What did you talk about?" Joanne asked, checking her desk one more time.

"We connected so fast my head was spinning. Let's see. The operation transformed his life. Bye, bye dialysis. Hello, lots of energy–like it should be at that age. For me, it is heart-warming to think he'll enjoy a long life with his wife and their new baby."

"Your grandchild. Imagine," said Joanne.

"Lord love a duck."

"Who knew you'd be a grandmother in your early fifties?" said Joanne, a twinge of envy rippling through her. While didn't spend time dreaming about being a grandmother, she liked the sound of it. Yet she knew it wasn't likely for the Cambridge family for a while: Emmaleigh was busy with endless wonderful projects, and Gretchen had denounced childbearing long ago. "Excited, Lu?"

"Yes, except they live in France. So, I'll watch my *petite-fille* granddaughter growing up on a video screen." Lucy's voice sounded both defiant and wistful. "You know what's weird?"

CHAPTER 32

"What?"

"He has no idea I'm his mother, but we're like two magnets that wandered into each other's path. KAPOW! Instant connection. He thinks it's because he has my kidney."

"How are you going to deal with that?"

"Avoid the topic as long as possible."

"Like you are doing with your family?" Joanne checked her watch. "You know, eventually all of this has to come out, Lucy." She heard Lucy's familiar gulp of air, preparing to launch into a long discussion. "Sorry Lucy, I shouldn't have raised that right now–we should continue this chat another time. I have to head out."

"Me too. Not that I can even concentrate right now. How's your dream about wrestling the flower shop from your loser cousin coming along?"

"Another time Lucy, okay?" she gasped, but then laughed.

"Love you too!"

Joanne smiled and turned off the phone. Relieved that Lucy didn't offend easily, she hoped her friend would do some more soul searching with this mess. For now, it was time to leave behind her concerns about Lucy's dramas.

She closed her laptop, picked up her bag and exited the office, hurrying past the workstations, chairs sticking out and bankers' boxes piled sky high. She wished a general good night to everyone without stopping for chats as she used to. Since returning from Europe, she didn't want to miss a minute of family time at home.

***

Joanne pulled into the driveway and parked the car. Besides her family improvements, she was feeling optimistic about her life and career plans. Something had changed, and she was working toward something new, but still figuring things out. Would it be Bev's flower shop? A new venture with Holly? The dreaming continued.

Since returning from Europe, she found Gretchen responding more positively, offering Joanne brief glimpses of hope. She didn't want to read too much into it but prayed it would continue. With several arms holding grocery bags with different handle lengths, she balanced a heavy bag on her arm while she unlocked the side door.

She pried open the door, held it with her foot, and made her way into the kitchen. After setting down the bags that gave her arms a good workout, she hollered out to Gretchen. Her happy greeting echoed around the hallway and fell flat. Somehow the lack of sound felt odd. "Hi Gretchen." Joanne called again from the banister downstairs. No response.

Joanne guessed she must be out doing errands, or upstairs and not in the mood for talking. While life improved in the household, Gretchen still switched between being nice and mean-spirited toward everyone, or "Sweet and Sour Gretchen" as Joanne sometimes described it to Peter in times of exasperation.

Joanne wouldn't have gotten away with that kind of behavior with her parents. Yet here she was tiptoeing around her daughter, wondering how and why she let Gretchen treat her with such contempt. While wandering the gardens at the clinic in Paris where she had endless time to think about her life, it occurred to Joanne that she had controlled her children's upbringing at every step.

While she meant well, she now pictured herself in hindsight, hovering over them. She jumped at every chance to solve minor kid skirmishes, school projects ignored until the night

CHAPTER 32

before they were due, and sports team disappointments—no obstacle was too small. She'd raised a sullen gal, always ready with a scowl in response to everything.

Joanne and her friends gradually realized they were the generation of parents who forgot to teach their kids resiliency skills. They issued participation ribbons to their offspring for simply showing up and awarded prizes for last place in the soccer tournament. Heaven forbid that any child had to face losing a game. In her mind, she didn't want them to deal with the insecurities of being female as she did in her teens, so self-esteem was the top goal for her children.

Whenever Peter tried to show some parental discipline, such as getting them to take responsibility for their actions, managing their finances, or facing obstacles, she invariably pushed back (and the girls figured out who to go to with their issues). Joanne realized she focused too much on building confidence, and she and Peter found it a challenge to deal with problems.

Emmaleigh blossomed with that approach. While she didn't experience adversity growing up, she somehow understood that life dealt some terrible blows which she witnessed in her volunteer work. She took pride in helping people to overcome problems. At university, she met a group of friends who were like brothers and sisters. They helped each other out, instead of focusing on themselves. She adapted quickly and soon embraced that attitude as a lifestyle.

As she put the groceries away, she realized Gretchen still hadn't responded to her shouts upstairs. She walked back to the staircase. "Honey? You home?" A whimper wafted out of the bathroom. Joanne's body burst with adrenaline. She reminded herself not to panic.

However, deep down she knew the room in the house with a bathtub and a medicine cabinet posed a certain danger. While she believed her daughter would not do something extreme, it didn't stop her from worrying about it.

She rocketed up the stairs, three at a time.

Chapter 33

Max

His nerves revved at the thought of getting to know a relative overseas who had saved his life. Who was she? And why had she chosen to donate a kidney to him? He had never even heard of the family connection before, and suddenly she was playing a major role in his life. But then again, his father wasn't much for family.

Max flipped open his laptop and smiled as Jane appeared on her screen. "Hello Jane."

"Morning Max. How's Katarin?"

"She'll be delivering her baby any day now."

"So exciting."

"There are many wonderful things in my life," he smiled at her. He didn't want to become too sentimental with her, but there was something about her that made him feel so connected.

"I understand you are an architect," she said.

"Yes," he beamed. "I have a firm with nine people." While he was proud of what he had achieved for his age, people sometimes implied that his family money enabled it.

"Wow, you're so young."

"I always knew, so I didn't waste any time!" he joked. "My parents understood Legoland was my ultimate vacation. First, we visited Legoland in Denmark, then Germany, England, and California. I built houses as soon as I could hold Lego bricks."

"Were your parents pleased?"

Max nearly scoffed, remembering his father's scorn. But there was no need to reveal family dynamics with her. "My father wanted me to be a lawyer at his firm, and my mother hoped I'd take over the family winery."

"And you?"

"Neither. I began university with law in mind because my father pushed hardest. He could be forceful. Did you find that?" Max noticed her face flushed, but she didn't reply. "Luckily, a professor in my class noticed my detailed drawings for buildings. He introduced me to an architect."

"And?"

"We met." He paused, his eyes filling with excitement as he recalled that special time. "We spoke the same language… and I felt like I belonged. I could talk all day about architecture."

"Did you feel you were letting your parents down?"

He shrugged. "Sure, but I couldn't stomach what my father did–he was either defending guilty people or hurting innocent people."

"Sounds like it wasn't your thing," said Jane.

"The pressure eased when my cousin Gilles became a partner at my father's company. What a relief. They talked non-stop about law."

"Did you and your father get along?"

Max wondered why she asked that question. Whatever, he didn't have anything to hide. "Not so much. I never lived up to his standards. He was bright and extremely critical."

"How long did you study architecture?"

"Seven years. I have a Master's, then there's an internship, exams, the usual hoops, and a designation in France called *HMONP*. And I'm fortunate, I have a very respected architect as my mentor with the company. He tried to retire, but it didn't take." Max enjoyed watching Jane laugh. It was loud and happy. She didn't hold back the way his parents did.

"So, do you specialize in a particular architecture?" she said.

"Tiny houses."

"Really?" said Lucy. "What are they called in French?"

"Tiny houses." He said in an exaggerated French accent, dropping the H in houses.

Lucy smiled. "Sounds fascinating," she said. "How did that go over with your parents?"

"My mother accepted it, but it embarrassed my father. 'Tiny' was not in his vocabulary."

"Maybe that's why you chose the opposite."

"Could be..." he trailed off, yet he couldn't stop his enthusiasm. Besides, she looked interested. "The movement is skyrocketing. With concerns about space, the environment, sustainability, cost of housing–it's the perfect solution."

"What's the name of your firm?"

"Lilliput Architecture."

Jane choked on her coffee. "Lilliput? As in the little people in *Gulliver's Travels*?"

"Makes sense, *non*?" He grinned at her. "We are not a traditional firm."

"No kidding."

"We make key decisions together and share profits. Of course, there are heated debates, We're artists."

"I'll bet your staff meetings are lively."

"Sure, but that's because they are during Happy Hour at the Narrow Café, a few steps along the street. It's about being true to yourself and hiring people who feel the same way." Max took a breath. "Sorry, I went on about my work. It's like we're old friends catching up."

"I enjoy hearing about your life, Max."

Normally, he noticed bored expressions within ten minutes when he talked about architecture and his philosophy with people outside of his usual circle. Not Jane. She appeared to hang onto his every word. He enjoyed himself but figured she too would soon tire of it. "Katarin says I'm too enthusiastic," he laughed.

"Is she an architect?"

"She's an interior designer with the firm. That's how we met."

"Life has treated you well," she said. "Well, I guess before your kidney woes."

"I'm grateful to be alive. Thank you."

"I wasn't fishing for compliments."

"I have a beautiful wife, a child on the way, and a career that brings me joy. It doesn't get any better."

Jane checked her watch. "Listen, Max, I'd love to chat more, but I have to go."

"I understand. Talk to you on the fifteenth?"

Jane nodded. "Take care and say hello to Katarin."

"Promise me one thing for next time?"

"What?"

"I want to know about you and your family, including how we are related. I've asked my mother several times, but she glosses over it. Will you explain it to me?"

"Well… ah… it's complicated," she smiled. "I'll do my best to connect the dots next time, okay?"

"Sure. All I meant was, enough talking about me, unless Katarin goes into labor. Then we'll talk about the baby. Deal?"

"Yes, Max. Talk soon."

Max watched Jane disappear from the screen. His lighthearted mood gave him a feeling that everything would be okay. He couldn't believe how his luck had changed. Less than a year ago, he worried he might not live long enough to watch a child grow up–a thought that nearly crushed him. He was so far down the donor list that the future didn't look bright.

Yet his dear mother had channeled her efforts into finding a kidney, and amazingly, she found an obscure family member. His mother sounded so relieved after the operation, he realized how stressful it must have been for her. While she was more relaxed, she sounded a little iffy when he talked about his conversations with Jane. Was she worried about Jane wanting something? He didn't sense she'd be a problem. As much as he loved his mother, she thought the worst about people–he didn't. Whatever. He enjoyed getting to know Jane and couldn't wait for the next session.

Chapter 34

Joanne

She arrived at the top of the stairs and wedged through the bathroom door, fearing the worst. Relief swept over her as she saw Gretchen sitting on the floor, sniffling. "Hon? What happened?" she yelped, gripped by fear.

Gretchen looked dazed. "I think I passed out."

"Whatever it is, we can work it out," said Joanne, her eyes darting around the room. There was no sign of the unthinkable with her daughter, and she felt stupid for even considering such a thing.

She pulled in a long breath because she needed to look at Gretchen's wounds and her daughter would resist. She had already battled her earlier about it, Gretchen insisting she would check them, not her mother. "Honey, I need to see this wound," she said, not even waiting for Gretchen to protest. She eased the bandage off and winced at the sight of the red bumps and puffy gash. "The big cut from your fall is infected."

She sat down and slid her arm around her, holding her tight. Gretchen clung to her mother, locking her into a position that prevented her from moving.

CHAPTER 34

After a few minutes, she gently removed Gretchen's two arms from around her shoulder. Joanne placed her palm on the floor to steady herself and eased to a standing position. She offered her hand to Gretchen. "We need to get this looked at. You might have an infection from your time in the hospital."

"I'm not going back to the hospital," Gretchen wailed.

Joanne shifted into full mother mode. "This is serious. You need help. NOW." Gretchen's face scrunched up and fear encircled her body. Joanne lifted her broken leg and pressed lightly to move. She remembered her friend's father had died of sepsis after a minor operation. Pushing back fear, Joanne eased her downstairs and grabbed her purse, the keys and two coats and sped to the hospital.

***

In the hospital room, Joanne, Emmaleigh and Peter stood around Gretchen's bed. Although miserable, she was healing after a few days of a nasty infection, likely picked up during her first hospital visit. Joanne fussed and made sure her daughter was as comfortable as she could be for someone who feared medical spaces.

Normally she would have felt the wrath of her daughter, but this time she felt wanted by Gretchen, so she stayed close by. "Peter and Em, you should go home and get some rest," she whispered as they huddled outside of the room. Before either of them could summon up the energy to argue, she added, "I just want to stay until she's out of danger and goes off to sleep."

She hugged them both, and they wandered off down the corridor lit up with flickering fluorescents. Joanne returned to the room and sat beside her daughter, whose eyes were closed, but tense. Every thirty seconds, a beep from the monitoring machine broke Gretchen's concentration. A patient on the other side of the curtain snored. This could be a long night.

Gretchen opened her eyes, turned her head away and mumbled, "You must hate me by now." Joanne looked at her withered daughter, exhausted from the strain. She held her hand. "Darling, I couldn't love you any more if I tried."

"That's a relief."

Joanne wasn't about to lose out on a moment for dialog. "We still need to talk about the rave and you taking drugs."

"Look, Mom, it was only something I wanted to try. No biggie. It didn't go well, so I don't plan on doing it again."

"What about Ally-Up?"

"What about him?"

"Are you still seeing him?"

"He said he doesn't want to see me anymore."

"Can you understand why?"

"I guess so."

"Well, he impressed me by taking a stand about going to the rave."

Gretchen sighed. "I can't do anything without somebody telling me what to do or how to do it."

"You mean me."

"His mother too. She is way, way too involved in every aspect of his life," said Gretchen.

"That's what you accuse me of, right?"

"There's a difference. You hover, she digs in and decides on our behalf. It makes me nuts."

"So, I only drive you half nuts!" Joanne joked, yet pleased with the back-handed compliment. She took a deep breath to organize her thoughts. "Gretchen, I thought about you a lot while I was in Europe." Her daughter's eyebrows lifted. This was hard for Joanne.

"Gretchen, I know I've tried to do too much. I meant well. However, that didn't work for you. From now on, you are in control of your own life. You'll make your own decisions. Some outcomes will be wrong, or not what you wanted," said Joanne, feeling uneasy. "But they'll be your choices. If you need my help, I'll be there. Okay?"

Gretchen nodded. "I realize the rave and drugs upset you. I need to figure out my next steps."

"You made a mistake. But I'm glad you are owning it." Joanne sat quietly, letting the conversation settle a bit. This was a lot for both to process.

"Do you think Ally-Up will take me back? I really care about him," she said, her voice quivering.

Joanne opened her mouth, ready to strategize solutions, but stopped. "Honey, I don't know. What do you like about him?"

Her daughter's face lit up. "Mom, he is doing wonderful stuff. You know, he invited all those immigrants out to the community garden and helped them to grow stuff like herbs, Bok choy and other produce they use in local restaurants. He delivers twice a week on his bike, and shares what he earns with the gardeners. Everybody loves him."

"Wow, I'm impressed. I guess the best thing to do is let you figure out if you two can make it work." Joanne sipped her water and smiled at her daughter. While Gretchen didn't exactly sound happy, she seemed… less miserable. Maybe she'd always be that way. Anyway, she'd take any small win.

In a half hour, Gretchen nodded off to sleep. Joanne pulled the covers up and kissed her forehead. As she walked back to the car, she felt better about life with her daughter. There would still be more landmines as she let Gretchen solve her own problems, but they had to start somewhere. Then she had her own next steps to figure out and resolve some unspoken issues with Peter. As Lucy would say, "one Massive Family Hairball at a time".

Chapter 35

Lucy

After her video call with Max, Lucy started mapping out the next steps to tell her husband and her kids about him. She could no longer bear the thoughts of keeping separate strands in her life and dreamed of bringing them together. There was no need for a big family reunion fuss because Max had grown up in France and that's where he would stay. While she dreamed of visiting him regularly, it wasn't necessary for everybody to do so. She'd take it one step at a time.

A series of texts buzzed on her phone. She scanned them and saw Riley's name mentioned over and over. Something big was up. *You must be so proud of Riley! Riley's rocks, What a kid.* On and on the texts danced with emojis. What happened? Perhaps he won a video game competition.

Often, she heard cheers erupt from the basement and when she asked him what was going on, he'd say they'd won a gaming tournament. Video games remained a mystery to her–she was the only one in the family who didn't play. Not once. The noise, the violence, the time to play and the treatment of women were all deterrents to her playing (although Riley always insisted that the females he competed against truly kicked ass). Lucy would sigh and retort how 'happy' that made her. It embarrassed her she wasn't aware of his news. She walked to the top of the basement stairs–headquarters for Riley and his buddies–and called him, but only heard the dryer rumble.

She texted Maggie, *What's up with Riley?* In seconds, her phone pinged. *Riley's APP!* Lucy could fess up to Maggie that she didn't get some technology, and she wouldn't judge her (other than occasional teasing). She'd patiently explain to her mother how something worked or fix a problem for her.

A doorknob rattling and a chorus of loud voices interrupted her text as Riley and his best friends piled through the front door. She called them the Bible Bunch because of their names: Ethan, Matthias, Noah and Jason. She had never heard them chatter like that as they removed their enormous running shoes in the entryway and a sweaty stench filled the house. Riley shouted his usual distracted "Hey Mom" as he and his buddies walked through the house. Lucy tugged Riley's sleeve before he headed to the cave. "What's UP with the APP?" she said, trying to sound light.

"Launch is on Thursday," said Riley. Lucy tried to hide her shock. "Thursday?" This was news to her. "You developed an app ready for market?" she said in a nobody-ever-tells-me tone, which made her cringe because she sounded just like her mother. She had been so wrapped up in her own world–with the trip, a kidney donation and Max, she missed the hoopla.

Matthias, with an over-stretched, lanky body resembling a telecom tower, paused at the top of the stairs. "Investors are already circling BandOnTour, Mrs. B."

She turned to Riley, fear of missing out rising inside her.

CHAPTER 35

"What's it do?"

Riley slipped into sales mode. "We help bands on tour. It's too expensive to buy and travel with a lot of stuff. Through this app they can rent equipment, instruments, gear, vehicles in any city and hire local crews and musicians. Then there are hotels, restaurants and other services catering to bands that could be helpful. We're adding new suppliers daily."

"And I thought you were playing video games all this time."

"Sometimes, but always working on this project," said Riley.

"I don't even remember you talking about it."

"You never asked."

Riley's sucker punch raised her irritation level. "Riley, how many times did I ask and got a one-syllable response?" He shrugged. "You didn't seem interested, or you were away."

Lucy didn't want to spoil the moment, but she felt hurt by his casual observation that boiled down to lack of interest. She needed to take the high road. "Anyway, Riley, fantastic news! Are you going to start a company? I can help you with the legal needs."

"Done. Noah's father is a lawyer."

"I'm not?"

"You do that advocacy stuff. He does actual business. We're officially DigiMo," said Riley.

Zing, he had just insulted his mother again. Maybe he didn't mean to, but he was sure pressing the hurt buttons. "As in Digital Monks?" Lucy hinted, trying to remind him she came up with the name.

"Yup."

"Got a website?"

He shot her a feigned look of exasperation and put his arm around her. "DigiMo dot DUH, Mom."

"I'll take that as a yes." Yikes. She was acting like a nagging mother with a checklist for her kid's summer camp. Clearly Riley and his buddies knew what they were doing, and when they didn't, they hired experts.

She wanted to be part of the excitement, but it was like she had arrived for a dinner party with the appetizer, only to find they'd moved on to dessert. Riley hugged her. "Have to run, they're waiting for me." He scooted past her, headed for the basement until a whiff from the kitchen grabbed him.

"Hey... chili. Awesome!" He walked to door and shouted, "Dudes, chili!" A rush of oversized sock feet pounded the stairs. Their home was the official hang-out for Riley and his friends that started in high school.

Lucy shook her head. In only a few words, he insulted her career, then praised her for an enormous pot of chili that she hadn't cooked. Her neighbor Patricia had opened a family meal delivery business. Lucy bought two slow cookers and every few days, Jennifer would drop by with stew, soup and ribs–and Riley's group performed "locust duty" as Lucy described it. Riley and the guys pulled out bowls from the cupboard and forks from the drawer–as if they lived there. But they also loaded the dishwasher, so Lucy never complained.

Lucy sat at the island and brought up their website. A pop-up ad invited her to join the subscriber list. Lucy opened the "About" section and saw the group shot she had taken on her phone on a frosty fall day in Nova Scotia.

Riley and his buddies walked toward the house, all wearing dark hoodies, the hoods up over their heads, their hands shoved into the side pockets, trying to keep warm. She had shouted at the guys who all looked up at the same time. A shaft of silver light illuminated Riley's face at the front of the line.

"What do you think, Mom?" said Riley, scooping chili from the pot.

"This is fantastic, Riley. I guess you liked the photo I took." Riley smiled. Lucy gave up trying to find out about the app. All she knew, it was huge. And now his life was blossoming.

Why hadn't she asked more questions over the past couple of years? She was proud of him, when not on his case about hiding in the basement. He was a curious hybrid personality, both introvert and extrovert. He liked his alone time, yet he attracted friends continuously. Lucy realized that his understated good looks benefited him. His stature wasn't tall, but his addiction to surfing from an early age blessed him with a sturdy body and healthy glow.

He was confident, yet sensitive to others. Girls found him irresistible, which he barely seemed to notice in high school (although he was likely acting on it, he didn't tell his mother). On one of the few occasions Riley invited his mom to watch him surf at Martinique Beach, she could see young women back on shore, eyeing him.

When he emerged from the ocean, he looked perfect with the sun highlighting his tanned face, melancholy smile, and salty tangled mess of hair. While he could have led part of the cool cliques at school, he avoided groups that humiliated people or made them feel left out.

Lucy remembered chatting with her neighbor Michelle, a lunchtime monitor at Riley's school. She described an incident when some guys were making fun of an autistic student, Richard. They chanted "au-tis-tic-Dick" as he shuffled by. Frightened, Richard scrambled to the corner of the cafeteria for safety. Riley picked up his tray, saying "not cool" to the bullies as he passed by. He walked to Richard and asked if he could sit with him. He nodded but didn't say a word, and neither did Riley.

From then on, Riley invited Richard to sit with his buddies, though it took weeks before they exchanged a few words. Gradually they learned he was a brilliant mathematician and did algorithms for fun (probably in his head). While he didn't spend time in the basement with the others, he became a key member of the DigiMo group. Riley's group loved Richard's technical talent. He did his work, sent it to them and waited for feedback. They'd test it together and say, "Holy shit, this guy is incredible". Richard liked the work but shied away from the buddy interaction.

As she sipped a glass of red in the kitchen, Dave arrived home. He kissed Lucy on the forehead, took a sip of her wine and smiled. "Proud of our son?"

"Better believe it. So, you knew about the app?"

"I've been helping them test it before it went live," said Dave.

"Guess I'm the only one who didn't know."

"Maybe you were wrapped up in your own little world there, Lucy."

"Aren't you supposed to be on my side?"

"I love you, but this one's on you."

"How can I do better?" she said, frustration lacing each syllable.

"Show some interest," he said, kissing her cheek.

She watched Dave head to the basement. In seconds, the guys howled with laughter as he shouted at them. She didn't speak geek. Annoyed, she returned to her email.

Maggie walked in. "Hey Mom."

"Hi," said Lucy, giving her a hug. "I'm getting caught up on the family news."

"Great isn't it? All my friends are texting me. Riley is Hali-famous!"

"Hali what?"

"Famous in Halifax, but not beyond. Yet."

"Listen, Maggie. I messed up. I've been focused on myself and missed all the buildup to this."

"Don't feel bad," said Maggie. "I only got it in bits. And I know all his friends."

"Really?" Lucy straightened up. She needed to do better, starting now. "What's happening with you these days?" Maggie broke into a big smile. Lucy could tell she was into something good.

"The prof says I'm a natural with numbers."

That wasn't quite what she was expecting, but she was ready for the curveball. "Where did you get that talent, Mags? Not me, sorry to say."

"Hard to say. I just love numbers," said Maggie.

"What does that mean for your studies?"

"Well, you might not like this—" Maggie shifted in her chair. "When I finish my business degree, I may study accounting."

Lucy swallowed her wine before choking on it. She remembered joking it was the career most likely to cause her to poke her eyes out. She hoped Maggie didn't remember.

"I get that you hate accounting," said Maggie.

Whoops, she did remember. "Listen, that's only because I'm so bad at it and envious of you. Power to you!" Maggie brightened and leaned toward her mother. "It sounds crazy, Mom, but there's genuine beauty in it. When I think about reviewing somebody's financials, I want to understand the story and how it fits together. I love making order out of chaos."

"Wow, I never thought of it that way. I support your dream, Maggie."

"You mean that?"

"Of course," said Lucy. Did her kids see her as close-minded or something? She only wanted them to be happy.

"Thanks Mom. I realize you may have had different ideas about what I should do with my life."

"I'm glad you're more sensible. What else do you enjoy about it?"

"It's fairly standard in the industry: Pay and benefits are great. There's a medical package, and I'd start with lots of vacation. Plus, I'd know how my career will unfold."

Lucy recalled what she was like at Maggie's age–and not one of those items was on her mind during job interviews. Where did these children come from? She understood that every generation wanted to differ from their parents–the exact opposite in fact–in a pendulum-swinging way. Yet happiness was what she dreamed of for her kids. "I'm so freakin' proud of you, Mags."

"You just want me to do your income tax," joked Maggie, hugging her Mom.

Chapter 36

Joanne

She moved around the kitchen like a choreographer, pulling items out of the dishwasher, making coffee, and monitoring the laundry. A multi-tasker in the morning, she understood how to get everybody out the door on time.

After Gretchen's health scare, she improved in tiny increments. She dodged landmine discussions with her, yet she saw signs of hope as the trauma eased. Joanne pictured even more wonderful things happening for her family. She picked up her keys and headed out the door, enjoying a wisp of optimism for the first time in months. Arriving at the office at eight o'clock, she poured a coffee, chatted with a few early birds on her team, and sat down to tackle a report before her meeting.

Mid-morning, a light knock nudged her from a daydream. Claire, her executive assistant, opened the door.

"Joanne," she whispered.

"Hi. What's up?"

"George would like to see you."

"Sure, but we have our senior leaders' meeting. Can you book something after that?"

"Sorry, but he said now."

This was her life, her job–that's what she had to do–respond on a whim to many unforeseen things happening daily. She loved the variety but dreamed of finishing her report without interruption. Not today.

She locked the document and grabbed a notebook and pen. "Okay, Claire. Be right there." She walked out of her office and down the hallway to the president's office, as George emerged from behind a closed door and looked surprised to see her. "Oh, hi George," she said smiling. "I guess this will be quick since we have our meeting." He muttered hello, his red face avoiding eye contact. In the outer meeting room, she spotted HR professionals from the top outplacement firm in Halifax.

She felt a sudden wallop to her stomach. In a split-second, she understood exactly what was about to happen: Her status was about to shift to unemployed. A flurry of thoughts raced through her head. She thought about the big financial hit, just as Gretchen was nearing university age.

Her long-standing daily work rhythm with lovely colleagues would soon vaporize, along with the pride she felt from working her way to the top of her field at that company. She would soon be rehearsing an awkward pitch to describe her status, shifting from HR professional to job seeker. Yuck.

***

It was over in minutes. She waited in the little office for one of her colleagues to bring her coat, purse and a few boxes of personal items and plans.

Bill, the security guard, who wore the same expression of shock as she did, escorted her out the side door. Bill helped her load the boxes and plants into her car. "I'm so sorry, Jo. We've been through a lot together."

CHAPTER 36

"Thanks Bill. Not your fault," she said, shoving everything into her trunk. For once, she didn't care where anything landed. She needed to get out of there as fast as possible.

"Stay in touch?"

"You bet," she said, welcoming his kindness. "See you around, Bill." She surprised herself by how calm she sounded.

She climbed into her car and drove out of the parking lot. Everything appeared oddly normal, yet there was nothing normal about this day. Her mind raced. Where to start? She had pushed through the roughest patch with Gretchen and had relaxed a little. Now jobless at fifty. She understood that's what happened in life–just when she dared to believe things were improving.

After a few minutes, she realized she was driving with no destination in mind. What should she do? Go home? Call Peter? Lucy? She couldn't decide. All she knew was that she needed down time.

Joanne drove across town to the South End, down Young Avenue, past Halifax's grandest homes, to Point Pleasant Park. She needed to be alone with her thoughts. The park skirted the edge of the city, overlooking the Atlantic Ocean. People walked their dogs, strolled, and chatted with friends as they followed the trails.

She didn't want to bump into anyone and immediately spotted someone from her swimming club. She slouched in the car until Brenda ran by. Joanne got out and opened the trunk which she called the "department of fun".

It was full of fitness and play gear in case she got the urge to walk, run, do yoga, play tennis or swim. She pulled out her yoga pants, jacket, and running shoes; and climbed back into the car, changing with no one noticing. She plugged in her earbuds and started walking, hoping to avoid eye contact with people. Dogs darted around her, chasing seagulls and squirrels.

She walked for several hours and thought about how things had been in the past few years. Now there was a fresh crisis to add to the mix. As an HR professional, she knew all about being downsized. While the session with her boss pinged around in her head like static electricity, she knew all the key messages: It wasn't personal, and by restructuring (or "rightsizing" the department, as they liked to call it), they could accommodate the budget cuts.

Then there were the outplacement firm's nuggets such as "Things will get better", "This will be the best thing to happen to you" and "There will be other jobs". Those were pep talk points she'd been saying to others for years.

She crawled under a gigantic maple tree and leaned back. Having a good cry seemed obvious, but she couldn't coax it out of her system. Why was that? Maybe the health problems with Gretchen felt so much bigger, and besides, she realized this would all pass, somehow.

Anger pulsed through her body. She was head of HR, so she understood the work required to eliminate her job without her knowledge. That was standard practice, yet it hurt. She put on a meditation track and stared at the harbor waves. They arrived in gentle breaks, as if to comfort her.

After an hour, she woke up, still feeling pangs of sadness. Although her career had suddenly derailed, she reminded herself it wasn't the end of the world. She would miss her colleagues the most. Of course, the loss of her title and salary scared her, and yet something inside her quietly cheered as she thought about no longer working so many hours.

CHAPTER 36

For a moment, she considered the unknown world opening for her. What if she was being offered an exciting new chapter in life? She had dreamt of changing her career for several years–she couldn't even pinpoint when it started–yet she didn't have the courage to pursue it. Isn't that what she had wanted–the chance to do something meaningful?

She had been standing at the edge of change but didn't have the courage to jump without a parachute and a perfect landing in sight. But that's not how it worked in life. Now she was free to do whatever the hell she wanted for work. The one thing she knew, it wouldn't be for another corporation.

Chapter 37

Lucy

The subject line, "It's a Girl!" caught her eye. Her heart fluttered as she viewed a photo of Katarin and Max holding a newborn accompanied by a note:

We are proud to announce the birth of our beautiful daughter, who weighed 3.1 kilograms. We are smitten with this baby girl who has wisps of curly red hair (must be from Katarin's Breton roots!). Katarin and the baby are doing well. We are still deciding on names. For now, we are going with her middle name, Margaux, in honor of Katarin's grandmother.

Lucy stared at the photo, her body pumping with joy. The red hair excited her beyond belief, and she was bursting to share the news. She forwarded the message to Joanne, who in seconds was on the phone.

"Congrats, Grandma. How does it feel?"

"Weird and wonderful. It's time to tell the clan."

"You think?"

"I have to run, Jo. I've got a call with Max set up," said Lucy, nearly breathless.

***

CHAPTER 37

Lucy sat on the sofa in her office and waited for Max to appear on the screen. She loved getting to know her son. As soon as his face appeared, her body settled. Just seeing him made her feel more complete as a mother. Although she did not watch him grow up, she wanted to know every detail of his life.

"Hi, Max," she almost shouted. "Congratulations! She's beautiful."

"Thank you, Jane. Have you checked out the other baby photos? There were so many visits online, we nearly crashed the server," he chuckled.

"She's perfect." Lucy felt warm inside, and full of love. "Tell me all about Margaux, which is a beautiful name by the way," she added.

"Yes… thank you." He drew a quiet breath, clearly high about his child. "Of course, the first thing you notice is her red hair. She's our little redhead, or *petite rousse* as we call her. Already she glows when people talk about it. I imagine you got lots of attention with your red hair when you were growing up."

"Yes, for better and worse," Lucy said, trying not to focus on her contribution to Margaux's hair color. "People remembered me because of my red hair, which worked well unless I was doing something bad," she added.

Max glanced at the photo, still bursting with enthusiasm. "And she's tiny, like her mother. Her sweet limbs waving in all directions, telling us she wants us to hold her. Everybody wants a turn. You know, since she was born, I realize nothing else matters. Not a thing. What a feeling."

"You sound like a natural father, Max." Lucy ached for a turn to hold her grandchild.

"Thanks. Of course, I could talk about her forever; but, we have so much to chat about."

Lucy jumped in. "I saw your website for Lilliput Architecture. I'm impressed."

"Thanks. You saw the plans for *Nanoville*?

"Yes. A community of tiny houses." Lucy loved his confidence. Here was a young man who was going to change things in his world. "Brilliant ideas. I love the eco-construction, shared bikes and cars. Amazing that it's intergenerational residents and every tenth house is designated for low-income families."

"It's been a dream for Katarin and me."

"How did you become so devoted to the tiny house movement?"

"Good question. Maybe it's because I wanted the opposite of what I had. I grew up in a spacious apartment in Paris, my father's family had a summer home, and my mother's family has a château and winery in the south of France. But you probably know all that…" He waved his hand. "Enough about the Morin family. Tell me about your life and family."

Lucy bubbled on about her husband and children, and their accomplishments and dreams. When she slowed down to take a breath, Max smiled.

"You are passionate too! They sound wonderful. If you want to bring them to Paris for a visit, we'd love to host them."

"That sounds fun."

"Tell me about Halifax. All I know is that my family ships in lobsters from there for Christmas dinner. They're the best!"

"It's a port city. The capital area, Halifax and Dartmouth, is connected by two bridges over a large harbor and Bedford Basin. The population is under half a million people."

"A good size."

"It's all about a relaxed lifestyle. People head to the ocean on a sweltering day–a beautiful beach is only thirty minutes away. And there are tons of lakes in the city. We have a home in the west end. It's not fancy or big, but an amazing neighborhood. We know everybody."

"Do you work?"

"I'm an executive director with an environmental organization. I fight the good fight of protecting our land and shoreline."

"Are you at work now?"

"I'm working from home. Let me give you a brief tour." Lucy walked out of the room with her laptop. She headed first to the garden, then the kitchen, living room and upstairs. Max asked endless questions about the materials used, the wood inside and others that Lucy couldn't answer. She returned to her office and moved over to her desk.

"That's the house and here we are back at my office," she said, sitting down at her desk.

His face soured. "Wait a minute…"

"What?" she said, puzzled by his sudden change.

"Jane, that painting behind you."

Lucy turned, almost surprised to see it. "What about it?" said Lucy. Max looked visibly shaken, as if stunned by it. "That's my father's work." She felt like she had just sat on a hornet's nest and they were encircling her. "You recognize it?" she asked, buying time to collect her thoughts. Don't panic, she coached herself, people know artwork. No biggie.

"Yes, he painted sunflowers all his life at his family's estate."

"He was an accomplished artist, eh?" She assumed a casual manner.

"May I ask how you acquired it?" he said, his tone over-polite.

Her mind raced. Maybe since his father's death, the artwork had disappeared, and they wanted them back. She did not understand what was going on. Did he think she stole it or something? Suddenly she wished she had turfed it when Joanne suggested it. She no longer wanted the thing in her life. "Sorry, that was decades ago. I'm trying to remember…. I must have admired it and he gave it to me."

His face remained neutral. "Not this painting."

Lucy needed some fast action to address the problem. "I'd be happy to give it back to you. I imagine since your father's passing these are more precious to you."

"Not at all."

The conversation halted. "What then, Max?"

Max stared at her without blinking. "Who are you?"

A prickly sensation shot through her, like she was sitting in an interrogation room with a French detective who was quiet and meticulous but preparing to pounce. Worse, she sensed she was in deep shit but didn't know why. "Why do you ask?" Lucy could feel her red hair and temper flaring. He looked directly at her on the screen. "That's not a painting he'd give to a cousin."

Now Lucy's ire and embarrassment rose inside her. If he thought she stole it, she was ready to ship it right back. She didn't like the implication. "Please explain yourself."

"My father's affairs were the worst-kept secret in our family. The sunflower paintings with his lovers were a symbol of his exceptional talent and manliness. After all, he was quite fond of himself."

Lucy's session was imploding. "Don't be ridiculous. Maybe

it's someone else's artwork."

"No."

"No? What do you mean?" She realized she sounded testy, as she always did when pushed into a tight corner.

"There's one way to identify if it's from his series *"Tournesols d'amour"* or "Sunflowers of Love," he said.

Lucy's shoulders pulled back as if readying to defend herself. She hadn't forgotten. That's exactly what Jacques had called it–except he didn't call it a series. He appeared to coin the title during their *grande seduction* weekend. "How?"

"His signature. The entire canvas is full of bright yellow sunflowers and in the right-hand bottom corner, you'll see two intense flowers inter-twined, it's as if the petals were on fire. With each lover, he declared it was a symbol of his deep passion and love."

"You sure?" She squeaked.

"I know several women–a couple of them were even family friends. And one is a lawyer at his firm. After he died, they showed me the painting. Each woman told me a similar story. I've seen four, this makes five."

"Oh?" Lucy said. She felt like she was floating high in a hot-air balloon, and someone had just shut off the gas valve.

"Louise Tremblay, a lawyer at his office, collects them. She had a long-term affair with my father, and she buys them to take them off the market."

Lucy burned with humiliation. Not only did she feel tawdry about the entire thing, but she believed she had inspired Jacques so much they had to paint together. And now she learned it was a damn series with all the women he bedded. How could she have been so stupid?

She saw Max's face shift. "I am going to ask one more time.

Who are—?"

"Your mother," she blurted and then gasped. She wasn't sure who looked more shocked.

"Why would you say that?"

Should she pretend it was a joke? But that wasn't something a sane person would do. She could claim temporary craziness from the heat, but that sounded worse. After the jolt of blurting it out, it also felt like the boulder she had been dragging behind her for decades had finally broken loose and was now hurtling down a steep hill.

"Max, that's why you were born in Montreal," said Lucy. "Sorry you had to find out this way, but it's the truth." The two sat without saying a word for what seemed like forever. Oh my god, how on earth did she land here? This wasn't how she wanted him to find out.

Tears welled up in his eyes. "I am very sorry, but I have to go."

"Max, I—."

"Sorry," he whispered. His image disappeared and Lucy realized their relationship had imploded in seconds. Why did things always go sideways for her, even when she was doing the right thing? She waited three days, hoping that Max and Elise would have a conversation and finally confirm the truth.

Lucy decided she could live with Elise still being the "mother", after all she had raised him, and now had a grandchild. But Lucy no longer wanted to miss out on knowing her son after all this time. While the revelation lacked finesse in terms of timing and context, maybe it was better to tear off the bandage in one quick snap.

The pain was intense, but over fast. She hoped he'd feel that way too. She checked her inbox constantly, scouring

CHAPTER 37

for a response. On the fourth day, she finally sent a message, trying to sound calm. "Hey Max, have you talked to Elise?" She decided not to say, your mother, now that the cat was out of the bag and running rampant.

After checking her email obsessively for days, she saw one from Max. "I spoke to my mother. She says you are Jacques' cousin, and you have issues. While I continue to be eternally grateful for the kidney, I can't accept your story. I am sorry."

Lucy's rage burned like a summer wildfire. Once again, she was being shafted by Elise and alienated from her son. She dialed Elise's number, but it went directly to voicemail. She emailed and called her a coward for not being honest and insisted she tell Max. Elise ignored her. Lucy started calling and sending emails daily, demanding a response.

No way. Not this time. Lucy refused to give up. Her resolve bounced back. She needed to convince Max that she was his birth mother and win his love.

***

Lucy got a text from Joanne with their NTT code: Need To Talk. Lucy agreed and they both sprinted toward the downtown terminal. During the work week, they could meet during lunch for a "Ferry Summit". They reserved it to reveal big news items during the twelve-minute ferry ride from Halifax to Dartmouth, and then a bonus twelve-minute wrap up to return.

Joanne and Lucy met on the top deck. The harbor pulsed with tankers, pilot boats, sailboats and kayakers all maneuvering around each other. The sun sparkled on the water from the mouth of the Bedford Basin into the infinite Atlantic Ocean. They sat on a bench sipping coffee at the back for more privacy.

Lucy was full of angst herself and wanted to blurt out her news, but it was Joanne's summit. She couldn't recall the last time Joanne had looked so bad.

"What's up, Jo?"

Joanne described her job being eliminated. Lucy let her vent without interrupting. As she wrapped up, she handed a letter to Lucy, asking "Should I accept?" Lucy read it, her left eyebrow lifting higher the further she read. She looked up at Joanne, "Take the money and run."

"Seems like a decent offer," said Joanne.

Lucy nodded, sipping her coffee. "This is perfect. You were ready to do something else, so celebrate."

"I wanted to do it on my terms," said Joanne, her voice cracking.

"Look, if you'd quit you wouldn't have gotten this little pot of gold, Jo," she said waving the letter. "Worse, if the job hadn't been eliminated, you wouldn't have had the courage to jump. You needed this." Lucy waved off a pushy seagull eyeing her cookie.

The massive grumbling engines slowed down, which signaled it was time to wrap up their conversation. They walked down the steps and waited for the ferry to settle into the dock. A uniformed man removed the oversized chain and nodded to the passengers as they disembarked. They showed their transit passes at the pay station, and prepared to get back on the ferry for the return trip.

"You've got a lot of stuff coming at you right now. How's Gretchen?" said Lucy.

"It seems like she's getting better… more of her old self," said Joanne. "But it's two steps forward, a few back. It's all about patience and time."

CHAPTER 37

Lucy admired her ability to stay positive and realistic at the same time. "Is she still with Ally-Up?" Joanne raised the coffee cup to her lips and paused. "I guess, but who knows? He's a nice guy, but it's up to them to work it out."

The shift in Joanne's attitude surprised Lucy. "Wow, that's different for you to say they need to work it out together. Normally, you'd have held a counseling session for the two of them."

"Ha, ha," said Joanne. "We had a long talk. I'm now trying to deal with Gretchen the way it works for her, not the way it worked for Em. It only took eighteen years to learn," deadpanned Joanne. "Enough about me. You look stressed, Lu."

Lucy's face changed to deep concern "No. This is your summit Joanne. I will not take over."

Joanne smiled. "It's okay. We talked about my job, you checked my legal letter, so I'm done. What's going on? Is it Max?"

Lucy's lip trembled as she thought about it. In fact, as she had obsessed about it for days. She breathed in the cool harbor air. "Everything was going so well. He asked about my family. I was giving him a tour of the house and wrapped up by my desk. And that's when he spotted the sunflower painting."

Joanne tilted her head. "So?"

"Apparently Jacques painted a series of sunflowers with his lovers, and Max knew all about his father's worst-kept secrets. Right in the middle of the conversation, he asks me who I am. It humiliated me beyond belief."

"What did you do?"

"I blurted out that I was his mother."

Joanne gasped. "Oh my god. What happened?"

"He looked confused and freaked out. He was polite but ended the conversation quickly."

"Newsflash: That wasn't the best way to introduce the topic."

Lucy felt the need to defend herself. "It slipped out. Elise had cooked up this elaborate lie about why he was born in Montreal, so that is what he believes."

"Don't judge him. That's what he's known all his life."

"I'm not, but it's hard to counter. He told me he was grateful for the generous kidney donation, but he couldn't continue a relationship with me," she sniffed.

"No!"

"I've waited twenty-seven years to see him. Elise pulled the rug from under me and my son, yet again."

"What are you going to do?"

"Do you think I should go to Paris?"

"No, you can't do that to your family. Why not call him?"

"He doesn't answer phone or emails. Elise probably told him I'm whacko and he should not communicate with me–that seems to be her *modus operandi*. And it works."

Lucy gulped her coffee, trying to hide her misery. "I've truly fucked up. Again." Lucy sensed Joanne's practical thinking going on in her head.

"Send him proof. You must have some paperwork from when they were awarded custody of Max."

Lucy winced. "There's a blue folder with everything in it, including the nasty letters Jacques and Elise's lawyers sent. I have no idea where it is."

"Sounds like we need a search party. I'm in."

"I don't know where to start," Lucy sighed. Yes, the paperwork was likely there. She vaguely remembered stowing it somewhere when they moved in years ago. Did she really want to rummage through the past and remember all the pain of losing her son?

"I'll help," said Joanne. "And ask Max for his mother to show him some newborn shots. She won't have anything. Remind me, how old was he when they took him from you—?"

"Two years, four months and ten days," she said, her voice quivering.

"What parent doesn't take endless newborn and baby photos?" said Joanne.

Lucy's expression picked up for the first time since arriving. "You're right. All his early photos are in the folder, and his birth certificate. If I can find it."

"We will."

Lucy's fight and resolve raced through her head. She had passed the point of no return and would not lose Max one more time. The photos and birth certificate were the trump cards she needed to thwart Elise's plan to keep Lucy out of Max's life.

She would unearth the items if it killed her (sadly, the state of the storage in her home might just do it). She didn't care. If Elise thought Lucy would give up that easily, she didn't know Lucy. She smiled at Joanne. "How about on Saturday? Everybody is out in the afternoon."

Chapter 38

Joanne

After lunch, she arrived at Lucy's determined to help her find a way through the mess with Max and Elise.

"Let's start with the basement first, so that we can eliminate it," announced Lucy.

"This looks like our basement," Joanne said, as she eased down the steps to a storage mess that afflicted so many Canadian houses. She scanned the room jammed with boxes, sporting gear and abandoned projects. Dave's work area resembled a giant octopus of long cables, twisted around sound equipment.

She noted Lucy cursing as she dragged out box after box, unlabeled and packed with useless items. They took turns picking a carton and rifling through it until it was clear the items weren't there.

Lucy shook her head. "What a pile of crap. We swear we'll get rid of it, but never do. I think we should pitch this to the reality show for out-of-control households. What's it called?"

"*Hoarders Anonymous?*" said Joanne.

"*Hoarders Unanimous* in our house." She opened the last

unmarked box. "Nope, nothing there. To the attic," said Lucy.

They went up to the second floor and pulled down the hidden ladder that turned into a set of stairs to the attic which was not tall enough to stand up in. Lucy offered Joanne a headlamp to better light the place.

Joanne climbed up the ladder steps and gasped as she each arrived in the hot, damp space, packed with boxes. "We could be here for weeks."

Lucy chuckled. "This is the sequel to the show–as soon as they finish in the basement, we take them upstairs."

"Egad, Lucy." She tried to think like Lucy and crawled to the far corner, which seemed logical for hiding something from the family. She opened ten boxes in a row, with unidentified items piled into each one. When she landed on Lucy's books from McGill, she was getting warm. "Why are you saving law textbooks, Lucy?"

Lucy shrugged. Joanne held up a group of purses, the leather and plastic cracking from the heat and cold in the attic. "Why don't you get rid of some stuff?"

Lucy groaned. "I need a big-ass dumpster outside the house where I can chuck things."

"Why not start now?"

"Not in the mood," Lucy said, closing the flaps on another one.

"That's what everybody says."

"Yup, Jo. And then we say, I'll do it later."

"Which means you are leaving this mess for your kids when you kick off."

Lucy grinned. "I consider it payback for all the crap I put up with."

Joanne opened a crate and found some diaries and photo

albums that looked like they were from the eighties. She lifted two or three books and saw the edge of a dark blue folder. Her hands trembled. "Lucy."

From the opposite corner, Lucy crouched in a squat position, moving across the joists. "That's it!" she shouted. She grabbed the decrepit elastic around the folder which snapped in her hands. They stepped down the ladder to the daylight and sat on top of the steps in the hallway. Lucy flipped through the legal letters. She lifted a tiny hospital band with Max's name on it.

Joanne squealed, "Aww."

"It's shocking to remember that a wrist could be so small," whispered Lucy.

Joanne watched Lucy's expression shift as she examined Max's birth certificate from the Jewish General in Montreal. There were pictures of Lucy and Max, and even a few with Joanne.

"I forgot I had these," said Lucy, gently touching the photos.

"He was a real cutie, wasn't he?" Joanne said, inspecting them. "I loved that little sailor outfit."

"Remember that lady from Westmount in the hospital with you? What was her name?"

"Hmm… Roz… something, with baby number four! Claimed it was her multi-tasking abilities that made it all possible. I don't remember why she gave me clothes," mused Lucy.

Joanne remembered exactly why. "She heard you fretting about having no baby clothes. When she went home, she shipped over three boxes to you at the hospital."

"That's right," Lucy said. "She sent enough clothes until—."

"I'm sorry, I know that was tough," said Joanne, knowing

CHAPTER 38

exactly where Lucy was going with this. She stared at a photo of Lucy and Max. Lucy's expression was sheer exhilaration and terror as she held her little boy. In the next shot, when he was older, she was holding Max high above her shoulders, tossing him in the air, to Max's delight. She turned the photo toward Lucy. "He was so adorable. We tried to get him to say JoJo, and he kept saying OH OH."

"That's right. And look at this," Lucy said, pointing to a head shot. "He had those tufts of dark black hair and olive skin tone. But it was the eyes, those beautiful dark eyes that sparkled and those crazy long lashes. He won everybody's heart in a blink. You know, I can still see little bits of him now. His eyes still shine when we talk on video."

"I can imagine," said Jo.

"You don't know how many times I wanted to show my family, especially Dave," said Lucy. "I have to sort things out with Max first. It would be weird if he shuts me out of his life, after I've told my family. I get the order wrong for everything."

"There's overwhelming evidence in here, Lucy. Also, I can talk to him–I was there during the entire mess."

"You sure were."

Joanne leaned her head on Lucy's shoulder. She felt dusty and sweaty from crawling across beams in the attic. But they got what they needed. That was all that mattered, yet she sensed her own pain rising.

Joanne knew Lucy would feel so many emotions as she faced this earlier chapter in her life. But it surprised Joanne was how much she was feeling. She had forgotten how much pain she had stored, or maybe she never even knew.

Further, she knew Lucy's trauma was always front and center, the few times they had discussed it. Pain suddenly flooded through her body when she pictured the toddler being turned over to Jacques and Elise. Of course, Lucy was the mother, that was clear. Yet they shared the child-rearing. By two, he had a personality. He reached to Joanne for hugs and kisses almost as much as his mother. Yet Joanne had never truly acknowledged how attached she was. Until now. But this pain had to wait. She glanced at Lucy, who beamed, clutching her buried treasure. "What now, Lu?"

"This is my only hope to set things straight," she said, waving the papers. "I know what I need to do."

Chapter 39

Lucy

She studied the various documents, still not quite believing her luck. She had in her hands, the long form birth certificate, which named Jacques Morin as the father and Lucy McGee as the mother. In Quebec, she could choose the last name. After the birth, she debated between McGee and Morin. Finally, Lucy gave him the last name Morin, since she knew it was his baby by the timing. And she might want to pursue childcare payments since he had refused any support.

She scanned the pictures and Max's hospital band and emailed them to Max. For the email subject she wrote "Here's proof." She recommended he ask Elise to show him baby photos from the first two years.

Now it was up to fate. She hoped he'd let her explain. Badgering him with emails would not yield the desired results. Reluctantly, she returned to her family life. Riley's app launch was a tremendous success. Joanne and Lucy teared up at the thought of Lucy's son doing so well as he reached adulthood. She checked her email often over the next week, looking for a response from Max. Finally, she spotted his note and held her breath as she read it.

Lucy McGee (from the birth certificate, I now know that it's not Jane Dough), your news came as a major shock. I am still recovering from the operation, and we have a new baby at home—so it's a lot to process.

If it's true, that means my parents have been hiding the truth for decades. Also, it means you didn't raise me as your child. There is so much I don't understand. I need time to take it all in and talk to my mother. Whatever the truth is or isn't, I remain deeply grateful to you for saving my life—that will never change.

Max

She burned as she reread the message and hints that she had abandoned her son. Since Elise and Jacques were masters of the cover-up, Elise would likely tell him Lucy's documents were a hoax. After losing Max in the eighties, she couldn't bear being shut out of his life again and missing out on knowing her granddaughter.

Lucy stood up and turned to look at the sunflower painting that got her into the mess with Max. Humiliation swept through her for believing Jacques wanted something more than a fling. Why had he made her feel so adored? Their *grande seduction* weekend in Montreal that resulted in that painting was like nothing she had ever experienced before or after in her life. It also resulted in a baby he refused to accept.

She recalled that weekend in fine detail, except in hindsight, she realized Jacques put considerable effort into appearing spontaneous. The sudden urge to visit the art supply store, followed by the music shop for CDs of his favorite musicians.

The prep for an all-night painting session, starting with drinks on her apartment balcony in the Plateau area. Playing Dexter Gordon's *'Round Midnight*, Jacques set up the canvas and sketched the sunflowers. His confident hand guided her shaking fingers as they outlined the petals. After her first sunflower, he declared her a natural artist and handed her a palette. They painted on and off for two days, with *Arthur H* blasting from the stereo, his boozy French voice oozing passion from the speakers.

When the track 'Loulou' came on, Jacques cranked the volume and sang right to her, calling her Loulou. She almost fainted from too much booze and desire, and no sleep.

Now she understood she was merely a conquest for Jacques–a way to prove he could attract women. How insecure. She wondered if Elise knew about her husband's affairs–likely yes, but maybe she didn't care. Wealthy in her own right, and from a powerful family, Elise could have whatever she wanted. Except a baby. Lucy figured since Elise couldn't conceive, at least with Jacques' love child, she got a half-pure Morin baby.

Decades later, Lucy still felt an unexplained longing for Jacques. Their time together had been swift, but memorable. After the mess with Jacques, she retreated for ages, trying to heal her pain. Gradually, she moved back to Nova Scotia and married Dave, who she knew immediately was a much better man and husband. They weren't the most romantic couple, yet he grounded her and loved her unconditionally, even when she was behaving stupidly. She knew she was a lucky woman.

As she read the note from Max, something shifted. She hated the painting. All these years, it hung over her head with Jacques' arrogant spirit looking down on her. No wonder she wasn't moving on. What was wrong with her? Why had she kept it? Why didn't she listen to Jo?

It had to go. Now. She thought about how to destroy it for maximum impact: a knife slicing through the canvas? A bonfire in the garden? Slash it into pieces and shove it into a garbage bag? What would make her feel better? She needed input and dialed Joanne's number.

"What's up?"

"I've been looking at that sunflower painting. I want it out of my life."

"About time—"

"Yes, you were right. I finally get it."

"What are you going to do?"

"How about slashing a utility knife through the canvas in a big X?"

"Very dramatic. Is this for YouTube or something?"

"I'm trying to make a freaking statement. Must you be so practical?"

"I thought you said Max knew someone who collects them, and they're valuable—"

Lucy snorted. "Sure, I'll call her up. 'Hey, Louise, heard you collect Jacques' paintings from old lovers who got sucked in by him, including you. How pathetic. And do you want to buy mine?'"

"Fair point," said Joanne.

Lucy looked at the painting, still stinging. "What do you propose, Jo?"

"How about donating it to a charity shop?"

Lucy sighed. "Where's the fun in that?"

"I guess that's the difference between us."

"What?"

"In dramatic situations, I like to bring order to chaos, you like to bring chaos to order."

CHAPTER 39

"Ouch," said Lucy. "I'd be more annoyed, except it's true. While destroying the canvas would help me with closure on the Jacques' chapter, I guess your idea makes sense—."

"Don't move," Joanne shouted. "On my way."

***

In minutes, Joanne pulled up to Lucy's house. Lucy placed an old blanket on the floor. She still felt an odd attachment to it, despite convincing Joanne of the opposite. They lifted the large canvas off the wall and laid it on the blanket, then wrapped and taped it. Lucy grimaced at the space. "Well, shit. Now I have to repaint this room. That's how home renovations start."

They carried it out the front door and walked to Dave's truck. Lucy opened the back and slid in the blanket. They drove it to the nearest charity shop. Lucy explained to the manager that it was valuable, and it should be auctioned off to maximize the revenue.

She handed her a slip of paper with the contact name of a woman at a law firm in Paris who collected these paintings and suggested a social media campaign to drive up the bidding. The manager looked both baffled and excited, as if she were either being duped or hitting the motherlode. As the two pulled out of the parking lot, they watched staff gathering around the painting, lifting off the blanket and pointing excitedly.

"That was fun," said Joanne.

"I need a cigarette and I don't even smoke," said Lucy. "Seriously, donating it was perfect. I get these moments of stupidity, Jo. Thanks for helping me to see the light."

Within days, the charity had posted a story about a mystery person who had donated a valuable painting, with rumors flying about her deceased lover. The media blew it out of proportion, assuming the donor did not realize its value. Soon people were guessing who the contributor was, with people trying to remember if they had seen this painting at a family or friend's place. Lucy ignored the hoopla. She didn't care if someone figured it out–it was now out of her life.

A week later, the manager called Lucy to report that traffic to the store had skyrocketed and a bidding war drove it to six thousand dollars. They agreed that the woman in Paris would get it at any price. Lucy laughed with her and wished her well.

With the painting sale in hand, Lucy turned her thoughts to larger burning issues like solving her own Massive Family Hairball.

Chapter 40

Joanne

Her new days opened with an infinite amount of daily time to be filled, which panicked her at first. She was used to racing non-stop from the moment she got up in the morning until she slumped in bed at night, exhausted and joyful for the chance to go horizontal. Joanne did that for years, decades even, which she accepted as part of her life. This time, she sat at the kitchen table with a notebook, pen, and a cup of coffee.

She opened it, bent the spine back to cracking point and stared at the page in front of her. After the downsizing months earlier, she was floundering. Several business acquaintances had contacted her to see if she was interested in jobs. Initially, she responded with excitement, yet days later, each job seemed more of the same. She realized she wanted something different for the last decade of her career. As a HR professional, she understood that enough time had passed for grieving. Now she wanted to map out her future.

She jotted her current situation on the first page. After another discussion with her cousin Bev, Joanne decided not to buy the family flower business. Bev wanted a fortune for a dying shop, and Joanne would have to do a massive renovation. It made no business sense. She needed a fresh beginning.

In half an hour, her notebook filled with doodles rather than notes, and she set her pen down. Each time she thought about next steps, she still liked the idea of something with Holly, a lifelong friend. She respected Holly's many years of experience as a successful businessperson.

In search of inspiration, she walked to downtown Dartmouth to the area that had livened up over the past five years. Portland Street now blossomed with retail optimism. Shops, restaurants and breweries sprouted up everywhere–some in new spaces, others retrofitted in heritage buildings. Young people and families flocked to the community. After a four-decade decline, it returned to its roots as a local shopping district. As she wandered, she saw only a few empty spaces, and each one had a "coming soon" sign for a business. Things were brisk.

As Joanne turned the corner, she bumped into Steve Mills, who owned the building with Henderson's Flower Shop. Steve's father had been the original landlord and the two families went way back.

"Hey Steve. How's it going?" she said, offering a quick hug.

"Heard the news about Bev?" He said, unable to hide his delight. "Closing down."

"Really?" Joanne's face burned. She hadn't heard.

"She's not renewing the lease. End of an era, I'd say."

"I offered to take over the family business many times. She wouldn't do it."

"You're better off without her."

"Yes, her customer relations were poor."

"And landlord relations," said Steve.

CHAPTER 40

Joanne sensed a glimmer of potential. "I guess you'll have lots of interest in that space."

He nodded. "You interested?"

"I am, but it sounds like it's a hot property." She explained about her idea with Holly, in the same building, and a tenant of Steve.

"If you are serious, let's talk."

"Really?" Joanne's stomach fluttered. What the hell was she thinking? She had little business experience. And yet, the urge to keep going stayed on her mind.

"Our families go way back! You're the most grounded of the Henderson clan."

"Thanks."

"It's still a business deal, and we need more than a handshake–even if that's what our ancestors did. However, you and Holly would make a talented team. Call my office and set up an appointment." His cell phone buzzed, and he shoved it in his jacket. "Hey, if you want any of the fixtures or anything, you can have them. Bev plans to close the door and walk away."

Suddenly Joanne felt more excited than she had in ages. Here was something creative she always dreamed of and a business partner she knew well.

***

She immediately dialed Peter at work. She spoke excitedly and started relaying the story. He had sounded distracted for the past few years whenever she told him something. This time, he said he'd be right home from work. In minutes, he walked in the door and set his lunch on the counter. He pulled a mug from the cupboard and poured himself a coffee, tossing in the two usual teaspoons of sugar–half in his cup, the rest on the counter. He sat down.

"Start from the beginning. What's going on with the flower shop?"

"Bev is walking away after her lease is up."

"It's about time," said Peter.

"Remember I told you Holly Weston is looking to do something different? We've been discussing a hybrid restaurant and flower shop. We came up with Botanica Café. She'd look after the restaurant and I'd do the flowers. We'd knock down the wall between the two shops and expand it, adding French doors between spaces, so they could be open like an indoor patio. In the shop, we'll offer an event space for rent."

"Such as?"

"Garden and book clubs, painting societies, and knitting circles. I mentioned it to Geoff and his partner, Roberto. They have an exclusive line of designer sweaters called Knit Picker and they work as a collective with local knitters. They sell for five hundred bucks and up."

"For a sweater? You're kidding me."

"Nope. They are looking for a place to hold knitting workshops and recruit knitters. I'd also have the retail shop. We'd display bouquets for sale outside the door, like they do in Paris." She knew he'd have no interest in the details, yet Joanne noticed Peter smiling. "What?"

"I haven't seen you this excited in so long," said Peter. "We need the best trades people. Call Larry Driscoll. He built the interior to the micro-brewery over on McIsaac Street, What Ales Ya."

"I love that place," said Joanne. She noticed him using the word "we" and felt excited.

"You know—" he paused.

CHAPTER 40

"What?"

"I have six weeks' vacation carried over. I could manage the contract and do some work to get it done quickly."

"Really?" She asked, wondering if this could be something to bring them together.

"I'll do the things I'm good at and leave the rest for the pros. I'd be the general contractor."

"That would be incredible, Peter." She was shocked because the idea hadn't crossed her mind. He seemed so... far away lately.

Gretchen walked in and smiled at her father. "Hi Gretchen," he said.

"Hey Dad. What brings you home for lunch?"

"I wanted to hear your mother's plans for the Botanica Café."

"Cool idea, eh?"

"Thanks darling, that means a lot to me." Joanne couldn't remember the last time her daughter complimented her.

"I'll manage the project," explained Peter.

"Makes sense. It's not Mom's forte."

Joanne's spirits soared. Things suddenly felt good.

Gretchen turned to her father. "Did mom tell you I want to be called Greta from now on?"

Joanne's shoulders dropped. That kid sure knew how to kill a joyful moment.

"I know you didn't like your grandmother's name," said Peter.

"See if you like being called Retchin' at school."

Joanne could see the pain on both their faces. "Greta is lovely," she said, checking Peter's and Gretchen's responses. "It honors your grandmother, but it's more elegant. Like Greta Garbo."

"Who?" Gretchen looked puzzled. "I meant Greta Lee."

"Umm… who's she?" said Joanne, not wanting to spoil the moment.

"You know, the movie *Sisters*? *Russian Doll*? *Spiderman*? You've heard of *Spiderman*, right?"

"Okay…. Greta," he said.

Joanne watched Greta exit the kitchen and climb the stairs. She heard the bedroom door close. "Are we getting our girl back?" said Joanne.

"Yeah, about that—" he said, shifting. "I know I wasn't supportive of you," he mumbled.

Joanne's insides churned. On the one hand, she felt like tearing into him, yet she knew he was hopeless with his feelings. "I realize emotional intelligence is not in your tool kit."

"What's emotional intelligence?"

Jo laughed. "Never mind, it's HR speak. Joanne returned to the project, and soon they were laughing. She heard Greta trundle down the stairs, one leg and one step at a time.

"What's so funny in there?" she yelled.

"We're having a couple of laughs at Bev's expense," Joanne said, leaning into Peter. She filled with hope, even though she knew Greta's recovery would be gradual with more bumps. For now, she was seizing the moment. She opened her arms and waved to her daughter.

"Ah jeez, I gotta leave before Mom starts hugging me," said Greta, nodding at her father.

Chapter 41

Lucy

"Let's talk" caught her eye in the email subject line. Excited but cautious, Lucy opened it, wondering what was coming. Everything had been going so well with Max until the sunflower painting debacle.

He finally agreed to talk later in the week, which made her restless as she counted down the minutes and hours. On Thursday, she opened her laptop and took a breath as if preparing for a major case to the Supreme Court. She had lived through many nerve-wracking scenarios in her lifetime–this one was way up there. Max's strained face appeared on the screen.

"Hi," said Max, his tone polite.

"How are you doing?" she said, matching his low-key tone. Her muscles tensed to the point of squeaking.

He paused. "I talked with my mother last weekend."

Somehow, she willed herself to nod without responding, allowing him to talk.

"It was an incredible conversation. She explained she couldn't have children. Given that Jacques was the father of your child and your life was a constant struggle, they saw it as an opportunity to make things right."

Her throat burned. "That's one way of putting it," she said, swallowing the burn but still making her point about Elise, who had an incredible knack for rationalizing things to suit her agenda.

"I listened to her story," he said calmly. "Now I'd like to hear yours."

Lucy was impressed with his maturity, knowing it was difficult for him to hear the story. She feared she might never shut up, but he also needed to hear her truth. "I had a brief affair with Jacques. In hindsight, it seemed exciting… until I got pregnant. Then it got ugly. He didn't want his life in Paris disrupted. Believe it or not, I daydreamed about us being together."

"What was his response?"

"He asked me to have an abortion and said he'd look after everything…." She felt weird talking about something that might have prevented Max from being born. But he wanted the truth. "I considered all options. I was young, and I knew a baby might prevent me from finishing university. Still, I couldn't go ahead. He unleashed his fury and said he had zero interest in me. That devastated me."

"What happened next?"

"I decided to give birth. And I'd figure out whether to raise you or give you up for… for adoption," she finally blurted out. She could only imagine what Max must be feeling to learn about his past, which had seemed so straightforward until his kidney acted up.

"And Jacques?"

"Angry with me, beyond belief."

CHAPTER 41

"Why?"

"I'm sorry to say this…. He said he didn't want children. Not with his wife, not with me." Here was another blow to Max. She halted but summoned up more strength. "And if I kept the child, he wouldn't help me out. He was true to his word."

"What happened after I was born?"

"I believed he should support the baby he'd helped create. I called his office, and the receptionist would say he was away." Lucy burned with the humiliation she felt when calling the law firm. It was clear they gave the receptionist strict instructions to protect Jacques. She even overheard the woman refer to her as *Madame Cinglé* and then laugh. It crushed her to learn *cinglé* meant "crackpot". "He never returned my calls or faxes."

"And?"

"I finally called his home and blurted the story to Elise. She called me a liar. But we both knew it was true."

"Did anything come out of that?"

Lucy shook her head. "No. Life was a struggle. I loved you dearly, but I had to go on welfare, which I detested. In those days, they treated single mothers like dirt. My friend Joanne helped me. We shared an apartment, and she even took a part-time job to help. Honestly, she saved me."

"Is she the one who accompanied you for the kidney transplant?"

"Yes," Lucy said, hoping that they were now past the hard part. "My best friend from way back–we've been through so much together."

"As I now understand it, my mother saw an opportunity to raise a baby with my father's genes."

"I guess. I met with Jacques once more when he returned

a year later to McGill. He said that Elise gave him an ultimatum–adopt the baby, or their marriage was over." Lucy wondered if she should have said that, but it was Jacques' exact words.

"Did they take you to court for custody?" said Max.

Lucy froze, there was no spinning this one. "It was headed for that. However, the lawyers called us to a meeting. They depicted me as a broke and incompetent mother with mental health issues. I'll admit, I did some pretty stupid things in my youth that worked against me being awarded custody."

She waited for Max to respond; he didn't. She explained it all–the suicide note at sixteen saying she was pregnant, which wasn't true. The many calls to Jacques and Elise, in which she sounded increasingly desperate. "I'm not proud of myself," she said, taking a breath. But there was more.

"I see," said Max.

Lucy winced; it was time for the kicker. "With that information, the lawyer knew I didn't have a chance. She advised me to avoid the stress of going to court." Her voice quivered. "The truth, Max, is that I gave you up for adoption to Jacques and Elise." She felt so torn up inside, she didn't even know what to say. His eyes spoke volumes of sorrow. "I am so, so sorry. You know, I still remember the day they pulled you out of my arms and..." Lucy choked up.

"It's hard to know what to say, Lucy—"

"They took you back to Paris and raised you as Max Daniel instead of Daniel Max. It's like they whisked you out of my life and left me with nothing."

"I am curious, Lucy. Did you ever try to contact me?"

Lucy's shame choked her vocal cords. "They had full custody. At one point, I thought of revisiting the case, but

I didn't have a hope. I was so ashamed for giving you up, I felt I had to move on in my life or I would never heal. Yet it's important for you to know, I never, ever stopped thinking about you–throughout your life."

"I'm so sorry for the pain you've suffered," he whispered.

"No, I'm the one who is sorry. I failed you and I've never forgiven myself. In hindsight, I should have borrowed money for better lawyers to dispute their stupid claims. And I should have worked harder to keep you."

"Nobody was a match for my father. But don't feel sorry for me. I was raised well and deeply loved by my mother," added Max.

Lucy smiled through her sniffles. "Yes, the only thing that comforted me was that your family had the means to give you the best. And it sounds like you've had a great life."

"Yes. And it explains so much. He wasn't fatherly. I don't know when it started, but I called him Jacques, not Papa. I felt I couldn't do anything right. One time, he berated me for something. I asked the typical teenage question: 'So why did you two even have me?' He didn't answer."

Lucy nodded. She felt sorry for Max having to learn this story about his father, but in some ways, he didn't seem surprised.

"I used to ask myself what I was doing wrong. Finally, I understand, it wasn't me."

"That's sad, Max. And your mother?"

"She made up for my father's lack of affection. I am deeply hurt by the long-term deception. Yet I know she always loved me. And she's been tireless in finding me a kidney transplant. I love her unconditionally."

"Of course," said Lucy, trying to sound reasonable, even

though she secretly hoped for a deeper divide between Max and Elise.

"So, when she got in touch with you for the kidney, did you want to tell her to go away?"

Lucy tensed up. "At first. However, I knew it was my chance to make it up to you." She added, "Actually, it was Joanne who reminded me."

"I must meet her."

"She wants to meet you too. She adores you!"

"So how are you with all this drama?"

Just when she felt like she had done enough to present herself as a jerk, she had more evidence. "Well, I've got my own problems."

"Oh?"

"I never told my husband or children about you."

"What?"

She saw Max's eyebrows shoot up. "It's crazy. I always planned to tell Dave, but it was still so raw when I met him. After we married, I wanted to tell him and the kids, but the time was never right. Years flew by, then it seemed too late."

"What about the kidney transplant?"

Lucy's shame welled up as she tried to explain her life to the son that she was just getting to know. What would he think of her? "It all happened so fast, so I didn't explain to my family why I was going to Paris. And I forced Joanne to be part of my cover-up, which was wrong too."

"That's kind of a mess, isn't it?"

"Totally agree." She wondered if he'd want to distance himself from her. Lucy glanced at her watch. "Max, I'm sorry, I have a meeting. But I need to ask one thing: are we good?"

"There's a lot to process with the adoption. But I'd like to work on it."

If she was going to build on this relationship, she needed to step up. This was the moment to show some maturity. "Look, you're an adult. Elise obviously loved you and is your mother–that won't change. I'd love to have an adult relationship with you and your family, that's all. It's my life dream."

"That's good to know, Lucy. I will work out things with my mother, but it may take time."

"Understood, Max." Lucy ended the call and curled up on the sofa, overcome with pain and relief. How many times had she dreamt of that conversation? With Jacques gone and Lucy being outed for the deception, her only hope was not being rejected by her firstborn.

Lucy started tapping a text to Joanne, then deleted it. It was time to stop dragging her friend into her endless problems. In fact, what she realized is that she needed time away from everyone to think–and therapy without a therapist. Instead, she needed her cure for everything: Vitamin Sea.

She jumped into her car and headed to Crystal Crescent Beach in the late afternoon, as families were returning to the city, SUVs brimming with kids, picnic coolers and floating devices squeezed into every corner. Several cars had Lab dogs sitting on somebody's lap in the passenger's seat, their ample heads bobbing out of windows with the wind flapping their lips and a couldn't-be-happier smile on their faces.

Lucy parked the car and put on her flip-flops, heading to the shoreline. An August breeze flared up, yet it was colder than she expected. She spread a towel and placed rocks at each corner to anchor it.

After ten minutes, she stepped into the rhythm of the

crashing waves. She walked out and lowered her body into an oncoming swell. A rolling wave of salty effervescence crashed directly into her face, stinging her eyes. Shivering, she plunged under again. This time, something welled up from deep inside her and she allowed herself to cry. She wept for those she had hurt in the past and her family she was about to hurt. Lucy felt relief as the ocean swept away her tears.

Another wave picked up momentum in the distance. Just as it moved in behind her, Lucy started swimming fast so the wave would lift and carry her. Once it took over, she relaxed as her body surfed toward shore. As the wave crashed, there was momentary underwater chaos. Then she bobbed to the surface. An ocean swimmer since childhood, she understood you had to be part of the wave, not fight it. Nature always won. She was freezing her ass off but couldn't stop because the ocean was washing away the misery she'd held inside for too long.

Teeth chattering, she came out of the water and sat in the late afternoon sun. The air smelled like a salt-water garden infused with tangy kelp. Now that things were being sorted out with Max, she had to tell her family. Would they live and let live? Would they want to meet Max? Would her parents come around? Her heart filled with possibilities, but she also knew she had caused a lot of damage. She worried about the massive next steps and made an elaborate plan to right some wrongs.

***

Lucy got a message from Max inviting her to meet her granddaughter and Katarin. She closed the office door and opened the laptop. The video came to life and her lovely son, his wife and baby lit up the screen. She wasn't sure if Katarin

CHAPTER 41

spoke English, but she figured Max would help.

"*Salut and hello*," Lucy said.

"*Allô*," Max and Katarin replied in unison, then exchanged glances and laughed.

"Lucy, this is Katarin."

"Nice to meet you!" said Katarin, with only a slight accent.

"And you." Lucy wanted to reach through the screen and hug them all. "Max is right, you are so beautiful!"

Katarin blushed. "Thank you so much for giving your son a new kidney."

Lucy gulped. She hadn't heard him referred to as her son. She had a good feeling. "I'm so happy to help. Max, is your body accepting the kidney?"

"Feeling better every day."

"That's the best news I could hope for," said Lucy like a proud mother. She couldn't keep her eyes off the baby. Max and Katarin held her up together. Lucy's heart revved up to an aerobic pace. The newborn had little tufts of red curls. "And you know who this is," said Max.

"She's so tiny and sweet," Lucy sighed, full of awe. She was a grandmother, and it blew her mind.

"Thanks," said Katarin. "Our little girl is perfect. My mother is helping us for a few weeks and our home is bursting with happiness."

"Look at her flaming curls," Lucy said, gushing.

"Now we know where she got her red hair," said Max.

"No kidding. From at least one of her grandmothers. Katarin, I understand you have Celtic heritage from Breton?" said Lucy.

Katarin nodded. "Yes, although we haven't seen red hair in several generations."

"Do you like it?" Lucy knew from childhood, not every redhead welcomed their lot in life. Max and Katarin smiled. "We love it! Red hair isn't so common in France," Max said. He held the baby and rocked her back and forth. She was sound asleep.

Max and Katarin exchanged knowing glances. "We have something to tell you," said Max. At first Lucy worried that something might be wrong. Yet their buoyant tone showed otherwise. "Oh?"

"As you recall, her middle name is Margaux, and we were waiting to find the right first name. We are naming her in honor of you and her lovely red hair. And Lucille is Latin for light, so that makes it even better," he said.

"She reminds us of Lucille Ball too," added Katarin.

"I… am…. speechless."

"The only difference, we will spell it L-U-C-I-E."

"Well, you are French," she joked. Then she wondered if it was too much of a "filter-less Lucy" comment that she was famous for. She was relieved when they both giggled. Just then, the baby woke up and laughed in response to her parents' laughter. "This is the nicest thing that's happened to me in so long. I can't wait to see her."

"Any time. You, your family and Joanne are welcome to visit," said Max.

The baby fussed. "Time to go. Great to meet you," said Katarin.

"You too. And thanks so much," said Lucy. She and Max chatted a little longer, but Lucy could hardly focus. They signed off and agreed to talk in a few weeks. She turned off the screen and sat quietly, full of gratitude and happiness.

And yet, fear roiled inside her.

Chapter 42

Lucy

Lucy cycled to her parents' house and stashed her bike in the bushes. While her stomach was usually in knots when she arrived, today was different. She was about to clear up the gritty relationship with her mother she had battled all her life.

She knocked, then pushed the door with her shoulder. It shuddered and creaked, barely letting her in. Mangy the cat peered out from the kitchen and returned to her bowl of water. The television blared in the living room.

Lucy shuffled down the dark hallway. She was about to revisit a conversation that ended twenty-nine years ago, triggering a lifetime of wrath from her mother. When she first called with the news that she was pregnant, her mother showed no concern about Lucy's health, or wellbeing. She fretted about what everybody else would think. She told Lucy not to return home to Nova Scotia with a baby. Her mother didn't want to deal with the neighbors' judgments.

After Lucy had given up custody of Max, her mother announced it was okay for her to come home. By then, Lucy no longer cared about her mother's rules; she was coming anyway. Although the tension had settled between them, her mother continued judging her only daughter.

In her mother's eyes, her brothers could do no wrong and Lucy could do no right–even though the boys did stupid things like driving under the influence, smashing up vehicles, and racking up divorces. When Lucy pointed this out to her mother, she said, "Boys will be boys." That imbalance in the McGee household was there from day one, and Lucy soon learned to fight for what she wanted. Not physically, but more of a never surrender attitude that shaped her life and got her into many tense moments.

The brothers grew up and settled into roles as plumbers, carpenters and decent parents. They teased Lucy for becoming a lawyer and attributed it to her fine arguing skills, yet they were proud of their little sister. They called on each other when in need. The siblings even combined resources to pay off their parents' mortgage for their fiftieth wedding anniversary, narrowly dodging a mortgage default in progress, though it was never acknowledged or discussed.

At the house, Lucy fidgeted, preparing to tell her parents the big news. It was business as usual: her father chatted nonstop, asking Lucy about her family, while her mother never took her eyes off the screen. Lucy pressed the mute button on the remote. Her mother looked shocked. "Who died?" asked her mother. Lucy wondered why her mother had to assume the worst about every situation. "Nobody. Why?"

"It must be serious if you are interrupting my favorite show."

Nice dig, she thought. Lucy opened her mouth to argue and caught her father's wink. He still had some fun in him, but her mother's joy disappeared long ago. She was killing time until what she described as "the good Lord taking me away from

CHAPTER 42

all this misery". Lucy couldn't imagine being that unhappy in life, yet her mother dedicated a lot of time to it.

"I donated a kidney," she blurted. Both parents looked puzzled. "To my firstborn son."

"Riley needs a kidney?" said her father, gasping.

"No. Daniel, or Max as he's now called." Lucy noted the look of regret on her father's face for thinking it was Riley. She understood; it was easy to forget because she never talked about Max, but only because her mother freaked out when his name came up. Right on cue, her mother's face twisted. "Don't start."

Things had to change; she refused to hold back about Max anymore. "He needed a new one, or he'd die." She waited for her mother's expression to soften. It did not. "I had an extra, so I gave him one," she joked. It fell flat.

"What? Where?" said Lucky.

"You know that Joanne and I recently traveled to France, right?" She didn't wait for a response. "Well, during part of the trip, we stayed in a luxury clinic/spa and the best surgeon in Europe did the transplant, paid for by Elise Morin."

"Who's she?" said her mother.

"Jacques' wife."

"Who's Jacks?" she asked, making him sound like he was plural rather than French.

Lucy sighed. It was the never-ending tango with her mother. She could never tell whether it was her mother's Alzheimer's kicking in, or her trying to pretend Lucy's past didn't exist.

The doctor told the family that there would be times when she was fully clear about everything, and other days, not so much. Gradually, the forgetful days would continue until they became most days. Lucy was never sure about her mother's status, so she had to treat her with some patience. "Jacques was the father of my child."

"The adulterer?"

Here we go, Lucy thought. Her mother liked words with the most negative impact. It used to upset Lucy terribly, but she didn't want a battle. "Yes, but he's dead now."

"No wonder. The way you two behaved during that time of fornicatin' in Montreal."

Where did she dig up a word like that? "I liked to call it the *grande seduction* weekend," Lucy said, knowing her mother would hate that phrase. Worn down by her unwillingness to accept her, Lucy no longer fretted about her past mistakes. Wasn't a parent supposed to love you unconditionally? That's how she lived her life with her husband and kids.

"It's a wonder God didn't strike you dead for that," said her mother.

"You probably wished he had," Lucy muttered under her breath, but not low enough. "Don't be daft, Luv," her father whispered, his Irish accent sneaking to the surface.

Her mother hissed, "You conceived your son outside of marriage, so I reject him."

"News flash, Mom: It's no longer a crime to be pregnant and unmarried." Lucy delivered the comment like an ace tennis serve. Her mother didn't flinch. Lucy looked at her worried father, whose expression detected brewing trouble between two strong-willed women.

Lucy wanted to shout at her mother: "You hypocrite, we all know you were three months pregnant when you married Pops." Although labeled a preemie, baby Owen miraculously arrived fully formed at nine pounds, ten ounces, only six months after the wedding. Everybody knew, and they also understood they shouldn't raise it with Mary, or they'd regret it. She neither forgave nor forgot anyone who questioned her. Instead, they gossiped behind her back.

It was only a few years earlier Owen learned that his mother and father "placed him in the family shopping cart before checking out" as his father described it. When a heart attack nearly took Lucky, he confessed to his firstborn son. He didn't want to die without telling him the truth. Owen promised not to tell a living soul.

For two weeks he kept the promise until a night of drinking when he called Lucy. She let it slip to her other brothers, one by one, each sworn to secrecy. In no time, every cast member of her crazy family knew and pretended to be the keeper of a secret that nobody else knew.

Lucy noted it was all part of the McGee Code of Dishonor. She joked that the McGees had so many family skeletons, they needed a walk-in closet. And nobody remembered who knew what, so they didn't dare say a word, except behind each other's backs. Somehow, the dysfunctional system served her family well.

With the latest news, Lucy aimed for a full-steam ahead approach. "Anyway, Max is doing fine. We've started a mother and son relationship and I'm over the moon. I'll tell Dave and the kids, but I'm telling you first since you already knew about the baby. We'll work through it as a family. Max and his wife would love to visit from France sometime and meet everyone."

Her father grinned. "As I always said, live and let live."

"And," said Lucy, beaming. "You have a great-grandchild."

"Is that so?" said Lucky.

Her mother scowled. "Who had a baby?"

"Max and his wife Katarin."

"Who are they?" Again, was it her mother's Alzheimer's or deliberate denial? Who knew? Besides, Lucy wondered if it even mattered. Max would be connected to the family; there was no turning back. Lucy stood up to leave. Her father's face communicated defeat, while her mother showed confusion.

Her mother's face, etched with age and pain, also looked vulnerable. It must have been exhausting for her to carry on with the lie for her adult life. Suddenly, Lucy got an unreligious epiphany, as her father called them.

She finally understood her mother's hostility toward her: almost thirty years ago, she watched Lucy repeating the same mistake. Maybe she didn't want her pregnant daughter heading down the aisle to marry a rogue like her husband with a philandering eye and an allergy to work. Perhaps that's why her mother buried herself in religion, to forget all the terrible things that befell her–and there were many.

While Lucy hadn't planned to get pregnant at twenty-one, she became smitten with little Max and decided she'd make it work. Yet her mother's anger and shame about the baby was the reason behind the secret. In hindsight, she regretted more than anything that she hadn't told Dave and her children.

Lucy wished that she and her mother could have discussed things over the years instead of staying locked in battle. Lucy knew her birth was unplanned. Further, it didn't take a genius to figure out after three brothers in a row and a big gap, she was a surprise or a mistake.

When she was a teen, Lucy overheard her mother on the phone in the kitchen, joking with her friend Nancy, while stabbing the boiling potatoes with a fork. She called Lucille "The Last Straw" baby and laughed as she described laying down the law with her husband. Lucille was officially his

CHAPTER 42

problem. Lucky surprised her by stepping up to care for his daughter, unlike his track record with the three boys. In fact, the two became inseparable. As she grew up, she sensed her mother's exasperation. Lucy figured it was nothing personal; her mother would have behaved the same way to any fourth child who arrived.

A wave of compassion welled up in Lucy's heart because she finally understood her mother. She wanted to hold her mother and cry, for the pain they both shared in an era that shamed unwed, pregnant women. But too much time had passed, with a catalog of endless arguments and hurt shared between them. It was as if her mother locked up all the unhappy memories and tossed away the key.

Lucy knew the crucial conversation would never happen, ever. It wasn't possible for her mother to admit to a mistake, or that she too, had kept a secret. Lucy figured in a weird way, Alzheimer's was a gift to her mother: when things got tough, she slipped into that world and no further discussion took place.

"Well, I have to get going," said Lucy, hugging her father. She knew he would visit her at her home, and she could tell him about Max and his family, which he'd eventually pass on to Mary. Her mother picked up the TV Guide to avoid Lucy's hug. It was the way the family rolled.

While staring at the screen, her mother stated: "Lucille, never bring that bastard into this household."

Lucy jerked, as if her mother had slapped her hard enough to knock her off her feet. Where did that nasty and loaded word come from? Was she saving it all these years to hurl at her daughter at the right moment? She had only heard her mother say that word once, when her father hadn't shown up at home for five days back in the day. It was a harsh word to describe such a beautiful young man like Max.

She stared at her mother whose body was charged with rage, built-up like static electricity that was ready to discharge like a bolt of lightning. Pity the poor person near her who accidentally touched her. Her father's worried eyes darted between mother and daughter.

Lucy glanced at the empty glass and read the verse stamped on the coaster beneath the tumbler: "Judge not lest ye be judged." She wondered if her mother had ever thought about the messages she foisted on everybody who sipped refreshments in her home.

As she walked toward her mother, she noticed her angry expression shift to that of a frightened child. Lucy felt sorry for her mother, trapped in a sad world. There was no need to battle anymore; somebody had to stop the cycle of anger and blame. Lucy wrapped her arm around her mother's shoulder, hugged her and kissed her on the forehead. "I love you too, Ma," she said, and stepped out the door into the bright sun.

Chapter 43

Lucy

She walked through the door at home and strolled into the kitchen to find Dave. Something felt weird in the house. Dave was just standing there by the counter, doing nothing, which was not like him. His expression scared her. In fact, she wasn't sure if she had ever seen that look on his face. It was a cross between seething anger and utter disgust. "What's wrong?" Lucy asked, taming her fear.

"Wrong, Lucy? Two things," he said, holding up his fingers, as if to make his case. "First, there was a weird call on the landline from some French doctor, Dr. Haber… Haberdasher… or something. Wants you to call back. Pronto."

Lucy gulped. At the clinic in France, they insisted on having two phone numbers on file for follow up. She reluctantly gave them the landline but asked for them to call her cell. "Yes, Dr. Haberling," she stated slowly, as if to slow down the conversation.

"And two, follow me," he said, turning from her and walking toward her office. Dave rarely, if ever, went into her office.

Lucy walked like a guilty child caught doing something

dire, except she didn't know what crime she had committed. "What's up?"

"Remember that shelf that you asked me to install a few months ago?"

Lucy nodded, but she had forgotten. He was sometimes slow getting things done, but he did them. Somehow, she sensed the shelf wasn't the problem.

"I set my tools on your desk and accidentally pushed this file onto the floor. And, after that weird phone call, I see this!" Dave opened the file from the clinic, containing papers covered in post-it notes and a brochure about kidney donation. "I just have one question Lucy: What the fuck?"

"Oh my god," Lucy gasped, nearly fainting. "Dave... I'm so sorry. I don't even know where to start." Deep remorse ripped through her because she hadn't told him (or felt she couldn't). Worse, she had taken him for granted. She often did that with situations, knowing he would be initially irritated, yet over it quickly. Not today. She had crossed the line with someone she cared about more than anyone in the world, other than her children. She hadn't shown him the respect that he so deserved. Here was a man who put up with so much of her drama, but this might have been the last straw. She felt sick. "Dave, can you sit down with me? I have a lot of explaining to do."

"No kidding," he spat out. They walked over to the sofa, away from her desk.

Lucy took his hand, but he pulled back. He had never done that before. Gathering her courage, she went back into her sordid history and explained everything from the time in Montreal, the baby, giving him up for adoption and finally, the kidney transplant.

CHAPTER 43

"I'm gobsmacked," said Dave.

He stared ahead, without looking at Lucy. She wanted to do or say something to get him talking but kept quiet. Dave didn't like her blathering during stressful conversations.

Finally, he turned back to her. "You know, I could have handled the fact that you got pregnant in Montreal–hell, it was before I knew you. And I know it wouldn't have been easy for a single mother at university, plus I can imagine your crazy mother and her guilt. I get that. And, I wouldn't have judged you for giving up a child for adoption. The kid sounds like he was well looked after. But I'm surprised, no, make it shocked, that you didn't bother to tell me back then."

"I know, I know, Dave. I don't even know …"

"But years later, you keep the secret and even put your life at risk, without telling me? Fuckin' selfish of you." David said, shaking his head. "Honestly, Lucy."

Lucy wanted to crawl under the sofa. "The risk is low for healthy people. I was up and walking the day after the operation."

Dave put up his hand like a stop sign. "So what? And for once, don't argue. That's not the point. Really Lucy, why the hell did you hide it all these years?"

"I don't know. Somehow, I pushed it deep down."

"Did you talk to anybody about it?" said Dave.

"Only with Joanne. My mother initially banned me from the family, then after the adoption, pretended nothing happened. Pops let it ride to get along."

Dave shook his head. "It's not what you did. It's that you didn't tell me. I'm not an ogre."

Lucy felt sick. "I know. I worried if I told you back then, I would lose you." She stopped, wondering if he believed her.

"You were the best thing that ever happened to me, Dave." She hung her head. "I wouldn't blame you if you walked away."

He released a big fat sigh. "I didn't say I was walking away. But make no mistake, I am fully pissed off," he said to the space in the middle of the room. "Funny, throughout our marriage, I'm the guy who always thought I'd lose you."

"What? Why?"

"You were the interesting one, crazy and usually up to something exciting. You were so attractive with your curly red hair and spicy personality. Everyone wanted to be around you. Me? I'm just the oaf with a lot of gear."

"Seriously, Dave, you are the best father. You're smart, funny and you put up with me," she said, smiling, tears trembling at the lids.

They said nothing for a few minutes, which felt like hours. Lucy knew to keep her foot out of her mouth and let everything sink in. Dave turned to her. "Look, this will be a shock for Riley and Maggie to discover they have a half-brother in France. You got to tell them fast. I will not lie for you."

"I realize that, but I knew it wasn't the right time to tell everyone, just before the operation. Do you understand?" Lucy looked at him, but it was clear he wasn't budging. Her motivations didn't matter. "Dave, I will do it this weekend so that we have time to talk. Is that okay?"

"You'd better," he said, getting up and grabbing his tools before storming out of her office.

Lucy wanted to beg and plead for a sign that he still loved her. Not this time. She accepted it would take some time for him to get over this, and maybe he never would. It was hard to tell. The best thing she could do to win back his trust was by doing what was asked.

CHAPTER 43

✳✳✳

Revealing a secret older than her marriage and children churned her up inside. Maybe the hard part was over, telling Dave, but she dreaded telling her kids for other reasons. She knew this would change the dynamic between them.

When they were growing up, Riley and Maggie adored her and saw her as a hero (with a few faults). Now, she was stripping bare her decades-old secret to reveal a major character flaw–a mother who had lied to her children. Not the little lies, like throwing out Riley's favorite teddy bear, then pretending it was left behind somewhere. Or forgetting Maggie's soccer game and leaving her waiting on the school steps for an hour. No, this was the big one, and she only had herself to blame.

Her kids were busy during the week, so she asked them to be at home on Saturday at two o'clock. When they questioned why, she requested they wait until then and she would reveal all. Then, with the meekest sounding voice she had ever heard, she asked Dave if he would be there. He shrugged and mumbled "yes, for the children". Despite minimal conversation between Dave and Lucy, tension rose in the household. Neither Riley nor Maggie asked what was going on. However, Lucy could hear muffled conversations in other rooms.

On Saturday, at one forty-five, Lucy waited for the family in the living room. At ten to two, Riley was still loafing in the basement. Lucy called him. There was a basket on the hall table, where everybody deposited their cell phones for family meetings.

Arriving early, Maggie appeared antsy without her phone. Riley emerged from the basement and eased onto the sofa, yet ready to bolt. Dave arrived at the last minute and sat in the occasional chair, some distance from the kids.

Lucy scanned their faces and noted they all looked like the Ashen Family instead of the Baxter Family. Nobody said a word. The calm before the shit storm.

She opened her mouth, nothing came out. Never had she been so nervous. She sucked in a breath. "I suppose you are wondering why I called you here today," she joked feebly, then realizing herself it wasn't funny. Painful silence.

"Are you two getting a divorce?" Maggie blurted out, impatient for information.

"No!" Lucy and Dave shouted together. Lucy was relieved to hear Dave join in.

"Are you sick… or something worse?" said Riley.

"Hell no. I'm going to live way beyond my best before date." She hoped they'd be happy it was a positive story to learn about Max. She took a deep breath. "When I was at McGill University in Montreal, and twenty-one years old, I had an affair with a visiting professor from France."

"Affair as in—" started Maggie.

"Yes, he was married," Lucy cut in.

"Before Dad?" said Riley.

"Of course."

"That it? No biggie." Riley stood up.

"I got pregnant."

Riley sat down. "Oh."

"Did you have an—" Maggie stumbled.

"Abortion?" she asked, knowing it was a tough question for her daughter to ask. "No, but I gave birth to a boy," she added. "My mother forbade me to return to Nova Scotia."

Maggie squirmed in her seat. "Why?"

CHAPTER 43

"Embarrassment. Ma's favorite saying: 'Better the trouble that follows death, than the trouble that follows shame,'" said Lucy.

"Because you got pregnant? Really?" said Maggie, her eyebrows narrowing.

"It was different back then," Lucy said. "Then Jacques Morin, the father of my child, refused to have anything to do with me for going through with it. In fact, my only friend was Joanne–she helped me more than I can explain."

"So, like, did you give it up for adoption?" said Riley, suddenly inquisitive.

Lucy held up a finger to show she was getting there. She wanted to think about how to explain this, but her two kids staring at her made her nervous. "At first, I dropped out of university and went on welfare to look after him."

"What's his name?" said Maggie.

"It is Daniel Maxim Morin on the birth certificate. He goes by Max now."

The questions ping-ponged around the room. Lucy had to regain control. "Listen. I started to raise him, but Jacques wouldn't support us. I was ready to do whatever it took to be a good mother. Jacques' wife found out about the affair and the baby. A year later, when she learned she couldn't have children, her desperation grew. Suddenly, from the father who refused to acknowledge our child, I got ambushed by a team of lawyers in Montreal going for custody of Max. They built a case and presented me as an unfit mother before we went to court."

"So, what happened, Mom?" Maggie said. Lucy could see her daughter was expecting her to be a hero in this story. She dreaded finishing the story.

"I allowed Jacques and Elise to adopt him," Lucy glanced at Dave's blank face. "Actually, I gave them full custody. They changed his name from Daniel Max to Max Daniel and raised him as their child. They never told him that I was his birth mother."

"Why did you hide it?" asked Maggie. Lucy blushed deep red. "I wish I knew, Maggie. I didn't plan it that way. But it got harder, the longer I left it."

"Single women have babies all the time," said Riley. "I mean, like, who cares?"

"Not then," she replied. "I suffered for ages about the situation. Eventually, I started over. I don't know where to start with an apology to you two."

"Do you think it was fair to keep it from us?" said Maggie. Lucy's heart broke to see her daughter look so hurt and deceived. "So many times, I wanted to tell you. It's hard to explain, but when things were going well, I wanted the happiness to continue, so I said nothing. And when things weren't going well, I couldn't bring myself to raise it. I kept digging a deeper hole."

"What about Granny and Grampy McGee? Do they ever ask about him?"

"No, honey, they don't," she whispered.

"Mom, I don't give a shit that you had a baby three decades ago, but I mind being lied to," said Riley.

"Second that," said Maggie.

Lucy twitched. She knew this was no time to put up a brave or arrogant front. She had messed up. "I hope you can forgive me."

"Where he is now?" said Maggie.

Lucy reminded herself she'd better get into the second

part before it got worse. "In Paris, where he grew up and continues to live, which leads me to the next part." Riley and Maggie expressed identical "oh shit" looks on their faces. "Elise contacted me last year. She told me Max had a serious kidney condition and would die without a transplant. No surprise, her kidney wasn't a match for him," said Lucy.

"So now she's in touch," said Maggie, sounding miffed.

"Exactly," said Lucy, picking up on Maggie's comment. "Plus, she hadn't told him she wasn't his mother."

"What about his father… Jacques, is it?" said Riley.

"He died four years ago. She begged me to donate a kidney and save her son's life."

"What did you decide?" asked Maggie.

"Yes, under one condition," explained Lucy. "Tell Max I was his birth mother. Elise absolutely refused. So, I said no deal. She was stubborn and kept searching for another family member. Finally, she came back and still insisted that I not mention the truth. We hit an impasse."

"Meanwhile, Max is sick," added Maggie.

"I was always going to donate one, I just wanted to make Elise feel some of the pain I felt," Lucy said, more defensively than she intended.

"When?" said Maggie.

"Uh… It's done. I donated a kidney to Max," said Lucy.

"Is that why you went to Europe?" Maggie asked.

"You could have died," squeaked Riley.

"Let me explain. They put me up at the most prestigious clinic in France and monitored me around the clock. All on Elise's tab. To be honest, I've never had such a luxurious week."

"Where was Joanne?" said Maggie.

"In an adjoining room where she received full spa treatment."

Maggie looked at her father. "Dad, did you know all about this?"

Dave shook his head. "I just found out a few days ago."

Maggie stared at her mother. "Mom, how could you?"

The dam burst. Lucy cried her heart out–for her kids, for Dave and the secret she had hidden for so many years. Oddly, despite all the pain, she felt better. The secret was out, and it didn't even seem so big and bad–why had she let it fester for so long?

Dave spoke first. "Riley and Maggie. Although I was upset learning this from your mother, let's keep in mind she's gone through a terrible time as well, trying to tell you the truth."

Both nodded. Lucy could tell they looked more shocked and unsure what to do. She felt the same way. "Kids, I only hope that you can somehow forgive me. I love you and your father more than anything in this world." Neither of them said a word.

"Could you give your mother and me a moment together?" Dave asked. Riley and Maggie nearly broke the speed of light bolting from the room.

Dave walked to the sofa and waved her over. She eased onto the sofa and sat near him, without cuddling up like she usually did. They sat quietly for a long time.

***

As weeks passed, instead of pushing details at Riley and Maggie, Lucy waited for questions to surface about Max. And when they did, she answered honestly. She explained to her kids he was grown up and didn't need her as a second mother.

She only wanted to know him and watch her grandchild

grow (which was yet another surprise for Riley and Maggie). For once, she was clear about her role and how she might go about fulfilling it without the many emotional potholes she normally created.

When Riley raised the idea of building a cottage on the piece of family land on the ocean, Lucy slipped in that Max was an architect of tiny houses. Riley said little, but after he checked out Max's website, he started asking more and more about him.

Before long, he and Maggie asked about Max and his family. Then they followed his blog about the kidney transplant. Other questions surfaced until it seemed like he was a connected member of the family. Distant for sure, but a tiny transatlantic connection was happening. Lucy felt some relief inside. It wasn't over, but the hardest part was now out in the open.

Chapter 44

Lucy

A month later, after she discussed it with David, Riley and Maggie, they agreed to meet their newly discovered family member. She arranged a time with Max. On the day of the video call, everybody piled into the living room. They looked awkward and unsure what to do, but still making an effort. It was not the usual atmosphere they enjoyed as a family in the living room while watching hockey or basketball playoffs.

Lucy wanted everybody to feel relaxed. "Riley, do you want something to eat?"

Riley perked up. "Hell, yes. I didn't know if that was okay."

"You bet," said Lucy.

Riley raced to the kitchen and returned with nachos, which Maggie described as gross to eat while talking to Max. She went to the kitchen and opened the Prosecco sparkling wine, which Maggie and her friends now drank for special gatherings. Lucy offered to grab a beer for Dave, and she poured a glass of wine for herself. When she came back, Lucy picked up the remote and clicked on a giant screen that Dave had bought as a surprise birthday gift for her, which she called an "indoor drive-in".

When Riley saw the screen flicker, he shouted, "WAIT!"

Lucy's heart skipped. "What now?" she asked Riley, wanting things to be perfect, but respecting that Maggie and Riley had their own point of view.

"Is this a TED Talk?" Riley joked, sending her his loving evil grin.

She was relieved by her son's humor. Somehow it broke the ice. "C'mon!" she lobbed back.

Riley winked at Maggie and said, "Mom, how many times during our childhood did you bait us with a 'cool video', then switch to a TED Talk?"

Lucy feigned hurt. "They were educational!"

"Eighteen minutes I'll never get back," he joked, high-fiving Maggie and their father. Insults shot around the room as the kids reminisced about their mother's goofball 'learning moments'.

"What an ungrateful bunch!" she scowled, smiling inside. They squished into the soft furniture, jockeying for their favorite spot. Riley scarfed down the cheesy nachos so fast, he requested another batch. Lucy offered to make more and headed to the kitchen. Maggie hollered out for a brie cheese and cracker tray, and David dove his meaty hand into the empty chip bag and waved it at her–his code for more chips. Usually, she shot them all a look telling them to get their own damn snacks, but this time she rushed to the kitchen full of excitement that things felt normal-ish. In the background, she heard some laughter as they waited for the session with Max.

By herself in the kitchen, she was awash in love. Suddenly she felt so happy that she wanted to run back and hug them all but figured it would shock them. As she paced, waiting for the broiler to melt the mound of grated orange cheddar on the nachos, she thought about each of them.

Maggie, who was so grown up for her twenties–way more mature than she was at that age. Her dear little girl marched straight down an even-keeled path of accounting. Lucy did not understand where Maggie got the need for structure and details–it wasn't from her or David. Perhaps their lack of structure motivated her need for it. But accounting worked for Maggie, and that was all that mattered.

Then there was Riley, the highly creative, funny and sensitive son, loved by everyone. He attracted friends like a giant magnet hanging around a pile of metal filings. His app would make him successful beyond what she could comprehend. She didn't understand what he was doing technically, yet she was bursting with pride.

And her beloved David, by his own admission, a big oaf. But she knew he was very smart. "I'm a simple guy," he'd state proudly. She used to find that description annoying. Why would someone be proud of that? Gradually, she realized he meant his principles were uncomplicated and nondramatic. They were downright admirable. He was the exact foil she needed since she supplied enough family drama to stage a Broadway production. With the need for continual excitement in her younger years, she chased unsuitable men which always ended badly. She was a slow learner. And she thanked her lucky stars she found Dave. She loved him even if he did wash in the bathroom like he was a statue in a large fountain, spraying water everywhere.

As part of their couple's recovery discussions, they agreed she was sometimes too busy with her life and David with his business. They still had some healing to do about the secret, and they needed more time. Yet it sparked some conversations they should have had years ago.

They agreed they'd do more things together, and she promised she wouldn't bug him to travel to Europe. Instead, she suggested taking that camping trip they had joked about doing for ten years. While she didn't relish the thought of putting up a tent–well, Dave putting up a tent–and sleeping on a blow-up mattress, what the hell. It was time for her to go out of her comfort zone for once.

Then there was Max and her dream of twenty-seven years to welcome him to the family, despite him living so far away. There would be occasional personal visits, she vowed. Her heart pounded as she recalled the light brush they had in Paris when she and Joanne walked by him as he headed to work. So close and yet so far. While video was all they had now, she would meet him in person one day and hug him so hard he'd squirm the way he did as a baby. She needed patience and promised herself it would happen soon.

Lucy wanted to lock this once-in-a-lifetime wave of happiness in a video and just keep pressing play. The stove timer jolted her from her thoughts. She loaded everything onto a tray and returned to the living room. The moment she dreamed of was finally here. She vowed not to mess it up.

She arrived with the snacks and surveyed her family settled on the sofa. It was a crazy scenario: meeting a new family member online. While it wasn't ideal, half the population had unconventional families these days, so who cared, other than her mother? A pang of sorrow swept through as Lucy recalled her mother's life shrouded in fear, shame and the grip of the church. Her choice, of course, but Lucy lived differently, pursuing happiness wherever possible, in case it suddenly disappeared. Maybe she didn't get everything right (hell, most things), but she sure had a fine family and a fine life. "Okay, everybody, we've got new family members for you to meet," she said.

She clicked the remote control. Everyone leaned in. Max and Katarin appeared on the screen. Together they lifted Baby Lucie, revealing her tiny red curls and a devilish smile.

"It's Lucy 2.0," shouted Riley. Lucy elbowed her son while everybody laughed. Lucy couldn't imagine what might unfold in the next few minutes. She hoped her children and husband would accept Max and want to visit his family. But one thing at a time, and only at the right time, with their permission. No more secrets.

As for her bigger family, Lucy wondered what her brothers would think about her earlier life. Probably they wouldn't care. They mostly shook their head when they heard about Lucy's surprises. That was fine. She knew her mother would never accept this chapter of her life and regretted that she would miss out on meeting Max.

If Max and family visited Nova Scotia, Lucy's father would sneak out to see his new grandson and great-granddaughter, and then report to Mary. Since her father's heart problem had grown, he no longer cared about grudges or resentment. She knew he'd melt when he saw Lucie, a replica of her at that age.

Max's eyes lit up and his smile expanded across the screen. As she got to know him, she sensed his excitement about meeting his family. Finally, the hole in her heart where her firstborn had been missing for decades was filling with motherly love. She heard Max say, "hello all" at the same time

CHAPTER 44

as David, Riley and Maggie said *"bonjour"* to him.

Lucy parked the hurt, the shame and mostly the loneliness that had plagued her for decades. It was not a pain obvious to the naked eye when people looked at her, but she felt it. She knew the sorrow in her soul wouldn't suddenly disappear just because she had finally revealed the truth, but it was a start. Ditto for her children, and David and Max.

This first meeting was more of an emotional down payment, and it was her deepest wish they could all stumble toward a truth that would allow them to move forward. Lucy ran a quick inventory of the contemporary family structure: Riley and Maggie had a half-brother and niece in France; David now had a stepson and family; and Lucy had a second son, a daughter-in-law and granddaughter she could acknowledge and celebrate.

During their trip in Europe, she recalled Joanne encouraging her to let the light in to heal her wounds. She didn't quite get it at the time, but today she felt different. In her mind's eye, she pictured a golden ray of sun with a gentle warmth that filled her heart.

And for the first time in more than half her life, she felt truly at peace.

About the Author

Born and raised in Nova Scotia, Gina N. Brown is a published writer of travel stories and feature articles. Following a career as a marketing specialist, she launched NovaHeart Media in 2020, an independent publishing platform dedicated to creative writing. She lives in her home port of Halifax, Nova Scotia. *Lucy McGee's Moment of Truth* is her first published novel.

You can connect with me on:
- https://www.novaheartmedia.com

Subscribe to my newsletter:
- https://www.novaheartmedia.com

www.ingramcontent.com/pod-product-compliance
Lightning Source LLC
Chambersburg PA
CBHW021438070526
44577CB00002B/212